TWENTIETH CENTURY VIEWS

The aim of this series is to present the best in contemporary critical opinion on major authors, providing a twentieth century perspective on their changing status in an era of profound revaluation.

Maynard Mack, *Series Editor*
Yale University

WALLACE
STEVENS

A COLLECTION OF CRITICAL ESSAYS

Edited by

Marie Borroff

A SPECTRUM BOOK

Prentice-Hall, Inc., *Englewood Cliffs, N. J.*

Second printing ...... August, 1965

© 1963 BY PRENTICE-HALL, INC.

ENGLEWOOD CLIFFS, N.J.

LIBRARY OF CONGRESS CATALOG CARD NO.: 63-19419

Printed in the United States of America—C

Preface

With the publication of *Transport to Summer* in 1947, *The Auroras of Autumn* in 1950, and *The Collected Poems* in 1954, the poetic achievement of Wallace Stevens stood essentially complete. The greatness of that achievement will become more and more fully apparent in the latter decades of our century. The essays collected here bear witness to it.

In the first essay, I have invited Stevens to speak for himself, since, as is generally acknowledged, he expresses his fundamental concerns as a poet more clearly and accurately in his prose writings than most of his critics do in theirs. For the rest, my concern has been to assemble essays by established and newer writers which reflect the present estimate of Stevens' poetry and provide enlightenment concerning it. Despite the difficulties he presents for the uninitiated, Stevens wrote not for critics and other poets but for men, offering strong and heartening counsel in a tragic world.

Poetry at its best takes on something of the nature of reality itself, in that it is endlessly subjected to interpretation and debate. The poetry of Stevens is of this order. Different, and at times disparate, opinions and points of view are represented by the essays collected in this volume, including my own. Drawing from them according to his needs and interests, the reader will, I hope, gain a fuller understanding of Stevens' poetic achievement and a deepened sense of its importance.

M. B.

Preface

Table of Contents

Introduction

Wallace Stevens: The World and the Poet

by Marie Borroff

> It is a theatre floating through the clouds,
> Itself a cloud, although of misted rock
> And mountains running like water, wave on wave,
>
> Through waves of light. It is of cloud transformed
> To cloud transformed again, idly, the way
> A season changes color to no end,
>
> Except the lavishing of itself in change,
> As light changes yellow into gold and gold
> To its opal elements and fire's delight,
>
> Splashed wide-wise because it likes magnificence
> And the solemn pleasures of magnificent space.

The Auroras of Autumn, p. 416[1]

This description of the terrestrial cosmos is a fitting epigraph for an introduction to Wallace Stevens. Since the publication of *The Auroras of Autumn* in 1950, his poetry has increasingly received due recognition as one of the great achievements of our time, a vast theater, running through endless transformations of setting and mood, in which the life of the mind, caught in its double fate of self and world, is the constant theme of the drama. This is a poetry of the most lavish variety and the most profound unity, of the most baffling obscurity and the most immediate power. The critic intent upon clarifying the obscurity must remember that the mysteries of the power are equally his concern.

The variety of the poems is apparent. They range in length from two lines to thirty-odd pages, taking the form of aphorisms, images, soliloquies, dialogues, anecdotes, parables, myths, invocations, lectures, pedagogical treatises, logical demonstrations. They are built of every sort of language, from the most common monosyllables to an arcane verbiage

[1] References giving page number only are to the *Collected Poems*. References to *Opus Posthumous* are preceded by *O.P.*

which sends the reader repeatedly to the dictionary, and frequently in vain. They freely use and discard such devices as metaphor and simile, rhetorical repetition and balance, meter, rhyme, patterns of consonant and vowel sounds. They are peopled by a host of characters, many nameless, others having such fictional, historical, or fabricated names as Peter Quince, Lady Lowzen, St. Ursula, Sister Eulalia, Redwood Roamer, Professor Eucalyptus, Mrs. Pappadopoulos, Nanzia Nunzio, Ulysses, Ercole, Liadoff, the Canon Aspirin.

Beneath this surface variety it is important to discover the limitations of Stevens' theater, limitations not of its immediately perceptible characters or settings, but of the human experience represented by them. Throughout the poems we find portrayed, directly or indirectly, the inner life of one man, a man characterized not merely by the content of his thought, but by his temperament and manners, by the range and occasions of his emotions, and by the ethical quality of his acts. He can be understood from the poems alone—they imply him as he implies them—and he is in that sense a fictional being; if I call him "Stevens" rather than "the Stevens of the poetry," I do not mean to imply that what is true of him is necessarily true of Stevens the insurance executive. To identify and describe this "man number one,"

> To lay his brain upon the board
> And pick the acrid colors out, . . .
>
> To strike his living hi and ho,
> To tick it, tock it, turn it true, (p. 166)

is an important part of the business at hand.

We find him dominated by two powerful and contending temperamental strains. His is a mind on the one hand fastidious and skeptical, a prey to restlessness, contemptuous of the esthetically vulgar and the intellectually pretentious. This is the Stevens of "The Poems of Our Climate," who recognizes in himself an "evilly compounded, vital I," a "never-resting mind" which must vent its bitterness in "flawed words" (pp. 193-194). Yet this same mind is constantly driven to find a possible basis for affirmation and acceptance, longs constantly for a "douce campagna" in which it can remain and be at peace. This is the Stevens of "The Solitude of Cataracts," who wants "his heart to stop beating and his mind to rest/In a permanent realization" (p. 425). The poetry of Wallace Stevens is the record of a lifelong attempt to discover what must be rejected and what can be affirmed. From *Harmonium* to the last short poems of *Opus Posthumous,* we see the possibility of affirmation becoming more and more a certainty.

An important manifestation of the skeptical strain, early made explicit, is the rejection of revealed religion. Systematic philosophy, too, is rejected insofar as it claims to arrive, through reason and logic, at a truth which must thenceforth be accepted as "the truth." For Stevens, truth is identified with one's own experience, and experience with one's state of consciousness at a given time. Experience does of course stem in part from a world external to and independent of the self but this world cannot be known as something apart from one's present awareness of it; it must remain forever the sum of perception and appearance. "Things seen are things as seen" (*O.P.*, p. 162).

It is of the utmost importance for Stevens to clear away all that intervenes between the perceiving mind and the world as presently perceived: "We fling ourselves, constantly longing, on this form" (p. 470). Thus Stevens, in contrast to the Yeats of "Sailing to Byzantium," can find neither consolation nor enlightenment in "studying/Monuments of [the soul's] own magnificence." Indeed, the monuments, all that may be called the authorized version of cultural history, are an active threat to the mind seeking to relate itself to the world of the present. Even though it is no longer believed in, the ancient myth of the sun-god may interpose itself between us and the sun, and the names and legends of the constellations may similarly obscure the stars. "The solar chariot is junk" (p. 332) and must be discarded. Language itself, in that it embodies the perceptions of the past in fossilized form, can take on this sinister aspect, hindering rather than furthering the vital activities of consciousness. In the opening section of "Extracts from Addresses to the Academy of Fine Ideas," the speaker is oppressed by a sort of claustrophobia of words, the real landscape of sea, sky, and mountains having been in effect papered over by stock descriptive terms:

> The sea is so many written words; the sky
> Is blue, clear, cloudy, high, dark, wide and round;
> The mountains inscribe themselves upon the walls.   (p. 252)

The past as foisted upon the present is suffocating and stultifying; our veneration of it is the object of Stevens' constant and endlessly resourceful attack. It is labeled "history," "doctrine," "definitions," "the rotted names"; it is a garbage dump, a junk shop, a theater beaten in by a tempest in which the audience continues to sit; it is the second-rate statuary on savings banks, the equestrian statues in public squares, the vested interests of the academies and the museums. To rid one's mind of it is "freedom," a redeeming "ignorance," "salvation," "health."

> The integrations of the past are like
> A *Museo Olimpico,* so much
> So little, our affair, which is the affair

> Of the possible: seemings that are to be,
> Seemings that it is possible may be.   (p. 342)

One must disassociate oneself even from the minds of one's contemporaries insofar as they carry the past into the present. It is Crispin's purpose in "The Comedian as the Letter C"

> to drive away
> The shadow of his fellows from the skies,
> And, from their stale intelligence released,
> To make a new intelligence prevail.   (p. 37)

The search for a truth acceptable in the present is equally impeded by the human craving for happiness, that "habit of wishing" which generates consoling falsehoods and leads us to take refuge from the tragedy of reality in sentimentalism. The concepts of a beneficent providence and of a personal life after death have their origins in this weakness; the truth is, as Stevens expresses it in "Sunday Morning," that we live in an "island solitude, unsponsored" in the vastness of space. Each human being is caught in a machine of constant operation, borne onward by the process of physical aging toward a total oblivion which is the last consequence of

> the unalterable necessity
> Of being this unalterable animal.   (p. 324)

The world is indifferent to our desires; beyond the consoling warmth of the summer sky there is "a barer sky that does not bend" (p. 108). Summer gives way to winter, youth to age, life to death, and peace to the ten-thousandfold catastrophe of war. To desire personal gratification in such a world is a kind of moral bad taste:

> *Encore un instant de bonheur.* The words
> Are a woman's words, unlikely to satisfy
> The taste of even a country connoisseur.   (p. 157)

We have already heard these "woman's words" in "Sunday Morning":

> She says, "But in contentment I still feel
> The need of some imperishable bliss."   (p. 68)

Stevens rejects Christianity as much on moral and emotional as on intellectual grounds, as is apparent in "Esthétique du Mal":

> The fault lies with an over-human god,
> Who by sympathy has made himself a man
> And is not to be distinguished, when we cry
>
> Because we suffer. . . .
>
> A too, too human god, self-pity's kin
> And uncourageous genesis.   (p. 315)

Throughout his poems there are flashes of contempt for the sentimental clinging to the past which vitiates our consciousness of the present:

> The sad smell of the lilacs—one remembered it,
> Not as the fragrance of Persephone,
> Nor of a widow Dooley,
> But as of an exhumation returned to earth,
>
> The rich earth, of its own self made rich,
> Fertile of its own leaves and days and wars.   (p. 491)

The stock subject matter of compassion is deliberately mocked:

> Beggars dropping to sleep,
> They pose themselves and their rags.
> Shucks. . . .   (p. 198)

Even the sacred subject matter of patriotism may be casually handled, with shocking effect:

> The paratroopers fall and as they fall
> They mow the lawn.   (p. 322)

These passages reveal an austerity of temper which is essential in Stevens. His is a poetry to which we can look neither for vicarious expression of the sufferings and yearnings of our daily existence, nor for escape from them on any but the highest plane. His earliest volume, *Harmonium*, includes in "Le Monocle de mon Oncle" a dismissal of sexual passion as a subject for public utterance:

> When amorists grow bald, then amours shrink
> Into the compass and curriculum
> Of introspective exiles, lecturing.
> It is a theme for Hyacinth alone.   (p. 15)

That is to say, it is a theme suitable only for the young and beautiful. The Stevens of "Le Monocle" is already forty; his attainment of the meridian of life is accompanied by a full and bitter realization of the effects of time upon himself and the woman he has loved. This bitterness frequently contorts the language of the poem into obscurity, yet nowhere in English is there a more vivid and searing expression of the humiliation of the aging body and the mind's attendant foreboding of death and decay:

> Our bloom is gone. We are the fruit thereof.
> Two golden gourds distended on our vines, . . .
> Distorted by hale fatness, turned grotesque.
> We hang like warty squashes, streaked and rayed,
> The laughing sky will see the two of us
> Washed into rinds by rotting winter rains.   (p. 16)

The situation dramatized in "Le Monocle" does not reappear in Stevens' poetry, from which, indeed, the personal plaint, whether erotic or elegiac, is almost totally absent. Even "Peter Quince at the Clavier," whose speaker is "here in this room, desiring you" (p. 90), is a meditation on desire and not an expression of it, just as "Another Weeping Woman" (p. 25) is a meditation on the grief in bereavement of an unnamed third person. The emotional range of Stevens' poetry excludes the obsessive horror at his own impending physical corruption of a Dylan Thomas, the frustrated lust and rage of the aging Yeats, the insistent eroticism of Whitman, reaching from the page for his reader's hand. Despite the frequently cited sun-as-Whitman passage of "Like Decorations in a Nigger Cemetery" (p. 150), and despite certain similarities in thought, the difference in temperament between the two is crucial. If the climate of Stevens' poetry demands a strength of mind which must occasionally flag, that of Whitman's has a lushness which ultimately surfeits.

The act of the mind, as we witness it in Stevens' poetry, becomes a way of life, in the sense of a deliberate and systematic control over one's emotional preoccupations. Insofar as this act involves a refusal to harp on personal pain, it has strength and nobility; our recognition of these qualities is an important part of our response to Stevens. For all his rejection of religious dogma, he too exhorts us to forsake the false happiness of this world and lay up our treasures where moth and rust cannot consume, nor thieves break in and steal. We are invited to participate in a kind of secular asceticism—one which, it must be admitted, allows for such refined pleasures as are epitomized by "Lobster Bombay with mango chutney" (p. 401) or a mango dressed with "white wine, sugar and lime juice" (p. 286). Its aim, like that of religious asceticism, is the achievement of a happiness invulnerable to the ravages of time, to personal tragedy, and the world-catastrophe of war.

The mind transcending personal tragedy, characteristically projected into the third person, is the dramatic subject of "World without Peculiarity" (pp. 453-454). The unnamed "he" of the poem has lost his father in death; he is afflicted by the contrast between the present physical image of his mother and what she was; he finds the woman he touches physically unresponsive. Reconciliation is possible insofar as he is able to widen the scope of his emotions, seeking satisfaction not from the "peculiarity" of his relationships to a few other human beings, but from his identity with the physical world to which he and all other human beings belong. He has willfully estranged himself from this true "mother" in denying it his love and refusing to seek knowledge of it. "He is the inhuman son and she,/She is the fateful mother whom he does not know." He thus resembles the infantile old men of "Questions Are Remarks" (pp. 462-463), who look at the earth and ask "Mother, my mother, who are you?" During the times when he can free himself from these limitations, he becomes truly human and the "difference" between himself and his world—i.e., his "peculiarity"—disappears.

An important part of our impression of what is characteristic in any poet is our sense of a certain degree of distance between him, as he appears in his works, and us as readers. In Stevens, we are made aware of a deliberate impersonality, a refusal to use the poem as a vehicle for the direct outpouring of emotion. This impersonality impresses us not as the bloodlessness of a shallow temperament, but as restraint, the reserve of a man who will accept us as fellows in a communal intellectual enterprise but has no interest in making us his confidants. The personal feelings of such a man are judged the deeper for the infrequency of their expression; in Stevens their expression is both rare and memorable. One thinks of the processional passage, beginning "Softly let all true sympathizers come," of "Esthétique du Mal":

> Within what we permit
> Within the actual, the warm, the near,
> So great a unity, that it is bliss,
> Ties us to those we love. . . .
>
> Be near me, come closer, touch my hand, phrases
> Compounded of dear relation, spoken twice,
> Once by the lips, once by the services
> Of central sense, these minutiae mean more
> Than clouds, benevolences, distant heads. (p. 317)

It is this same restrained and profound tenderness that suffuses "To an Old Philosopher in Rome."

Sexual passion is of course not excluded from the subject matter of Stevens' poetry. But almost invariably the physical relationship symbolizes the relationship between the world and the imagination, between "male reality/And . . . that other and her desire" (*O.P.,* p. 99). This is the subject of "The Hand as a Being," "The World as Meditation," and that "mystic marriage in Catawba/Between a great captain and the maiden Bawda" of "Notes toward a Supreme Fiction." On the literal level, the emotions which are an implicit part of the poet's experience and memory appear unexpectedly to enhance the power of a descriptive passage, as in "Prologues to What Is Possible":

> A flick added to what was real and its vocabulary, . . .
> The way the earliest single light in the evening sky, in spring,
> Creates a fresh universe out of nothingness by adding itself,
> The way a look or a touch reveals its unexpected magnitudes,   (p. 517)

and in "The Bouquet":

> A pack of cards is falling toward the floor.
> The sun is secretly shining on a wall.
> One remembers a woman standing in such a dress.   (p. 450)

I have said that of the two contending strains in Stevens' temperament, it is the drive toward affirmation and acceptance that ultimately prevails. Refusal to venerate the stale past, rejection of the consolations of wishful thinking and sentimentalism—these are steps toward a state of "exactest poverty" in which all the false wealth of the spirit has been cast away. "Stanzas of final peace/Lie in the heart's residuum . . . Amen" (p. 258). Upon this poverty is predicated "the imagination's new beginning,"

> the yes of the realist spoken because he must
> Say yes, spoken because under every no
> Lay a passion for yes that had never been broken.   (p. 320)

Although the grand design posited by religion no longer commands acceptance, the mind's desire for order and meaningfulness in its world remains and must be satisfied. A new order must be discovered and affirmed, a valid order having its sources in man himself and the reality of his experience. In it the "crude collops" of being, once united as proceeding from a supernatural Author of all things, will again come together, and as an integral part of this order man will find his place under the sun.

The constant attempt to piece the world together in Stevens' poetry takes many forms. It may be represented as a process of induction, the accumulation of exact particulars of knowledge from which the mind can generalize, so that they become "a pack on a giant's back" (*O.P.*, p. 103). It may be represented as a metaphor or analogy, an affirmation of intuited resemblance. It may be represented as synecdoche, in which contemplation of the part leads to an apprehension of the whole, as when a lemon stands for the relationship between all visual objects and the eye. It may take the form of a fiction, an all-inclusive mythic vision of a "green queen" of the landscape, a "giant of the weather," a "glass man" or gigantic shadow-shell of ice or air who becomes a spokesman for the imaginative power of all men of a certain time. We believe in these fictions not as we formerly believed in the persons and events of the Christian myth, but with "the nicer knowledge of/Belief, that what it believes in is not true" (p. 332).

The affirmed order must be valid, stripped of habitual and sentimental falsification; its discovery presupposes "the naked man in a state of fact" (p. 263). But the mind is an essential part of that reality in which order is to be found. A resemblance, like any other relationship, is an aspect not merely of things-in-themselves; it is also a perception, and as such stems from an observing intelligence. It is impossible to conceive of a resemblance apart from the judgment that a resemblance is present. In "The Idea of Order at Key West," the woman who personifies the idea of order sings "beyond the genius of the sea" (p. 128)—i.e. the sea without human spectators. Here, as frequently in Stevens, order is symbolized by language, which is sound given intelligible form. The singer utters the sea "word by word," transforming its inarticulate cry, its "dark voice," into the rhythmic and expressive language of the "maker" or poet. The resultant order is founded on reality, expressive of "the veritable ocean," but it is equally the creation of the "single artificer" who makes the world in which she sings.

An early version of "the imagination's new beginning" as it searches for a truth to replace the discarded truth of religion appears in "Sunday Morning," notably in two passages which have often been superficially read. In the first of these, the speaker of the poem imagines for the meditating woman an alternative to that "divinity" of "silent shadows" to which she has for the moment committed her thoughts:

> Divinity must live within herself:
> Passions of rain, or moods in falling snow;
> Grievings in loneliness, or unsubdued
> Elations when the forest blooms; gusty
> Emotions on wet roads on autumn nights;
> All pleasures and all pains, remembering
> The bough of summer and the winter branch.
> These are the measures destined for her soul.   (p. 67)

Stevens' adoption in this poem of the cadence and idiom of Tennysonian and late nineteenth century verse, for all his mastery in the handling of it, has proved an invitation to misunderstanding. It is easy to be lulled by the music of the words, the imagery of misty fields, silken weavings, and plucked lutes, the "whence" and "whither" and other instances of archaic-biblical diction, into reading the above-quoted passage as an invitation to escape from present reality into a poetic never-never land of refined sensations and beautiful emotions. But the satisfactions outlined are not escapist; they are positive and of the present moment, disciplinary "measures" whose aim is to restore health to the mind, to bring it about that our blood shall not fail. The woman is exhorted to practice a complete identification of the self with the natural landscape in its seasonal changes. She is to experience "passions" not "in rain" but "of rain," directly reflecting and in a sense consisting of the weather itself. Her "moods" of winter will similarly be both occasioned and defined by watching the snow as it falls. Her curriculum emphasizes grief as much as joy, and it is to be pursued in solitude, "within herself," "in loneliness." Her "elations" or liftings-up of the heart will have their sufficient cause in the upward surge of life in the spring trees. The wording of the last item in the series, "gusty/Emotions on wet roads on autumn nights," is especially significant. So closely here is emotion united with landscape that it can be described only by an adjective properly belonging to the landscape itself. The result is metaphor: a perception of relationship which is a valid step toward piecing the world together.

The second passage follows Stevens' famous apothegm "Death is the mother of beauty," and constitutes a gloss upon it.

> Is there no change of death in paradise?
> Does ripe fruit never fall? Or do the boughs
> Hang always heavy in that perfect sky,
> Unchanging, yet so like our perishing earth . . . ?
> Why set the pear upon those river-banks
> Or spice the shores with odors of the plum?
> Alas, that they should wear our colors there,
> The silken weavings of our afternoons,
> And pick the strings of our insipid lutes!
> Death is the mother of beauty, mystical. . . .   (p. 69)

Stevens is expressing here not the cliché that the transient things of earth become more precious, hence more beautiful, as we feel them to be transient, but the profounder idea that all the beauty we as human beings can know is born of the process of change which is one with the process of death. Ripeness itself is beauty in death, the beauty of the fruit that has come to the end of its life upon the bough. It is this same ripeness, in its malign aspect, that portends the rotting away of the fat squashes of "Le Monocle de mon Oncle." Man has never imagined, nor can he imagine, any heaven but his own perishing earth in which all things change and ultimately die. "Alas!" Stevens exclaims, addressing himself ironically to those who look toward the world to come and thus disregard the world around them, "How unfortunate that the landscape of paradise will be only the insipid landscape of earth, which you so despise!" His question, "Do the boughs/Hang always heavy in that perfect sky,/Unchanging," carries a further implication: such a paradise is not desirable —it would be tedious and oppressive. Here in germ is the second major theme, "It Must Change," of "Notes toward a Supreme Fiction."

The mind can find satisfaction only if what it affirms is felt as true, but the truth itself is perpetually changing in both its aspects, the perceiving consciousness and the world as perceived. It is obvious that such conditions of the landscape as the seasons, the weather, and the time of day are important constituents of the minor fictions of Stevens' shorter poems. One thinks of titles like "The Sun this March," "July Mountain," "Last Looks at the Lilacs," "In the Clear Season of Grapes" (this last a title specifying both season and weather), "A Fading of the Sun," and "God Is Good. It Is a Beautiful Night." The setting of "The House Was Quiet and the World Was Calm" is "summer night"; that of "The Dwarf," September; that of "Human Arrangement," "evening rain"; that of "Ghosts as Cocoons," the season when "the grass is in seed" and "the young birds are flying." One is not surprised at Stevens' rhetorical question in "Waving Adieu, Adieu, Adieu":

> What is there here but weather, what spirit
> Have I except it comes from the sun?   (p. 128)

Yet this is also the poet who asks, in "The Man with the Blue Guitar"

> What is there in life except one's ideas,
> Good air, good friend, what is there in life?   (p. 175)

Though the terrestrial cosmos, including man, does ultimately "come from the sun," yet for man the outer fluctuations of weather and season are only half the truth. The other half is the self, and the self has its own cycles, its seasons of high and low vital energy, its weathers of bright and dark. These changing inner conditions are as important in Stevens' poetry as the changing conditions of the external world, but they are not as frequently noted because they remain for the most part implicit. They appear to us as the sense communicated by the successive poems of particular states of being, exact barometric levels of the psyche. These dramatized moods and emotions range from sullen torpidity or fretful dissatisfaction, at one extreme, to visionary exaltation and rapture at the other.

The mind in its lowest state speaks in "Depression before Spring," which opens with the lines

> The cock crows
> But no queen rises.   (p. 63)

Morning comes, but the rising of the sun fails to elicit a responsive sense
of majesty and beauty in the landscape which might be expressed as a
fictive "green queen." The failure is stated—for that day—as final and
categorical; the mind attempts to compensate for it by a flight of rhetoric,
a deliberately fabricated simile which ends in bathos.

> The hair of my blonde
> Is dazzling,
> As the spittle of cows
> Threading the wind.
>
> Ho! Ho!

The speaker's bravado then subsides. He complains that the crow of the
cock has failed to bring the peaceful *rou-cou* of the dove, repeating the
onomatopoeic syllables as a fretful child repeats the name of the thing
it wants and is denied.

Akin to this depression, though less torpid, is the state of spleen in
which, obsessed by all that is distasteful in the surrounding world—the
monotonous, the vulgar, the banal, the pretentious, the sentimental—the
mind lashes out in satire or vents its irritation in flippancy or rudeness.
The language expressing this phase of experience frequently seems designed less to communicate than to baffle and mock; the diction tends to
be quirky and bizarre, the syntax difficult, the imagery fantastic or seemingly nonsensical. One is reminded of Stevens' remark, at the end of "The
Poems of Our Climate,"

> Note that, in this bitterness, delight . . .
> Lies in flawed words and stubborn sounds.   (p. 194)

"Loneliness in Jersey City," for example, opens with the statement that
"the deer and the dachshund are one" (p. 210). We discover that the
speaker is looking out of his hotel window, which is "plenty of window"
for him. From it he sees all too much of a world in which the "Polacks"
drive around in their automobiles, "play concertinas all night," and
"think that things are all right." The grace of the deer and the ungain-
liness of the dachshund are confounded in this world, and its gods reflect
its people. The speaker's comment, "Encore, encore, encore les dieux,"
implies irritation and boredom.

The activity of the mind in this phase is essentially destructive. The
statement in "Loneliness in Jersey City" that "the deer and the dachshund
are one," repeated verbatim three times, expresses a false synthesis which

is not replaced by a true one. In "A High-toned Old Christian Woman," one of Stevens' most brilliant splenetic outbursts, the supernal masque with its setting of "palms,/Squiggling like saxophones" (p. 59) is designed rather as an offense to the woman addressed than as a vision which can in itself be a source of satisfaction.

Such a title as "Depression before Spring" suggests that the speaker's state can be accounted for by the season. But the mind at a higher level of vital energy is able to respond more constructively to essentially the same external conditions. The first two stanzas of "Poesie Abrutie" (p. 302) resemble "Depression before Spring." The speaker looks out at a February landscape which at first appears monotonous and dreary.

> The brooks are bristling in the field,
> Now, brooks are bristling in the fields
> And gelid Januar has gone to hell.

> II

> The water puddles puddles are
> And ice is still in Februar.
> It still is ice in Februar.

Yet the brooks are moving; the ice is partly melted. The imagination here is capable of envisaging the beginning of change:

> III

> The figures of the past go cloaked.
> They walk in mist and rain and snow
> And go, go slowly, but they go.

> IV

> The greenhouse on the village green
> Is brighter than the sun itself.
> Cinerarias have a speaking sheen.

The effectiveness of the last line illustrates Stevens' power to create an image of whatever sort the occasion requires. The metaphor "speaking sheen" successfully conveys the heightened vitality of the speaker's mind at the end of the poem. Like "gusty emotions," it is a constructive metaphor which arises from a true sense of the landscape rather than being foisted upon it like the cows' spittle simile of "Depression before Spring."

In "Poesie Abrutie" we see a change taking place in the speaker's state of consciousness. His mind ceases to be dominated by negative emotions and moves toward satisfaction, affirming a limited but valid relationship among certain parts of its world—in this case the sun, the sunlight reflected on the greenhouse roof, and the sheen on the leaves of the plants within. Such a level of imaginative capability is frequently represented in Stevens' poems. It is characteristically attended by a calm and lucid strength, as distinguished from visionary fervor or exaltation, and the language of the poems portraying it is correspondingly simple and clear. The mind in this phase of experience is the diligent scholar of its world and of itself, absorbed in the disciplines of observation and meditation.

The subject matter of these poems is varied. In "The Snow Man" the speaker studies an adverse landscape of ice and snow with an intense concentration from which all thought of human "misery" is rigorously excluded. The fruit of this study is the perception of a unifying keynote of sound,

> the sound of the wind,
> In the sound of a few leaves,
>
> Which is the sound of the land
> Full of the same wind . . .   (p. 10)

Here the act of the mind takes the form of synecdoche: the valid apprehension of the immediate scene leads to an equally valid apprehension of a larger whole, the speaker's land. "Study of Two Pears" (pp. 196-197), one of the best-known disciplinary poems, is an exercise in visual perception. All senses save sight are excluded; compare the opening of "A Dish of Peaches in Russia" (p. 224), in which the speaker tastes, touches, and smells the peaches. The field of sight itself is rigidly circumscribed; only at the end of the poem, after prolonged study has yielded a sense of the "glistening" and "flowering" of color, is it expanded to include the shadows of the pears and the tablecloth on which they rest. Thoughts of other objects resembling the pears in shape but not identical with them are prohibited, as hindrances to the attainment of an exact knowledge of their appearance. The shadows have no form at all, and therefore no description implying it may be imposed on them; they must be accepted as "blobs."

In other poems, the mind is seen practicing the apprehension of keysounds or other pervasive qualities in such near or remote landscapes as the "place of perpetual undulation" which is the home of the solitaires (p. 60), or that of the river Swatara, "a swarthy presence moving,/Slowly, to the look of a swarthy name" (p. 429). A series of affirmations of relationship may be run through as a pianist practices scales:

> There are men of the East, he said,
> Who are the East.
> There are men of a province
> Who are that province.

> There are men of a valley
> Who are that valley.   (p. 51)

The disciplines of observation and meditation are means toward apprehending an order in which satisfaction can be found. But such apprehensions are not entirely under the control of the will. A sense of order and meaningfulness in existence can descend upon the mind unanticipated, flooding it with joy.

> Some things, niño, some things are like this,
> That instantly and in themselves they are gay
> And you and I are such things, O most miserable. . . .   (p. 248)

In these spontaneous remissions of human misery we experience "a gaiety that is being, not merely knowing." The title of the poem from which the above lines are taken, "Of Bright & Blue Birds & the Gala Sun," suggests that for Stevens, the gaiety of such moments has its source in the external world. Beneficences of weather and season can indeed make us forget the essential tragedy of our condition.

> After a lustre of the moon, we say
> We have not the need of any paradise,
> We have not the need of any seducing hymn.
> It is true. Tonight the lilacs magnify
> The easy passion, the ever-ready love
> Of the lover that lies within us. . . .   (p. 394)

A similar affirmation, "complete in a completed scene" (p. 378), is the theme of "Credences of Summer." But joy may also come to us on a surge of inner vitality, as when

> medium man
> In February hears the imagination's hymns
> And sees its images, its motions
> And multitude of motions
>
> And feels the imagination's mercies.   (p. 439)

The great moments of experience transcend a merely intellectual apprehension of relationships among parts of the world or an order uniting them. In the "gaiety that is being," we see into the life of things, and in response to this vision "the voice that is great within us rises up" (p. 138) and speaks in hieratic accents.

Out of my mind the golden ointment rained,
And my ears made the blowing hymns they heard.   (p. 65)

To express the awakening to full life of both consciousness and landscape,
Stevens uses dramatically appropriate images of motion, breathing,
speech, and the flashing of light. In "Martial Cadenza," for example, the
speaker tells of finding in the evening star a symbol of spiritual triumph
amid the catastrophe of war:

Only this evening I saw it again,
At the beginning of winter, and I walked and talked
Again, and lived and was again, and breathed again
And moved again and flashed again, time flashed again.   (p. 238)

Like other recurrent images in Stevens, the flash of light has multiple
significance. As the highlight seen on an object, it implies the inseparable
unity of the perceiving consciousness and the world as perceived, since it
appears to each man according to his position relative to the object and
the source of light. As the highlight in painting, it is the means by which
the artist expresses the three-dimensional reality of the object on a flat
surface, and can serve as a focal point of composition. As a phenomenon,
the flash of light implies vital motion, either of the object or of the perceiving eye. Finally, the flash of light is an event which, like any other,
comes to an end. The transience of the moment of imaginative triumph
is inevitable in a poet who sees the essential principle of life as change, for
whom the vital power of the mind and the vital presence of reality coexist
in a process of perpetual transformation. The visionary experience, once
it takes place, belongs to the past; it may be renewed but it cannot be
preserved. "The poet speaks the poem as it is,/Not as it was" (p. 473). The
imagination, for Stevens, is a destructive force in that it is constantly
saying farewell to its ideas, abandoning its integrations of a present become the past. In the difficult but important fourth section of "The Pure
Good of Theory," he describes the process whereby the "destroying spiritual" moves perpetually between the parts of its world and the visionary
whole, the alpha and omega of "An Ordinary Evening in New Haven."
Its motive is the need of a definitive union with reality—in Stevens' words,
the need

Of final access to its element—
Of access like the page of a wiggy book,

Touched suddenly by the universal flare
For a moment, a moment in which we read and repeat
The eloquences of light's faculties.   (p. 333)

The experience of revelation is fleeting; it must be sought afresh every day.

> And yet what good were yesterday's devotions?
> I affirm and then at midnight the great cat
> Leaps quickly from the fireside and is gone.   (p. 264)

The poetry of Stevens records from day to day the life of a changing consciousness in a changing world. Because it is a human record, it presents contradictions which cannot be resolved in logical terms. Its inconsistency reflects those fluctuations of inner strength whereby the adversities that depress us at one time exhilarate us at another. But more importantly, it reflects the fact that, while the goal of the mind remains constant, our progress toward it takes different forms according to our inner state or the conditions of the external world. The disciplines of reason and will may be appropriate in the adversities of winter,

> But what are radiant reason and radiant will
> To warblings early in the hilarious trees
> Of summer, the drunken mother?   (p. 124)

The mode of visual perception decreed in "Study of Two Pears" is an expedient, an exercise for a certain time and a certain state of mind. It no more represents Stevens' fixed doctrine than a physician's directions for a regimen of toast and tea. A comparison with "Poem Written at Morning" (p. 219) will help to make the point clear. In this poem, the patient is much stronger; his eye has the freshness of the "morning" of the title, easily taking in "the complete Poussiniana" of a sunny day. In this state, he is able to "paint" a pineapple by metaphor confidently and with success. But it should be noted that the metaphors that occur to him— "the pineapple was a leather fruit. . . . The juice was fragranter/Than wettest cinnamon"—are subtler and more arresting than the resemblances to viols, nudes, and bottles listed in "Study of Two Pears." In giving us a fresh and vivid sense of the pineapple, they demonstrate the potency which is their justification.

In the distinction between that which has its source in creative vitality and that which is merely fabricated, we have the key to an understanding of the contradictory attitudes toward metaphor, images, and rhetoric expressed in Stevens' poems. A typical example is "Add This to Rhetoric" (pp. 198-199). The speaker of this poem rudely derides the "poses" of the landscape as represented by second-rate poets and painters, the trite pathos of "beggars dropping to sleep" in their rags, the trite beauties of pearly clouds in "lavender" moonlight.

> Pfft . . . In the way you speak
> You arrange, the thing is posed,
> What in nature merely grows.

He goes on to reject these outworn images in favor of a new apprehension of reality.

> Tomorrow when the sun,
> For all your images,
> Comes up as the sun, bull fire,
> Your images will have left
> No shadow of themselves.

"Bull fire," of course, is itself an image. Clearly, what Stevens disapprovingly labels "images" in the poem are what he sees as expressions of the deadened consciousness entrapped in the stale past. The following magnificently rhetorical passage, from "Repetitions of a Young Captain," serves as prelude to a similar contradiction:

> A few words, a memorandum voluble
> Of the giant sense, the enormous harnesses
> And writhing wheels of this world's business,
>
> The driver in the wind-blows cracking whips,
> The pulling into the sky and the setting there
> Of the expanses that are mountainous rock and sea;
> And beyond the days, beyond the slow-foot litters
> Of the nights, the actual, universal strength. . . .   (pp. 308-309)

If Stevens now confounds the reader by adding "Without a word of rhetoric—there it is," this is because by "rhetoric" he means language whose elaborations are conventional and contrived. His own description has a power that transcends such "mere rhetoric"; it arises spontaneously from the speaker's "giant sense" of the scene and expresses his oneness with his world. Stevens is here exploiting an ancient device: the master-rhetorician's professed ignorance of his art. In using it, he shows himself the heir of the poetic tradition he revitalizes.

I have attempted in the foregoing pages an account of the range of experience dramatized in Stevens' theater of transformations and of the "man number one" to whom all that experience can directly or indirectly be referred. In the space that remains, it is necessary to give some account of his power as a poet, of the means whereby the fictional experiences of the poems are made to come alive and to remain in our memories. In one sense, this power must be measured by the poems individually, each considered as a separate assault on the stronghold of the reader's intellect and emotions. In this sense, Stevens' achievement is no greater than the best pages of the *Collected Poems.* And it must be admitted that even for the devoted student that volume has its arid stretches, poems or passages which do not of themselves compel a response, or in which obscurity declines into obfuscation. But in another sense, the achievement of the *Collected Poems* is a whole greater than the sum of its parts, an imaginative edifice of interrelated concepts, images, and symbols which acquire a cumulative power as we gain familiarity with them in the course of our reading. To such an edifice the lesser poems, like the *longueurs* of *The Faerie Queene,* make an indispensable contribution.

In Stevens, if in any poet, we see power lavishing itself in change. Persons, settings, and plots are poured forth with unflagging inventiveness in poems that display a Protean diversity of form in all its aspects: meter and rhyme, stanzaic patterns and line length, syntax and word order, diction, imagery and allusion. This virtuosity of technique may be illustrated by a detailed analysis and comparison of "Anything Is Beautiful If You Say It Is" and "Puella Parvula," two poems which, while alike successful, differ in every conceivable respect. Each is intelligible and effective in itself; each makes use of certain recurring elements of Stevens' poetic vocabulary and can thus be read as part of the larger imaginative edifice of the poetry as a whole.

"Anything Is Beautiful If You Say It Is" (p. 211) falls into two sections, the first concerned with the concubine, the demi-monde, the bees and the parrots, the second with the Johannisberger, Hans. The wording of the opening stanza fools the reader into taking a literary pratfall. The first line, with its setting of blooming honeysuckle, suggests the spring love-lyric of literary tradition. In cadence, "Under the eglantine" resembles Shakespeare's "Under the greenwood tree." In this setting, we encounter the concubine or mistress, who is, however, neither amorous nor coy, but "fretful." (It has been suggested to me that in "the fretful concubine" Stevens may be alluding to the "fretful porpentine" of *Hamlet* I:v, in which case an implication of prickliness is presumably intended.) In the third and fourth lines, all pretense of literary elevation is suddenly discarded as the concubine gives vent to her inelegant exclamations. The effect of absurdity is enhanced by the verb *whispered,* which leads one to expect a tender confidence.

The slangy exclamations of the concubine not only play a stylistic joke on the reader, they also throw into relief the remoteness from actuality of the "eglantine," causing the literary past with which the word is associated to seem faded and artificial. The fretfulness of the concubine seems justified in such a setting. Her reaction is echoed by the "demi-monde," who inhabits an indoor scene suggested by "mezzanine," "chandeliers," and "marblish." This scene aligns itself in artificial elegance with the faded pastoral prettiness of the subverted opening; *mignon*—i.e., "dainty and petite"—must be ironically intended with reference to the "marblish glare" of the chandeliers.

What is notable about the entire first section is its disjointed, fragmentary character. The "Hey-de-i-do!" of the demi-monde breaks in unexpectedly after her "Phooey!" with a strident and false gaiety. From the outdoor setting of the eglantine we move abruptly indoors to the "mezzanine." Then, again abruptly, the scene shifts back to the eglantine, where an unheralded "bee" is now gathering honey, then back to the mezzanine, where we hear the complaints of equally unheralded "parrots." The level of style traces a similar zigzag, from the opening down to the "Phooeys" and then back, in the third stanza, to cadences reminiscent of literary tradition. "From the eglantine-O" suggests such lines as "Green grow the rashes, O!" and "Among the leaves so green, O." In the fourth stanza, there is an effect of strangeness and disparity in the descriptive terms and their application. *Mignon* is a word rarely used in English, and *marblish* is a nonce formation. *Neat* is an odd word of praise for chandeliers, and it does not seem to follow that a "debonair" place would make one "cold."

From this world, where dissatisfaction predominates, we turn to "the Johannisberger, Hans." We notice that his name is contained in the name of his locality, and this at once suggests that he is rooted in, rather than alienated from, his surroundings. The names *Johannisberg* and *Hans* are of German affiliation, and thus contrast with the conspicuously French diction of the first section. In fact, Hans's relationship to his world contrasts in every way with that of the concubine, the demi-monde, and the parrots. Unlike them, he loves the objects that surround him, and he perceives these objects directly and starkly, without intervening literary associations. The use of *metal* as an adjective describing the brightness of the grapes avoids all suggestion of sentimentality (compare "the softly gleaming grapes"). "Metal grapes," "rusty shapes," and "lemon light" are all expressive and potent metaphors. Hans's feeling for his environment is "the very will of the nerves": it includes both sensitivity and deliberate attention, and involves acceptance of what is flawed and ugly. In the last lines of the poem, the concealed rhyme (a favorite trick of Stevens') between *will* and *sill* seems to stand for the latent harmony in an unpromising scene which reveals itself to the attentive observer.

The concubine, demi-monde, and parrots of the first section and the Johannisberger, Hans, of the second, are typical manifestations of Stevens' dramatic inventiveness, through which points of view and states of mind are transformed into fictional beings, and logical relationships into actions. The title of the poem gives us the theme: it is possible to find in whatever is around one a reality which can be felt as beautiful. In the poem we see this state of imaginative capability succeeding a state of frustration. The change is expressed, as in "Mrs. Alfred Uruguay," in terms of a shift from feminine to masculine. The world of the first section is fragmentary and false; it is significant that the word "demi-monde" literally means "half-world" (cf. the "mangled, smutted semi-world" of "Ghosts as Cocoons," p. 119). It is significant too that the light of this half-world is described as a "marblish glare," a harsh and unvarying light which is the opposite of the vital "flash" of reality. The parrot's cries are similarly harsh, and they represent a kind of speech which is mechanical rather than genuinely expressive.

In "Puella Parvula" (p. 456), the mind speaks at the outset in a state of high and triumphant vitality. The setting is autumn, "when the leaves fall like things mournful of the past." In the opening stanza, the end of summer is identified with the geological dissolution of continents and landscapes in images reminiscent of, though not directly allusive to, the Old Testament. But the destructive forces of the natural world, the tempestuous energies of wind and water, are seen here as subject to the greater power of the human imagination. The triumph of this power is dramatized in terms of sound. Over the inarticulate "roaring" and "blaring" of the beasts that symbolize the wind, the "gnashing" of wind-whipped branches, and the inarticulate "declaiming with wide throat" of the "vacant sea," rises the trumpet-voice of the imagination, speaking appropriately in the imperative mode. Its command is addressed to the mind dominated by passionate memory, which is personified as a "wild bitch"—an animal responding senselessly to the fury of the symbolic animals of the preceding stanzas. On behalf of the imagination, the speaker of the poem orders this creature to become human; "Be what he tells you to be: *Puella*." The mind now divides into a feminine and a masculine principle as it becomes receptive to the voice of its own imaginative potency. This voice speaks of destruction, but a destruction which is "composed," given order as a tale of sound and fury signifying not nothing but everything. The final action of the poem is one of reconciliation —"Write *pax* across the window pane"—and courage—"Hear what he says,/The dauntless master." The allusion in *"summarium in excelsis"* to such biblical phrases as "hosanna in excelsis" and "gloria in excelsis" implies that the revealed truth of imaginative vitality can fully compensate for the lost truth of religious revelation.

The student of Stevens will recognize in "Puella Parvula" images he has met in other poems. The threads to be unwoven by the coming of autumn compose the fictive garment of the imagined summer landscape, the dress of "carefulest, commodious weave" which lies cast-off on the floor in "The Beginning" (pp. 427-428) as we hear the first syllables of the tragic speech of autumn. The elephant and the lion appear in Section 1 of "Notes toward a Supreme Fiction" (p. 384) as representatives of

the red blood-world of nonhuman energy and violence which is to be
tamed by the "heroic children" of mankind. The "flame" of the final
stanza is that of "The Auroras of Autumn," the aurora borealis seen by
the meditating "scholar of one candle" from the door of his house (pp.
416-417). And the "dauntless master" whose tale begins at the end of the
poem is a human embodiment of the mythical cosmic imagination of "The
Auroras," the "master seated by the fire" of the sun (p. 414), who "in the
midst of summer stops/To imagine winter."

The triumph of the imagination over the forces of cosmic destruction
in "Puella Parvula" is implicit from the beginning of the poem in the
majesty of its language and the comprehensiveness of its vision. The
formal contrasts with "Anything Is Beautiful If You Say It Is" are instructive. The latter poem is made up of lines of from four to seven
syllables, and there are seven sentences in the first fifteen lines. The word
order is that of prose and everyday speech. The chopping up of the content of the poem into short prosodic and syntactic units is a device of
equal value in the two contrasting sections, contributing to the disjointed
effect of the first and the terseness of the second. In contrast, "Puella
Parvula" is composed of lines of from ten to fifteen syllables; the first
thirteen lines contain only three sentences, of which the third is ten lines
long. The word order shows the inversions characteristic of poetry and
elevated prose, particularly in the third sentence, in which a series of
parallel adverbial phrases precedes the main verb *triumphs*. Against this
long and elaborate *inquit* is deliberately played a succinct and simple
command ending in the startling appellation "O wild bitch." Here, as
throughout both poems, Stevens chooses forms which are appropriate for
the expression of dramatic content, and handles them with technical
mastery.

One of the finest poems of Stevens' last collection, *The Rock*, is his
tribute to George Santayana, "To an Old Philosopher in Rome." Here he
visualizes the philosopher as "on the threshold of heaven" in a city which
is at once real and imagined.

> The threshold, Rome, and that more merciful Rome
> Beyond, the two alike in the make of the mind.   (p. 508)

The clearly perceived objects of the immediate scene,

> The bed, the books, the chair, the moving nuns,
> The candle as it evades the sight,

merge with a sense of the life of the city as the sound of its bells drifts
in through the window. The old philosopher, having arrived at a poetic
vision of reality in which nothing of the poverty of the human condition

is denied, becomes an "orator . . . with an accurate tongue" in whose voice each man can hear his own. His life has taken on "a kind of total grandeur at the end," the "total grandeur of a total edifice."

The achievement of such a "total edifice" is, with characteristic modesty, claimed by Stevens not for himself but for another. His final view of his own achievement is expressed in "The Planet on the Table," whose Ariel is grateful that his poems possessed

> Some affluence, if only half-perceived,
> In the poverty of their words,
> Of the planet of which they were part,   (p. 533)

and in the second of the "Two Disquisitions that the World Is What You Make It," whose artist leaves to mankind

> only the fragments found in the grass,
> From his project, as finally magnified.   (p. 515)

Even Santayana is on a threshold, and the object of his vision is "the celestial possible." The tribute to his achievement that concludes the poem is expressed in Stevens' favorite mode of the possible actual, the conditional clause in the indicative.

> He stops upon this threshold,
> As if the design of all his words takes form
> And frame from thinking and is realized.

In the world as Stevens imagined it, it is inevitable that the "poem of the whole" or "supreme fiction" to which he refers with increasing frequency in his later volumes should remain forever in process, to be sketched in notes, affirmed of a possible present, predicted of a possible future. "They will get it straight one day at the Sorbonne" (p. 406). Yet the experiences portrayed in his poetry, the day-to-day rejections of the false and affirmations of the true, the recedings and returns of inner vitality, the efforts of the will and the flashes of vision, do in their entirety form such a "total edifice" as Stevens attributed to Santayana, one whose complicate and amassing harmony sounds in *The Collected Poems* and the last short poems of *Opus Posthumous*. In these volumes he continues to read from the purple tabulae of the imagination, and we in our need gather about him like the ghosts of "Large Red Man Reading" as they listened to

> the literal characters, the vatic lines,

> Which in those ears and in those thin, those spended hearts,
> Took on color, took on shape and the size of things as they are,
> And spoke the feeling for them, which was what they had lacked.

Three Academic Pieces: I

by *Wallace Stevens*

The accuracy of accurate letters is an accuracy with respect to the structure of reality.

Thus, if we desire to formulate an accurate theory of poetry, we find it necessary to examine the structure of reality, because reality is the central reference for poetry. By way of accomplishing this, suppose we examine one of the significant components of the structure of reality— that is to say, the resemblance between things.

First, then, as to the resemblance between things in nature, it should be observed that resemblance constitutes a relation between them since, in some sense, all things resemble each other. Take, for example, a beach extending as far as the eye can reach, bordered, on the one hand, by trees and, on the other, by the sea. The sky is cloudless and the sun is red. In what sense do the objects in this scene resemble each other? There is enough green in the sea to relate it to the palms. There is enough of the sky reflected in the water to create a resemblance, in some sense, between them. The sand is yellow between the green and the blue. In short, the light alone creates a unity not only in the recedings of distance, where differences become invisible, but also in the contacts of closer sight. So, too, sufficiently generalized, each man resembles all other men, each woman resembles all other women, this year resembles last year. The beginning of time will, no doubt, resemble the end of time. One world is said to resemble another.

A moment ago the resemblance between things was spoken of as one of the significant components of the structure of reality. It is significant because it creates the relation just described. It binds together. It is the base of appearance. In nature, however, the relation is between two or more of the parts of reality. In metaphor (and this word is used as a symbol for the single aspect of poetry with which we are now concerned —that is to say, the creation of resemblance by the imagination, even though metamorphosis might be a better word)—in metaphor, the resemblance may be, first, between two or more parts of reality; second, between something real and something imagined or, what is the same thing, between something imagined and something real as, for example, between music and whatever may be evoked by it; and, third, between two imagined things as when we say that God is good, since the statement involves a resemblance between two concepts, a concept of God and a concept of goodness.

We are not dealing with identity. Both in nature and in metaphor identity is the vanishing-point of resemblance. After all, if a man's exact double entered a room, seated himself and spoke the words that were in the man's mind, it would remain a resemblance. James Wardrop, in *Signature,* said recently:

> The business of the press is to furnish an indefinite public with a potentially indefinite number of identical texts.

Nature is not mechanical to that extent for all its mornings and evenings, for all its inhabitants of China or India or Russia, for all its waves, or its leaves, or its hands. Its prodigy is not identity but resemblance and its universe of reproduction is not an assembly line but an incessant creation. Because this is so in nature, it is so in metaphor.

Nor are we dealing with imitation. The difference between imitation and resemblance is a nicety. An imitation may be described as an identity manqué. It is artificial. It is not fortuitous as a true metaphor is. If it is an imitation of something in nature, it may even surpass identity and assume a praeter-nature. It may very well escape the derogatory. If it is an imitation of something in metaphor, it is lifeless and that, finally, is what is wrong with it. Resemblance in metaphor is an activity of the imagination; and in metaphor the imagination is life. In Chinese metaphor, there is a group of subjects to which poets used to address themselves, just as early Western painters and etchers used to address themselves to such a subject as the Virgin crowned by Angels. The variations in these themes were not imitations, nor identities, but resemblances.

In reality, there is a level of resemblance, which is the level of nature. In metaphor, there is no such level. If there were it would be the level of resemblance of the imagination, which has no such level. If, to our surprise, we should meet a monsieur who told us that he was from another world, and if he had in fact all the indicia of divinity, the luminous body, the nimbus, the heraldic stigmata, we should recognize him as above the level of nature but not as above the level of the imagination. So, too, if, to our surprise, we should meet one of these morons whose remarks are so conspicuous a part of the folklore of the world of the radio—remarks made without using either the tongue or the brain, spouted much like the spoutings of small whales—we should recognize him as below the level of nature but not as below the level of the imagination. It is not, however, a question of above or below but simply of beyond. Level is an abbre-

viated form of level of resemblance. The statement that the imagination
has no level of resemblance is not to be taken as a statement that the imagination itself has no limits. The imagination is deceptive in this respect.
There is a limit to its power to surpass resemblance and that limit is to
be found in nature. The imagination is able to manipulate nature as by
creating three legs and five arms but it is not able to create a totally new
nature as, for instance, a new element with creatures indigenous thereto,
their costumes and cuisines. Any discussion of level is a discussion of
balance as well. Thus, a false exaggeration is a disturbing of the balance
between reality and the imagination.

Resemblances between one object and another as between one brick
and another, one egg and another, are elementary. There are many objects which in respect to what they suggest resemble other objects and we
may include here, as objects, people. Thus, in addition to the fact that
one man resembles all other men, something about one man may make
him resemble some other particular man and this is true even when the
something about him is detached from him, as his wig. The wig of a particular man reminds us of some other particular man and resembles him.
A strand of a child's hair brings back the whole child and in that way
resembles the child. There must be vast numbers of things within this
category. Apparently objects of sentiment most easily prove the existence
of this kind of resemblance: something in a locket, one's grandfather's
high beaver hat, one's grandmother's hand-woven blankets. One may
find intimations of immortality in an object on the mantelpiece; and
these intimations are as real in the mind in which they occur as the mantelpiece itself. Even if they are only a part of an adult make-believe, the
whole point is that the structure of reality because of the range of resemblances that it contains is measurably an adult make-believe. Perhaps the
whole field of connotation is based on resemblance. Perhaps resemblance
which seems to be related so closely to the imagination is related even
more closely to the intelligence, of which perceptions of resemblance are
effortless accelerations.

What has just been said shows that there are private resemblances. The
resemblance of the baby's shoes to the baby, by suggestion, is likely to be
a resemblance that exists for one or two alone. A public resemblance, by
contrast, like the resemblance of the profile of a mountain to the profile
of General Washington, exists for that great class of people who co-exist
with the great ferns in public gardens, amplified music and minor educa-
tion. What our eyes behold may well be the text of life but one's meditations on the text and the disclosures of these meditations are no less a
part of the structure of reality.

It quite seems as if there is an activity that makes one thing resemble
another (possibly as a phase of the police power of conformity). What the
eye beholds may be the text of life. It is, nevertheless, a text that we do

not write. The eye does not beget in resemblance. It sees. But the mind
begets in resemblance as the painter begets in representation; that is to
say, as the painter makes his world within a world; or as the musician
begets in music, in the obvious small pieces having to do with gardens in
the rain or the fountains of Rome and in the obvious larger pieces having
to do with the sea, Brazilian night or those woods in the neighborhood of
Vienna in which the hunter was accustomed to blow his horn and in
which, also, yesterday, the birds sang preludes to the atom bomb. It is
not difficult, having once predicated such an activity, to attribute it to a
desire for resemblance. What a ghastly situation it would be if the world
of the dead was actually different from the world of the living and, if as
life ends, instead of passing to a former Victorian sphere, we passed into
a land in which none of our problems had been solved, after all, and
nothing resembled anything we have ever known and nothing resembled
anything else in shape, in color, in sound, in look or otherwise. To say
farewell to our generation and to look forward to a continuation in a
Jerusalem of pure surrealism would account for the taste for oblivion.

The study of the activity of resemblance is an approach to the understanding of poetry. Poetry is a satisfying of the desire for resemblance. As
the mere satisfying of a desire, it is pleasurable. But poetry if it did
nothing but satisfy a desire would not rise above the level of many lesser
things. Its singularity is that in the act of satisfying the desire for resemblance it touches the sense of reality, it enhances the sense of reality,
heightens it, intensifies it. If resemblance is described as a partial similarity between two dissimilar things, it complements and reinforces that
which the two dissimilar things have in common. It makes it brilliant.
When the similarity is between things of adequate dignity, the resemblance may be said to transfigure or to sublimate them. Take, for example,
the resemblance between reality and any projection of it in belief or in
metaphor. What is it that these two have in common? Is not the glory
of the idea of any future state a relation between a present and a future
glory? The brilliance of earth is the brilliance of every paradise. However, not all poetry attempts such grandiose transfiguration. Everyone
can call to mind a variety of figures and see clearly how these resemblances
please and why; how inevitably they heighten our sense of reality. The
images in Ecclesiastes:

> Or ever the silver cord be loosed, or the golden bowl be broken, or the
> pitcher be broken at the fountain, or the wheel broken at the cistern—

these images are not the language of reality, they are the symbolic language of metamorphosis, or resemblance, of poetry, but they relate to
reality and they intensify our sense of it and they give us the pleasure of
"lentor and solemnity" in respect to the most commonplace objects. These

images have a special interest, as a group of images in harmony with each other. In both prose and poetry, images come willingly but, usually, although there is a relation between the subject of the images there is no relation between the images themselves. A group of images in harmony with each other would constitute a poem within, or above, a poem. The suggestion sounds euphuistic. If the desire for resemblance is the desire to enjoy reality, it may be no less true that the desire to enjoy reality, an acute enough desire today, is the desire for elegance. Euphuism had its origin in the desire for elegance and it was euphuism that was a reason in the sun for metaphor. A school of literary ascetics denying itself any indulgence in resemblances would, necessarily, fall back on reality and vent all its relish there. The metaphorical school, in the end, does the same thing.

The proliferation of resemblances extends an object. The point at which this process begins, or rather at which this growth begins, is the point at which ambiguity has been reached. The ambiguity that is so favorable to the poetic mind is precisely the ambiguity favorable to resemblance. In this ambiguity, the intensification of reality by resemblance increases realization and this increased realization is pleasurable. It is as if a man who lived indoors should go outdoors on a day of sympathetic weather. His realization of the weather would exceed that of a man who lives outdoors. It might, in fact, be intense enough to convert the real world about him into an imagined world. In short, a sense of reality keen enough to be in excess of the normal sense of reality creates a reality of its own. Here what matters is that the intensification of the sense of reality creates a resemblance: that reality of its own is a reality. This may be going round a circle, first clockwise, then anticlockwise. If the savor of life is the savor of reality, the fact will establish itself whichever way one approaches it.

The relations between the ego and reality must be left largely on the margin. Yet Narcissus did not expect, when he looked in the stream, to find in his hair a serpent coiled to strike, nor, when he looked in his own eyes there, to be met by a look of hate, nor, in general, to discover himself at the center of an inexplicable ugliness from which he would be bound to avert himself. On the contrary, he sought out his image everywhere because it was the principle of his nature to do so and, to go a step beyond that, because it was the principle of his nature, as it is of ours, to expect to find pleasure in what he found. Narcissism, then, involves something beyond the prime sense of the word. It involves, also, this principle, that as we seek out our resemblances we expect to find pleasure in doing so; that is to say, in what we find. So strong is that expectation that we find nothing else. What is true of the observations of ourselves is equally true of the observations of resemblances between other things having no relation to us. We say that the sea, when it expands in a calm and immense reflection of the sky, resembles the sky, and this statement gives us pleasure. We enjoy the resemblance for the same reason that, if it were possible to look into the sea as into glass and if we should do so and suddenly should behold there some extraordinary transfiguration of ourselves, the experience would strike us as one of those amiable revelations that nature occasionally vouchsafes to favorites. So, when we think of arpeggios, we think of opening wings and the effect of the resemblance is pleasurable. When we read Ecclesiastes the effect of the symbols is pleasurable because as symbols they are resemblances and as resemblances they are pleasurable and they are pleasurable because it is a principle of our nature that they should be, the principle being not something derived from Narcissism since Narcissism itself is merely an evidence of the operation of the principle that we expect to find pleasure in resemblances.

We have been trying to get at a truth about poetry, to get at one of the principles that compose the theory of poetry. It comes to this, that poetry is a part of the structure of reality. If this has been demonstrated, it pretty much amounts to saying that the structure of poetry and the structure of reality are one or, in effect, that poetry and reality are one, or should be. This may be less thesis than hypothesis. Yet hypotheses relating to poetry, although they may appear to be very distant illuminations, could be the fires of fate, if rhetoric ever meant anything.

There is a gradus ad Metaphoram. The nature of metaphor is, like the nature of a play, comic, tragic, tragic-comic and so on. It may be poetic. A poetic metaphor—that is to say, a metaphor poetic in a sense more specific than the sense in which poetry and metaphor are one—appears to be poetry at its source. It is. At least it is poetry at one of its sources although not necessarily the most fecundating. But the steps to this particular abstraction, the gradus ad Metaphoram in respect to the general sense in which poetry and metaphor are one, are, like the ascent to any of the abstractions that interest us importantly, an ascent through illusion which gathers round us more closely and thickly, as we might expect it to do, the more we penetrate it.

In the fewest possible words since, as between resemblances, one is always a little more nearly perfect than another and since, from this, it is easy for perfectionism of a sort to evolve, it is not too extravagant to think of resemblances and of the repetitions of resemblances as a source of the ideal. In short, metaphor has its aspect of the ideal. This aspect of it cannot be dismissed merely because we think that we have long since outlived the ideal. The truth is that we are constantly outliving it and yet the ideal itself remains alive with an enormous life.

Walt Whitman and Wallace Stevens:
Functions of a "Literatus"

by Joseph N. Riddel

The influences of Whitman on modern literature have been diverse and, like his nature, contradictory. Almost every American poet has had occasion to pay homage to the gray bard or holy barbarian: for reasons as incommensurable as Ezra Pound's grudging "pact" with the primitive innovator of natural poetic language, or Hart Crane's apostrophe to the cosmic spirit in the "Cape Hatteras" poem of *The Bridge*. Even Wallace Stevens, nurtured by the sophisticated aesthetics of France, has revealed an affinity for Walt's native *élan* if not for the rough-hewn style. Stevens' urbanity has long misled his critics, who hesitate to admit the wisdom of Samuel French Morse's claim ("The Native Element," *Kenyon Review*, 1958) that we must begin with Stevens on this side of the Atlantic and not in France. It is not a little ironical that his debts to the *Symbolistes*—and they are many—have been studied exhaustively to the neglect of his American roots, for Stevens has been an articulate spokesman of the poet's essential identity with his native soil.[1] This connection is not simply nostalgic or sentimental, but is rather basic to his epistemological theory of poetry. Stevens is not an heir of Whitman in the sense, say, of Crane or the more recent Beats; yet he has absorbed his Whitman piecemeal if not swallowed it voraciously. There are revealing identities in their respective aesthetics, and just as revealing contrasts. One might suggest that on points of difference they dramatize a century of change in the American conscience: which might be described here as the movement from so-called cosmic consciousness to an existential consciousness.

"Walt Whitman and Wallace Stevens: Functions of a 'Literatus'" by Joseph N. Riddel. From *The South Atlantic Quarterly*, LXI, No. 4 (Autumn 1962), 506-520. Copyright © 1962 by the Duke University Press. Reprinted by permission of *The South Atlantic Quarterly*.

[1] This essay was written before the appearance of Roy Harvey Pearce's *The Continuity of American Poetry* (Princeton: Princeton University Press, 1961), which placed Stevens clearly and firmly in the American tradition. The reader is referred to that book for a profound, and controversial, treatment of Stevens' relation to and difference from the idealist, egocentric poetry of the Transcendentalists and post-Transcendentalists in particular.

In his only explicit reference to Whitman, Stevens characterizes the American mythmaker as an incarnate cosmic voice, the oracle of vitalism:

> In the far South the sun of autumn is passing
> Like Walt Whitman walking along a ruddy shore.
> He is singing and chanting the things that are part of him,
> The worlds that were and will be, death and day.
> Nothing is final, he chants. No man shall see the end.
> His beard is of fire and his staff is a leaping flame.

Whitman's identification with the sun is derived at once from his poetry and his historical image, as they relate to Stevens' conception of the poet. In Stevens' view of nature, organic rhythm and recurrence enact an order that is the only viable metaphor for the reconciliation of permanence and change. All is process, nothing final, and man's spirit, neither divine nor eternal, does not pass into an Absolute—as Whitman in essence held—but is returned at death with the body's sensorium into the fundamental energy of the cosmos. Nature's economy offers secular comfort, not divine assurance. Man and his world stand in dramatic opposition, not in symbolic embrace, and poetry is the record, his song, of the self-seeking re-union:

> The clouds preceded us
>
> There was a muddy centre before we breathed.
> There was a myth before the myth began,
> Venerable and articulate and complete.
>
> From this the poem springs: that we live in a place
> That is not our own and, much more, not ourselves
> And hard it is in spite of blazoned days.

Whereas Whitman thought of himself as "kosmos," Stevens was always the poet singular. Both celebrated poetry as a reconciliation of opposites and thus an articulated experience of symbolic and ultimately divine import. Their irresolvable difference lies in Stevens' skepticism, which rejects transcendental answers and finds, in sympathy with Santayana, resolution in an aesthetic view of life. Stevens' theory of poetry (and by his claim in the later poems, a "theory of life") is the naturalistic end of Whitman's vision. One might see their conflicting embrace of the prevailing spirit of their times in William James's metaphor as opposed to Emerson's: the self moved to the edge of nature rather than existing at the center.

The most revealing points of reference between Whitman and Stevens are a mutual indifference to traditional disciplines and an unqualified faith in poetry. But Stevens is heir to an age in which Whitman's democratic vistas—both ideal and real—have been sorely abused. In Whitman's grand design, poetry replaces religion as Revelation: "View'd, today, from a point of view sufficiently over-arching, the problem of humanity all over the civilized world is social and religious, and is to be finally met and treated by literature. The priest departs, the divine literatus comes." Literature, indeed, is the "non-subordinated Soul" which leads to the final integrations—a spiritual "Passage to India"—espoused at the end of "Democratic Vistas," where "Man . . . dilates beyond the sensible universe, competes with, outcopes space and time, meditating ever one great idea." And he continues: "Thus . . . does a human being, his spirit, ascend above, and justify, objective Nature, which, probably nothing in itself, is incredibly and divinely serviceable, indispensable, real, here. And as the purport of objective Nature is doubtless folded, hidden, somewhere here . . . it is here the great literature, especially verse, must get its inspiration and throbbing blood." The poet-priest begins with the world's body, reads its symbolic "purport," and from its printed notes sings the secret of the macrocosm. The Soul—he calls it "Santa Spirita" in "Chanting the Square Deific"—binds the metaphysical "solid" of the universe, embracing "all life on earth, touching, including God, including Saviour and Satan,/Ethereal, pervading all. . . ."

For Stevens, little more than half a century later, poetry was no less important, but considerably less transcendental: "In an age of disbelief, or, what is the same thing, in a time that is largely humanistic, in one sense or the other, it is for the poet to supply the satisfactions of belief, in his measure and in his style. . . . I think of it as a role of the utmost seriousness. It is, for one thing, a spiritual role." And in the midst of the 1930's, when polemicists were crying out for social commitment, Stevens could fall back on a poetry of order as the remaining stay against external chaos—moral, spiritual, even social: "Poetry/Exceeding music must take the place/Of empty heaven and its hymns. . . ."

There is, however, caution and reserve in Stevens' hope for poetry: no passage of the finite soul to God, no "Hegelian formulas" as Whitman insisted. Even the grandest designs of the human imagination—its mythologies and religions—are ultimately fictive and profane: ". . . if we are able to see the poet who achieved God and placed Him in His seat in heaven in all His glory, the poet himself, still in the ecstasy of the poem that completely accomplished his purpose, would have seemed, whether young or old . . . a man who needed what he had created, uttering hymns of joy that followed his creation." Stevens' poet exists in a naturalistic world, creating not through Emerson's "transparent eyeball" but with a self-awareness that inverts the creative ratio of God to man.

Here are a few relevant examples of their mutual faith in poetry:

(1) The poet for each is a creative center of vision, cultural prophet, and myth-maker, if not exactly the oracular bard of old. Whitman called him "equable" man, the axis away from whom things were "grotesque,

eccentric," an "arbiter of the diverse," an "equalizer." A "kosmos" containing "multitudes," he is Whitman's image, in sum, of the single man dilating outward from the center, absorbing both sensible and suprasensible universe. For Stevens, on the other hand, he is "central man," yet one of the many foci of reality in a Godless world, the "ultimate Plato" who inverts the master's plan by creating the ideal out of the real. In a phrase, he is the "transparence of the place in which/He is." Like Whitman's poet he is the voice of the "commonal," yet a "comedian" who cannot bring the world "quite round" in his eccentric eye. He is "central" only in the physical world, but without his imaginative perceptions there is no significant reality: there "is nothing until in a single man contained."

(2) Each is fascinated by process. Whitman saw in nature's organic order a dramatization of divine laws, nature always *becoming* in the bosom of the One. Stevens less ethereally found change a primal law working out its own destiny indifferent to man and his search for permanence. Whitman's professed "Materialism" is an adjunct of transcendentalism. Stevens' is a cousin to Santayana's: the material world is not transcended "except in crystal," that is, in the magical (symbolic) order of poetry. The "crystal" is Stevens' symbol for poetry's "transparence," at once abstract and vital: "the more than rational distortion,/The fiction that results from feeling."

(3) Each rejects reason for imagination as a way to truth, but whereas Whitman celebrates the poet's spiritual flights, Stevens can offer only his single vision. Whitman as "kosmos" is at one with nature and sings both its immediate and transcendental truths; Stevens subjectively engages an alien and profane nature, seeking in poetry a satisfaction for man's "rage for order," finding spiritual order, not divine revelation, in a secular imagination.

(4) But most important is their mutual acceptance of evil and death as realities to be engaged by the poet. Their near obsession with death in particular is a most convenient point of departure in any comparative view of their aesthetics.

In section eight of "Passage to India," Whitman announces his primary theme of "Time and Space and Death," an abstract extension of his earlier proclamation in "Starting from Paumanok" that he contained all contradictions:

> Omnes! omnes! let others ignore what they may,
> I make the poem of evil also, I commemorate that part also,
> I am myself just as much evil as good, and my nation is—and I say there is in
> fact no evil. . . .

Evil and death are incipient realities to a "kosmos," parts of immortality, as he says in "Song of Myself":

Has anyone supposed it lucky to be born?
I hasten to inform him or her it is just as lucky to die, and I know it.

I pass death with dying and birth with the new-wash'd babe . . .

This is not sentimental bravado but the egocentric faith of one who "contains multitudes" and reconciles all conflicts. In one of his greatest poems, "When Lilacs Last in the Dooryard Bloom'd," Whitman most fully articulates his eschatological vision. Like Emerson, he finds death resolved in the dialectical union of the many and the One, a truth which comes to him as an epiphany out of nature. In the poem's opening lines, images of process dramatize both increase and dissolution, and the perenially blooming lilacs portend in their intense cycle at once death and "ever-returning spring." The dominant theme, though elegiac, is death itself. "O sane and sacred death," inevitable and disturbing. Thus, Whitman introduces his theme in part as a developing psychological argument, with the recurrent "thought," or acute fear, of death regularly intruding into his vital and harmonious world of sensation. Section eleven presents this tension effectively, as the poet seeks a "perfume," or mystical palliative, to "adorn the burial-house of him I love." What he discovers is a vital life-death continuum in which the commonplace "scenes of life" and "growing spring" provide the mundane complement for death's sublimity.

The poem's recurrent symbols—lilacs, thrush, and western star—enact, each in its special and meaningful way, the cycle of "ever-returning spring," with death in the form of a dark, amorphous "cloud" obtruding incessantly into the forms of life. But at the conclusion, when the poet has read the drama of nature's holiness, the three symbols are "twined" into a total "knowledge" that death leads without contradiction to eternal union. This is the revelation of the climactic fourteenth section, in which the poet discovers that the "cloud" is inevitable in the cosmic sequence, and this "knowledge of death" takes its place by his side, companion with its opposite, the haunting "thought of death." Then only can the thrush, or poetic soul, sing its lambent affirmations: that death is the mysterious juncture in the universal spiral, a *"Dark mother"* from whose womb issues constant rebirth. This is "death's outlet song": within the All death is the essential moment in cosmic passage. The poem, in effect, is one realization of what Whitman later called for in "Democratic Vistas": ". . . great poems of death" which are "poems of the purports of life, not only in itself, but beyond itself." For him, the *"Dark mother"* becomes the essential antithesis of life in the drama of "Hegelian formulas."

The "mother" figure is particularly relevant to Wallace Stevens, who in a time less visionary found death "absolute and without memorial." His most famous poem, "Sunday Morning," is a direct engagement of this spiritual enigma in terms of an unremitting paganism that is neither Whitman's "barbaric yawp" nor his divine vision:

> Death is the mother of beauty; hence from her,
> Alone, shall come fulfilment to our dreams
> And our desires. Although she strews the leaves
> Of sure obliteration on our paths,
> The path sick sorrow took, . . .
> She makes the willow shiver in the sun
> For maidens who were wont to sit and gaze
> Upon the grass, relinquished to their feet.
> She causes boys to pile new plums and pears
> On disregarded plate. The maidens taste
> And stray impassioned in the littering leaves.

The above is the pivotal stanza of an eloquent lyrical "argument" against the consolations of Christianity. The poet, who provides a rhetorical voice for the inner conflicts of his indulgent lady, had previously established the center of reality—both physical and spiritual—within the single self, by abusing her lingering nostalgia for the "holy hush of ancient sacrifice":

> Divinity must live within herself:
> Passions of rain, or moods in falling snow;
> Grievings in loneliness, or unsubdued
> Elations when the forest blooms; gusty
> Emotions on wet roads on autumn nights;
> All pleasures and all pains, remembering
> The bough of summer and the winter branch.
> These are the measures destined for her soul.

The poet dictates an either/or choice for his lady who would have an eternity of pleasures, and in choosing for her sensation necessarily rejects permanence. The primitive cry of resolution in the penultimate stanza cannot but recall Whitman's Adamic devotions to the sun. But the pagan "chant" is ritualized and restrained, and the suppliants yearn for no heavenly diadems:

> Supple and turbulent, a ring of men
> Shall chant in orgy on a summer morn
> Their boisterous devotion to the sun,
> Not as a god, but as a god might be,
> Naked among them, like a savage source.
> Their chant shall be a chant of paradise,
> Out of their blood, returning to the sky . . .
> They shall know well the heavenly fellowship
> Of men that perish and of summer morn.
> And whence they came and whither they shall go
> The dew upon their feet shall manifest.

The poem's final stanza underscores this restraint. By inverting the Christian imagery which haunts the lady's divided conscience in stanza one, the poet adopts Christ as his symbol of mortality and Palestine as the holy land of man's temporal martyrdom. There is no redemption, and we live immediately in the "chaos" of time where pleasure and pain are necessary complements:

> We live in an old chaos of the sun,
> Or old dependency of day and night,
> Or island solitude, unsponsored, free,
> Of that wide water, inescapable.

Isolation is the human condition and death man's lone sponsor. The poem's concluding metaphor, of natural life describing in "Ambiguous undulations" a ritualistic circle around the center of darkness, dramatizes Stevens' basic figure of the relation of life and death: the tension produced by life's vital resistance to the insensible center toward which all mortal things are drawn.

One can skip apace through Stevens' poetry and find the same sense of finality and meaningfulness in death: from the wit of "The Emperor of Ice-Cream" to the farewell utterances of *The Rock*. He used death in the 1930's to mock the promises of idealists and utopians, just as he had excoriated the Christian illusion of "haunted heaven," but the tone is more rhetorical and urgent:

> In a world without heaven to follow, the stops
> Would be endings, more poignant than partings, profounder,
> And that would be saying farewell, repeating farewell,
> Just to be there and just to behold.
> .   .   .   .
> What is there here but weather, what spirit
> Have I except it comes from the sun?

In the 1940's he felt compelled to elaborate an "Esthétique du Mal," premised on the repudiation of all heavens and the embrace of violence, pain, and death as fundamental to life lived in the "physical world." And in one of his very late poems, "The Owl in the Sarcophagus," he toyed with the necessity for a "mythology of modern death," compounded of the knowledge that death is final but that the human sensibility needs mitigations of that knowledge. His "mythology," of course, is the consolations of a poetry which celebrates death as fundamental within our life's rhythms, a final punctuation just as sleep and rest are intermediate punctuations, pauses relative to the sense of rhythm itself. Or in another and more obvious figure, death is the static center around which the motions of life circulate. Both are rather commonplace metaphors, almost rationalizations, but they reduce life's enigma to the simplest level of process and serve Stevens' purpose of elevating life above immortality. If Stevens sings life's vital pulsations, it is not as Whitman did to propound from its rhythms cosmic prophecy.

To the very end of his career, Stevens refused to compromise with sentimental desire, rejecting what he called the spirit's "habit of wishing." He took his position with Santayana, whose intellectual alchemy of materialism and idealism offered the imaginative soul a new dignity in a skeptical age. This is Stevens' eloquent homage to Santayana in his throes, a noble sensibility refusing to defer to the insensible, finding the "afflatus of ruin":

> In the warmth of your bed, at the edge of your chair, alive
> Yet living in two worlds, impenitent
> As to one, and, as to one, most penitent,
> Impatient for the grandeur that you need
>
> In so much misery; and yet finding it
> Only in misery, the afflatus of ruin,
> Profound poetry of the poor and of the dead,
> As in the last drop of the deepest blood,
> As it falls from the heart and lies there to be seen . . .

By his rejection of idealist teleology, Stevens gives death a place in the blood's economy which is closer to Emily Dickinson's poetic vision than to Whitman's. But he shies away from Miss Dickinson's passive faith in immortal rewards. Stevens' reconciliations come not in a vision that outraces the poem, not in Whitman's "Suggestiveness" of transcendental experiences, but in a heightened present where sensation is intensified and formalized by the imagination. For Stevens and Whitman poetry is motivated by a similar feeling of alienation—from nature and God—and for each poetry offers the miraculous reintegrations, however different for each, that once were the office of religion. Thus for each poetry could be and is, in Stevens' words, the "subject of the poem."

The most significant of Whitman's poems about poetry is "Out of the Cradle Endlessly Rocking," which offers his vision of cosmic flow and recurrence as a poetic harmony, to be sung, and thus to be realized, by the "chanter of pains and joys, uniter of here and hereafter," the poet. Following upon a formal introduction of the theme as process and discovery, the second stanza picks up the development proper, with the poet-child moving among fertile "lilac scent" and "Fifth-month grass," discovering two inseparable love birds who symbolize for him the unity and harmony of nature. It is, of course, a child's vision, and the unity he sees is that which Wordsworth attributed to the child, the unmediated vision of innocence. And the birds sing periodically for him their lyric of unity, of *"Two together"* against the diverse elements.

The idyll, it is obvious, cannot last, as the child cannot remain child. And in the subsequent development, the poet's maturity is dramatized in the inevitable split of the harmonious lovers, a symbolic division of the self, of finite self from World Soul, which comes with consciousness of one's alienation from nature and its source. This experienced division, and its attendant pain, is more authentic than Whitman's usually uncritical body-soul identification. The division which comes with loss of innocence not only lends valuable tension to the poem but heightens the urgency of aesthetic reunion, which in the end resolves both poem and man's tragic state. The identification of the poet and the now "lone singer" —the single, mortal bird—is achieved in the poet's sympathetic recognition of loneliness as the mortal's fate:

> He call'd on his mate,
> He pour'd forth the meanings which I of all men know.
>
> Yes my brother I know,
> The rest might not, but I have treasur'd every note. . . .

This especial sympathy parallels the love bird's eloquent lament for his departed love, and the song, translated by the poet, reflects his similar sense of loss. More important is the long central lyric, which radiates outward from nature's primary antinomies—land-sea; day-night; sun-moon —each of which in the eternal flow of things cancels the other. In short, the lyric gives voice to the tragic sense of alienation and isolation to which man in his consciousness of self is heir; yet it intimates in the ceaseless confluence of opposites (the drive of sea into shore or the evolution of night) an innate cosmic unity:

> *Low hangs the moon, it rose late,*
> *It is lagging—O I think it is heavy with love, with love.*
>
> *O madly the sea pushes upon the land,*
> *With love, with love.*

One cannot miss the sexual overtones here; the key to reintegration is "love"—in "Song of Myself" he asserts that a "kelson of the creation is love"—but there is no easy resolution of mortal conflicts in the bird's song. His passionate lyric captures not a vision of eternity but only despair for his lost love. The bird remains, as the poet says in the last section, a "solitary" singer, but the poet intuits the song's wisdom and thus can redeem despair:

> Demon or bird! (said the boy's soul,)
> Is it indeed toward your mate you sing? or is it really to me?
> For I, that was a child, my tongue's use sleeping, now I have heard you,
> Now in a moment I know what I am for, I awake,
> And already a thousand singers, a thousand songs, clearer, louder
>   and more sorrowful than yours,
> A thousand warbling echoes have started to life within me, never to die.

This is the birth of a poet, his assumption of the prophet's mantle, born out of innocence and the rude cognizance that nature's division is prologue to reunion. The drama of the "solitary singer" symbolizes a poet's *rite de passage,* yet a rite unfulfilled. What is missing, of course, is the link of time and eternity, the "clew" to which the unreflective bird is deaf. The poet in his newly found glory, however, can obtain that "clew" in the mystical suggestiveness of the world's flux, the oracular whisper of the ever-drifting sea:

> A word then, (for I will conquer it,)
> The word final, superior to all,
> Subtle, sent up—what is it?—I listen;
> Are you whispering it, and have been all the time, you sea waves?
> Is that it from your liquid rims and wet sands?
>
> Whereto answering, the sea,
> Delaying not, hurrying not,
> Whisper'd me through the night, and very plainly before daybreak,
> Lisp'd to me the low and delicious word death,
> And again death, death, death, death,
> Hissing melodious, neither like the bird nor like my arous'd child's heart,
> But edging near as privately for me rustling at my feet,
> Creeping thence steadily up to my ears and laving me softly all over,
> Death, death, death, death, death.

Just as the wave forced in upon the shore to consummate a universal pact of love and union, so does this "clew" come as a baptismal "laving" in cosmic knowledge. The poet, initiated in the rites of nature's "word," attains a vision of Logos and fulfills Whitman's prophecy of the emerging "literatus." The pain of consciousness which motivates his sense of human finitude and loneliness is absorbed into the All, and the poet's songs, by including death, celebrate at once his alienation from nature and the eternal union toward which all is drifting.

"Out of the Cradle . . ." is, as its opening lines state, a "reminiscence," by which the poet discovers in the cycle of his own being mythic patterns of movement and return which fuse all reality. Integral to reunion is poetry, for alienation is, as it were, the loss of poetic harmony, or a loss of the *sense* of cosmic harmony. Pain and evil and ultimately death lose their intimidating sublimity when seen *sub specie aeternitatis.* Yet the pain of isolation is a prerequisite to poetic vision which, if it overcomes all contradictions, must first experience contradiction.

Stevens shares with Whitman what many critics have been at pains to define as the "American experience," which may be called here, without attempting definition, a search outside tradition for some kind of personal order: moral, spiritual, even aesthetic. Increasing studies of myth and literature focus attention on the search by America's individual talent for a meaning and order invested in our mythic past. Whitman has become, now, one of our myths, just as he embodied the ancient and ageless one of Adamic man. There are vestiges of this in Stevens, but he is sobered by his age and finds in the old conflicts of man and nature not so much a cosmic drama as the universal sanction for poetry. One has only to look at an early programmatic work like "To the One of Fictive Music" to discover his distinctive variation on the theme of man's separation from nature and reconciliation through poetry.

The poem opens with a rather conventional and hortatory invocation to the muse of poetry, divine but "Most near, most clear, and of the clearest bloom." She is strangely like nature, real yet ageless, sensuous yet ideal. But the poet is not concerned with personal epiphany, or with metaphysical revelation. The second stanza is startlingly similar to Whitman's theme, yet characteristically Stevens' in compactness and detached assertion:

> Now, of the music summoned by the birth
> That separates us from the wind and sea
> Yet leaves us in them, until earth becomes,
> By being so much of the things we are,
> Gross effigy and simulacrum, none
> Gives motion to perfection more serene
> Than yours, out of our imperfections wrought,
> More rare, or ever of more kindred air
> In the laborious weaving that you wear.

Here is the man-nature split viewed as the motive for poetry: the happy fall into imperfection which inflames our rage for order. The two remaining stanzas, however, turn metaphysical hypothesis into a theory of poetry. First, human truths like poetic images must spring from things of this world: "That apprehends the most which sees and names,/ . . . an image that is sure." But the final form, poem or vision, must be "not too like" its object:

> . . . not so like to be
> Too near, too clear, saving a little to endow
> Our feigning with the strange unlike, whence springs
> The difference that heavenly pity brings.

All this by way of asking for a return of the "imagination that we spurned and crave" in a world that has forfeited the miraculous subjective powers for the divisive powers of reason. "To the One of Fictive Music" is not Stevens' most engaging or successful poem, but it does offer in capsule his aesthetic and, moreover, relates poetic experience to our very essential life of sensation. Though poetry has its special province and particular qualities apart from other forms of expression, all experience in Stevens' view is incipient poetry, a conviction he never tired of expressing, from "The Comedian as the Letter C" to "An Ordinary Evening in New Haven." Rather than promote a philosophy of nature, Stevens is interested in returning poetry to its spiritual place in the economy of coherent experience, until it becomes inseparable from the life we live among things: "The poem is the cry of its occasion,/Part of the res itself and not about it."

In almost every poem, and particularly those of his later years, it is not so much the engagement of man and world that provides his subject matter as it is the implications of that engagement. His often quoted assertion that "Poetry is the subject of the poem" is not without meaning when seen in the context of his total achievement. Poetry, the mediated product of man's attendance upon his world, is a "reality" in its own right, for "a poet's words are of things that do not exist without the words." It would be incorrect to say that Stevens defines a theory of language, but he everywhere reflects the concern of the symbolist with the magical evocation of words: ". . . said words of the world are the life of the world." Order begins in the word: "In the way you speak/You arrange, the thing is posed,/What in nature merely grows." Such metaphors proliferate in both essays and poetry and suggest an elemental vision by which one can once more like the old Adam possess the world in naming it. The poet at least re-enacts this ritual every time he approaches the mundane with a fresh vision and a refreshing word. If poetry cannot penetrate to Logos, as Whitman believed, it can and does bring order and delight by the very act of renewing our cognizance of the human condition. Far from uniting us with God, it reminds us constantly of man's existential drama. Stevens has stated it very well in one of his last poems, "The Course of a Particular":

> And though one says that one is part of everything,
>
> There is a conflict; there is a resistance involved;
> And being part is an exertion that declines:
> One feels the life of that which gives life as it is.

One feels identity with his world by sensing his separation from it, by feeling the "resistance involved." The final resolution is not transcendence but the insensible blending of man and world in the dark sarcophagus; for Stevens knows that Whitman's "clew" is not the secret of passage but the "final finding." The differing convictions find a way into the very heart of their respective styles. Whitman's prophecy is returned to earth by Stevens, and the self redeemed in its mortality. "Death is the mother of beauty," but the enchanting discovery which emerged from "The Idea of Order at Key West" in mid-career remained the inflexible pivot of his belief:

> She was the single artificer of the world
> In which she sang. And when she sang, the sea,
> Whatever self it had, became the self
> That was her song, for she was the maker. Then we,
> As we beheld her striding there alone,
> Knew that there never was a world for her
> Except the one she sang and, singing, made.

Stevens makes no claims, philosophically or aesthetically, to the sense of cosmic oneness with nature and the universe that informs Whitman's ecstatic flights. The world we sing and make remains momentary and provisional, yet ever-renewable in the ritual of living "as and where we live." Whitman's "literatus" is Platonic, Stevens' Promethean, yet each provides a revealing example of the American poet's ordeal in the chaos of history.

NOTE

The most convenient source for both the poetry and prose of Whitman quoted here is the Rinehart edition of *Leaves of Grass and Selected Prose,* 1891-1892 edition, or Whitman's last supervised edition. It therefore includes the poems as they evolved from first inspiration and recording through the revisions of the more self-conscious "literatus."

The Genre of Wallace Stevens

by Hi Simons

Reviewing *Parts of a World* by Wallace Stevens in the Autumn 1942 issue of *Accent,* Mr. Horace Gregory raised the question: "Is Mr. Stevens a philosopher? Can we hook ladders to his Prester John's balloon with the hope of landing safely on a terrain peopled by Zeno, Plotinus, Socrates, George Santayana, William James, John Dewey and Professor White-head?" Gregory thought not. "I would go further," he wrote, "and insist that Mr. Stevens is not an intellectual, and that the value of his poetry cannot be measured in intellectual terms. . . ."

The same week when that criticism appeared, Mrs. Mary Colum reviewed the same volume in *The New York Times Book Review.* "The mind that the author projects into such careful and measured language," she complained, "is the philosophic speculative mind where the passions are of the intellectual rather than the sensuous order." She quoted as representative a short passage which she doubted had in it "enough sensuous delight to be poetry," and said: "It reads a little like a piece of Thomas Aquinas."

It goes of itself, as the French say, that Gregory and Mrs. Colum cannot both have understood their subject matter correctly and yet have construed it so differently. It is irresistible to try to set one or another, possibly both, of them right. Presumptuous as it will seem, the effort is worth making because it offers an opportunity to define the genre of Stevens' poems, something that has long needed doing.

We cannot argue Mrs. Colum's strictures profitably because she did not give us their basis in reason. Gregory's premises, however, are clear enough. For him, "intellectual poetry" and "philosophical poetry" are interchangeable terms, and he uses "philosophy" in "the sense which implies the creation or the furtherance of a philosophic system." He grants Stevens' poems intelligence and evidences of "a finely tempered and inquiring mind." But he seems not quite to have exhausted those evidences; for the only philosophic substance in Stevens which he discusses is the tendency toward skepticism which he finds in "Sad Strains of a Gay

"The Genre of Wallace Stevens" by Hi Simons. From *The Sewanee Review,* LIII, No. 4 (Autumn 1945), 566-579. Copyright 1945 by The University of the South. Reprinted by permission of *The Sewanee Review* and the estate of Hi Simons.

Waltz" and "Examination of the Hero in a Time of War"—this latter, a poem of affirmation if any such has been written in our distraught times.

Even on his own grounds, we must dispute Gregory's position. Stevens' six books present consistently developing attitudes toward at least four distinctively philosophic subjects; and for those to whom his poetry is worth the effort to comprehend it I list the four themes and, after each one, a few poems that mark the stages of its evolution:

1. The socio-esthetic problem of the relation of the artist to his environment. "The Comedian as the Letter C" (*Harmonium*); "Academic Discourse at Havana" and, by strong implication, "Farewell to Florida" and "Sailing after Lunch" (*Ideas of Order*); "The Man with the Blue Guitar," XII, XV, XVII, and XXVIII; "Of Modern Poetry" (*Parts of a World*), and the fourth poem and the epilogue of *Notes toward a Supreme Fiction*.

2. The esthetic-epistemological problem of the relation of imagination to reality. "Colloquy with a Polish Aunt" and "Another Weeping Woman" (*Harmonium*); "The Idea of Order at Key West" (*Ideas of Order*); parts v and vi of "A Duck for Dinner" (*Owl's Clover*); "The Man with the Blue Guitar," I-IV, XXII, XXIX, and XXXI; "Connoisseur of Chaos" and "Poem with Rhythms" (*Parts of a World*); and the poems on pages 12, 25, 29, 31, and 38-39 of *Notes toward a Supreme Fiction*.

3. The problem of belief, in both its metaphysical and theological aspects. "Sunday Morning" (*Harmonium*); "Sad Strains of a Gay Waltz," "Lions in Sweden," and "Evening without Angels" (*Ideas of Order*); parts ii and v of "The Greenest Continent" (*Owl's Clover*); "The Man with the Blue Guitar," V, XVIII-XXI, and XXIV; "On the Road Home," "The Latest Freed Man," and "Asides on the Oboe" (*Parts of a World*); in general, all of *Notes toward a Supreme Fiction*.

4. In connection with the preceding, a peculiar humanism most recently personified in "the hero" and "the major man." First clearly adumbrated in "A Duck for Dinner" (*Owl's Clover*) and "A Thought Revolved" (*The Man with the Blue Guitar*); the principal subject of "Montrachet-le-Jardin" and "Examination of the Hero in a Time of War" (*Parts of a World*); re-sketched in the poems on pages 17-19 of *Notes toward a Supreme Fiction*.

Any reader who will follow that outline as a guide for his own analysis of Stevens' characteristic preoccupations will conclude, I believe, that he is reading a poet quite as philosophical, in Gregory's sense, as any in our language.

Is it necessary to add that one need not "approve of" Stevens' ideas to recognize them as ideas? One need no more share all his thoughts in order to evaluate justly the independence, constancy, and intensity of ratiocination embodied in his poems, than one must believe in John Donne's theology, ethics, or astronomy to regard him as the classic type of the intellectual poet.

II

Yet if Gregory should ask me pointblank, "Is Stevens, then, a philosopher?" I would answer: "Certainly not—Mrs. Colum to the contrary. He doesn't purport to be one. He is a poet." Of course, he doesn't transport his readers to a terrain peopled by Zeno, or Santayana, or Thomas Aquinas. He keeps them always in the realm of poetry.

This whole question of intellection and poetry was set in an illuminating frame of reference twenty years ago in connection with the revival of interest in Donne. A more realistic conception of the intellectual poet than Gregory's was worked out by Mr. T. S. Eliot in his essay on "The Metaphysical Poets." "In Chapman especially," he found, "there is a direct sensuous apprehension of thought, or a recreation of thought into feeling, which is exactly what we find in Donne." Then, on the contrast between a passage by the elder Herbert and one by Tennyson, he remarked:

> The difference is not a simple difference of degree between poets. It is something which had happened to the mind of England between the time of Donne or Lord Herbert of Cherbury and the time of Tennyson and Browning; it is the difference between the intellectual poet and the reflective poet. Tennyson and Browning are poets, and they think; but they do not feel their thought as immediately as the odour of a rose. A thought to Donne was an experience; it modified his sensibility.

Those phrases so full of insight, "a direct sensuous apprehension of thought, or a re-creation of thought into feeling," precisely define the quality of Stevens' poetry that has confused readers like Mrs. Colum and Gregory. According to Eliot's definition, Stevens is an intellectual poet. For that reason, though "the value of his poetry cannot be measured in intellectual terms" *alone,* neither can it be appreciated without an equal understanding of both its intellectual component and its element of sheer sensibility. Most of those who have written about his work have assumed that he was a lyricist in the nineteenth century tradition. To the contrary, not the least of his distinctions is that he created for himself a genre that was new in its time, except insofar as Ezra Pound and Eliot did likewise: a type of poem that may be called a lyric of ideas, an intellectual lyric. Stevens is one of the originators of the Metaphysical trend in the poetry of our time.

To illustrate that view of his work I should prefer to use his latest book, the *Notes toward a Supreme Fiction.* Instead, I restrict myself to one of the shorter pieces in the volume Gregory and Mrs. Colum reviewed. Any

of fifty poems might be chosen; "Asides on the Oboe" is sufficiently representative.

In our outline, this piece was listed as important in the development of
Stevens' attitude toward the problem of belief. Its thesis is stated in a
short prologue:

> It is a question, now,
> Of final belief. So, say that final belief
> Must be in a fiction.

If men's ultimate beliefs have always been in some fiction or another,
the crisis of faith today may be due to the fact that our traditional myths
have ceased to be credible. Thus, the

> fiction of the wide river in
> An empty land; the gods that Boucher killed;
> And the metal heroes that time granulates—

are all "obsolete." "The wide river in/An empty land" evokes vague
religious associations—the Jordan, the river of light in Dante's paradise,
a stream of spirit fructifying an otherwise desert world. Following the
principle of reading each poem as in the context of its author's work as
a whole, we may recall here "the struggle of the idea of god/And the idea
of man," in "Mystic Garden & Middling Beast." The present poem as-
sumes a need to substitute some "idea of man" for "the idea of god." So
there is presumptive warrant for taking the first of the obsolete fictions
as the common current acceptation of religion. "The gods that Boucher
killed" may be considered to refer to all anthropomorphic mythologies
so familiarized and rationalized since the eighteenth century as to lose
their force as objects of veneration. And I imagine that "the metal heroes
that time granulates" are such ethical absolutes as Stevens satirized in
"Lions in Sweden,"

> those sovereigns of the soul
> And savings banks, Fides, the sculptor's prize,
> All eyes and size, and galled Justitia,
> Trained to poise the tables of the law,
> Patientia forever soothing wounds
> And mighty Fortitudo, frantic bass.

In contrast with those, or whatever other doctrines and deities the
reader may regard as no longer efficacious for belief,

> The philosophers' man still walks in dew,
> Still by the sea-side mutters milky lines
> Concerning an immaculate imagery.

This "philosophers' man" is a personification of "the idea of man," a prototype of Stevens' humanism. The three images by which he is presented—"walks in dew," "milky lines," and "immaculate imagery"—suggest pristine purity and thus emphasize the antithesis that, whereas other fictions of faith are obsolete, this concept is new and unblemished. To say he "still walks in dew" implies that he is in the morning of his career. "The sea-side" may be accepted as mere setting; but the sea as a metaphor for life is one of Stevens' oldest symbols, and the impression we get here is that of a contemplative person dwelling close to the common life of his time yet not engaged in the thick of it. He "mutters milky [sweet and sustaining, as well as fresh] lines/Concerning an immaculate imagery," that is, concerning an inviolate, vital conception of life.

Is the humanistic ideal, then, simply an apotheosis of the poet? Stevens is too realistic to think that. Ever since the winter of 1936-37, when he wrote "The Man with the Blue Guitar," he has held to the idea of total reality as a combination of the reality of things-as-they-are and the reality of imagination. Here, the poet is not to take precedence of ordinary men, but all of us are to live ever more and more by the imagination: as in every humanism, the ideal is not humanity as is, but a regenerated humanity. So,

> If you say on the hautboy man is not enough,
> Can never stand as god, is ever wrong
> In the end, however naked, tall, there is still
> The impossible possible philosophers' man . . .

You may argue skeptically that man as god still remains man, yet there is an *ideal* of humanity to believe in and aspire to. "If you say on the hautboy" means "If you write in your verses" or "If you imagine"; for the oboe is one of many instruments—guitar, harmonium, piano, banjo, an old horn, and so on—in which Stevens has likened poetry and its source, the imagination, to music. "Naked" stands for stripped of superficial falsities; and "tall" is another metaphor, for moral stature or loftiness.

Now, the gist of the concept having been given, further predicates are added. "The impossible possible philosophers' man" is

> The central man, the human globe, responsive
> As a mirror with a voice, the man of glass,
> Who in a million diamonds sums us up.

"Central" as a metaphor for the essence, as distinguished from irrelevant superficialities, of humanity offers no difficulty. The next four images— "globe" (probably light-globe primarily, though spherical map, also, by second intention), "mirror," "glass," and "diamonds"—all suggest bright light, emitted, reflected, or transmitted. Their meaning is summarized in the next line, "He is the transparence of the place in which/He is"; and, lest there be any doubt that the substance of the thought is spiritual insight, we may refer back to "The Greenest Continent," where it is said that, although "The heaven of Europe is empty" now, there was a heaven once

                          in which the mind
        Acquired transparence and beheld itself
        And beheld the source from which transparence came . . .

So the ideal man, embodying the essence of the finest in humanity, possessing especially a capacity for living by the imagination, would be a source of illumination for the rest of us. He would not live aloof, but would be "responsive/As a mirror with a voice." Responsive to our common impulses and aspirations. Like a mirror in reflecting them back, sharpened and clarified. Using his voice to keep before us the "immaculate imagery" of life at its best. In that complex sense, he would be an effulgent "man of glass,/Who in a million diamonds sums us up."

The short second section of the poem, that expresses the satisfaction inspired by belief in this humanistic fiction, scarcely needs such close analysis as what has preceded. Part III applies the conception to events current in the world of things-as-they-are, for "Asides on the Oboe" was written in the summer following the outbreak of the Second World War.

        One year, death and war prevented the jasmine scent
        And the jasmine islands were bloody martyrdoms.

"Jasmine" was chosen, I think, because of its sweetness: death and war expunged the sweetness of life, and the good lands of the earth were turned into places of slaughter.

        How was it then with the central man? Did we
        Find peace? We found the sum of men. We found,
        If we found the central evil, the central good.

We have not *over*-idealized man—we recognize the inexpugnable evil— yet we insist no less on the inherent good.

        We buried the fallen without jasmine crowns.
        There was nothing he did not suffer, no; nor we. . . .

But wherein is the efficacy of a belief so qualified by acknowledgment of its antithesis? Merely in a hope that the good will some day return? No,

> But we and the diamond globe at last were one.
> We had always been partly one. It was as we came
> To see him, that we were wholly one, as we heard
> Him chanting for those buried in their blood,
> In the jasmine haunted forests, that we knew
> The glass man, without external reference.

More clearly than ever before, we see the ideal in its failure. We know it now, not as a figment of speculation, but immediately, as a vital part of ourselves, that has failed through our failure, that must be restored through our reconsecrated belief.

III

Thus, "Asides on the Oboe" yields to (not exorbitantly difficult) analysis a meaning for which "intellectual" is the precise adjective. But the poem is not truly understood when those ideas have been abstracted from it: they must not only be known as ideas but also felt in the terms, the imagery, the *poetry*, in which they are given. Therein are both Gregory and Mrs. Colum confounded. For if ever a piece of writing fulfilled the description, "a direct sensuous apprehension of thought, or a re-creation of thought into feeling," this one does.

Intellectual intensity or, as Professor H. J. C. Grierson put it, a "strain of passionate paradoxical reasoning" is the quality which Donne introduced into English verse; and a similar "blend of argument and imagination" appears in some of the poetry of our time, that of Stevens included. Intensity of thought is evident in "Asides on the Oboe" from two different but, as the poem proves, not incompatible signs. The first is the directness and vigor of the rhetorical movement, and the "simple, sensuous, masculine" diction, especially noticeable in the three-line prologue and in the concluding section:

> How was it then with the central man? Did we
> Find peace? We found the sum of men. We found,
> If we found the central evil, the central good.

No less indicative of passion in reasoning are the richness and deep feeling of the imagery, particularly that in which the idea of "the philosophers' man" is developed and that of "the jasmine haunted forests" of war and death. Passages like those are the expression, not of a mind in which rhetorical figures blur and dispel or replace ideas, but of one to which ideas come in such figures, so that to think them is also to feel them. In *The Donne Tradition,* a brilliant elaboration upon Eliot's essay on the Metaphysicals, Mr. George Williamson says: "This intellectual in-

tensity derives its peculiar power from the unified sensibility which makes
it impossible to isolate the faculties of Donne. . . . His unified sensibility makes his images the very body of his thought, not something added
to it. . . ." Had Williamson been describing Stevens instead of Donne,
he could not have chosen better terms.

Gregory feared for Stevens the danger of "the *reductio ad* whimsy of
his totally serious and critical consideration of the relationship between
two aspects of reality." I imagine such a line as "But we and the diamond
globe at last were one" fairly represents what Gregory objected to as
"stating an intellectual problem in terms of fancy." If so, he would probably find much of Donne and Vaughan, to say nothing of Crashaw,
George Herbert, and Cowley, equally frivolous. For the central images
of "Asides on the Oboe" and of countless others of Stevens' compositions
are conceits quite of the Metaphysical order.

A useful definition of the conceit is, a figure in which two terms of a
comparison meet on limited ground but are otherwise incongruous. The
Metaphysicals used this device functionally, not decoratively. To quote
Williamson again: "The conceit is one of the principal means by which
Donne chained analysis to ecstasy." Exactly so, the figure of "the philosophers' man" and the others connected with it are not whimsies added to
the rational structure of the poem, but the means, and the only means, of
defining and conveying the essential conception. So far as this one poem
is concerned, all we know of "the idea of man" is what that series of
images tells us—and how adequate that is we have seen. Not only does
this conceit serve the author as an instrument of analysis, but we have
been able to analyze its evolution from the simple personification, "the
philosophers' man," to the paradox, "The impossible possible philosophers' man," on through the complex of "central man," "human globe,"
"mirror with a voice," and "man of glass/Who in a million diamonds
sums us up," to the final symbolic paradox, "We and the diamond globe
at last were one." Thus, the conceit is intellectual in intention and in-
tellectual-imaginative in genesis and development. In addition, it performs the important function of investing the poet's thought with the
"sensuous delight" which Mrs. Colum properly demands of poetry yet
apparently fails to recognize sometimes when she has it before her.

Much has been written of Stevens' wit. Too often the word has been
used derogatorily, as if in total ignorance of the great tradition established
by poets who were celebrated in their own day, though subsequently
chided, as wits. At other times the intention behind the term is equivocal,
as when Gregory refers to Stevens' "comic genius," yet leaves the net
impression that he may amuse us as a funny-man but not seriously interest
us as a "philosopher" who might "occupy Bishop Manning's pulpit or
write a supplementary volume to Professor Whitehead's *Reality and
Process.*" (*sic!*)

Stevens *is* a wit (as well as, occasionally, a humorist), and this would suggest that we might understand him the better by studying his work in relation to our leading tradition of poetic wit. In discussing Andrew Marvell, Eliot defined Metaphysical wit as "a tough reasonableness beneath the slight lyric grace." Expanding that idea, Williamson demonstrated the part of reason, first in the evolution of Donne's conceits, then in the construction of his poems: "Nothing is more characteristic of Donne than the way in which thought gives a mathematical basis to the music of his emotions." Hence, the ruggedness of his verse; hence also, in part, the difficulty, the occasional obscurity, of his poems: "It is a result of the reassertion of subject-matter in poetry." If our abstract of the meaning of "Asides on the Oboe" proves anything, it is that intellection provides the whole basis and form for its structure. Similarly, we traced the element of reason in the elaboration of one of its principal conceits. And if this poem is typical of its author's work in confronting the reader with seemingly cryptic obscurities, that is in consequence of what Williamson designates "the astringent effect of intellect on the facility of verse." Stevens' wit, like his rhetoric, is of the same general nature as that of the Metaphysicals. And thus it helps to define his genre: it is the factor of reasonableness underlying the lyric graces of his peculiarly characteristic poem of ideas.

IV

Every poem Stevens has written, not only in his latest period, but since about 1919 when his experimental phase finally issued in the first pieces definitely in his own kind and manner, is susceptible of the same sort of analysis we have applied to "Asides on the Oboe." Most of them disclose a similar content of ideas. The exceptions are pieces like "Variations on a Summer Day" and "The News and the Weather," in which the lyrical component takes precedence of the component of thought. Yet in these as well as the intellectual lyric, the same sensibility is at work, though upon a different kind of subject matter: Stevens' unified sensibility accounts for the singular uniformity of tone that, as many critics have observed, prevails throughout his writing.

All Stevens' poems do not equally exemplify all of Williamson's criteria of Metaphysical poetry. But neither do all those, for example, in Grierson's collection of *Metaphysical Lyrics & Poems of the Seventeenth Century*. As Eliot himself acknowledged, "Not only is it extremely difficult to define metaphysical poetry, but difficult to decide what poets practise it and in which of their verses"—the more one reads of recent criticism of the school of Donne, the more one feels that it applies to Donne but not to any school. Yet we can say of Stevens that each of his mature poems exhibits at least one Metaphysical trait and all Metaphysical characteristics are present somewhere in his work.

I know of no evidence, however, that Stevens has been influenced by Donne and his successors. In associating him with their tradition in order to emphasize his specifically intellectual quality, we should not minimize the differences between him and his distant predecessors in the line. There is, to begin with, a vast divergency of subject matter and of psychology, grounded in all the differences between the epoch that was nearing its end when Donne wrote and the civilization that is committing suicide now. Scarcely less important are the dissimilarities of diction and prosody produced by the social and literary vicissitudes of two centuries. Also, there is a fundamental rhetorical difference, and, since its rhetoric is one of the prime features of the Metaphysical mode, this must be defined.

Contemporary criticism has not yet agreed on a suitable name for the distinctive rhetorical device of contemporary poetry. It is the metaphor rather than the simile, but a peculiar usage of metaphor. The figure is employed not as an embellishment but as the means of discourse, and its communicative possibilities are stretched to the utmost—often, in fact, to the point of obscurity. Sometimes the emotive force of the vehicle, the written word, is stressed; again, the tenor, the idea to be conveyed. In either case, the latter is left to implication, and the distinction between traditional practice and the modern technic lies in the strictness with which that is done.

Stevens was not a master of the rhetoric of implication from the beginning of his career as a publishing poet, but the style by which he is now known was not mature until he had mastered it. "Asides on the Oboe" is as good an example as any of both the technic and the style resultant from it. The metaphor, "the diamond globe," is logically engendered, and explained, by the associated figures that precede it. But "the wide river in/An empty land," "the transparence of the place," and "the jasmine islands" stand as pure metaphors, affording a minimum of support to inference. For the clues to precise interpretation, we must resort to earlier poems treating analogous subject matter. Implication could scarcely be carried further than it is in these figures; and this method of making ideas into images is a basic characteristic of Stevens' art.

I doubt that there is any parallel to that in the practice of Donne and his followers; in the half-dozen volumes of their verse through which I have pursued the question I have not found a single instance of the extreme form of implication peculiar to the more advanced poetry of our time. If we consider the simile broadly, as a comparison in which both terms are given, no matter in what grammatical relationship, that and not the metaphor is the chief rhetorical resource of the Metaphysicals, as of most English poets.

It is generally accepted that what I would call "the radical metaphor" came into American poetry from French Symbolism, partly by direct influence, partly *via* the Imagists. Stevens is one of those who introduced and naturalized it. The combination, an intellectual lyric framed on the

Symbolist principle of implication, is a twentieth century extension of the Metaphysical tradition. No one did more than Wallace Stevens to create it; and no one has done more to manifest its potentialities as an expression of intensely felt thought and a medium of formal elegance. It is his genre.

Metamorphosis in Wallace Stevens

by Sister M. Bernetta Quinn, O.S.F.

What is constant in Wallace Stevens' poetry, as well as in his theory of poetry, is emphasis on change, or—as he expresses the principle with greater nicety in the first of "Three Academic Pieces"—on metamorphosis. He concerns himself first of all with the structure of reality; secondly, with the way in which man knows his world; and finally, with the transfigurations of that world as imagination acts upon it. Each succeeding year of his critical prose and his verse further defines metamorphosis as it functions in the areas of metaphysics, epistemology, and aesthetics, the latter term including life itself considered as the highest of the arts.

A primary aspect of metamorphosis in Stevens is the effect of the senses on extra-mental reality. No one sees quite the same rose as anyone else does; there is, in fact, a semantics of perception, wherein sense "is like a flow of meanings with no speech/And of as many meanings as of men." What connotation is to a word the action of the senses is to a physical object. In "Sombre Figuration" Stevens remarks that reality is that about reality which impresses us: "As a church is a bell and people are an eye,/ A cry, the pallor of a dress, a touch"; such a point of view relates him to impressionistic painting, a kinship made doubly clear by his habit of giving lyrics titles which might equally well apply to pictures ("Study of Two Pears," "Girl in a Nightgown," "Landscape with Boat," "Woman Looking at a Vase of Flowers," "Man Carrying Thing," "Large Red Man Reading," to mention only a few). This variety of synecdoche is a consequence of the selection made by the senses from the ineffably multiple phenomena comprising the flux which overwhelms human consciousness from instant to instant.

In "Bouquet of Roses in Sunlight," Stevens phrases the metamorphosis of perception thus:

"Metamorphosis in Wallace Stevens" by Sister M. Bernetta Quinn, O.S.F. From *The Sewanee Review*, LX, No. 2 (Spring 1952), 230-252. This article appears in a different form in *The Metamorphic Tradition in Modern Poetry*, by Sister M. Bernetta Quinn, Rutgers University Press, 1955. Copyright 1952 by The University of the South. Reprinted by permission of *The Sewanee Review*, Rutgers University Press, and Sister M. Bernetta Quinn.

> Our sense of these things changes and they change,
> Not as in metaphor, but in our sense
> Of them. So sense exceeds all metaphor.
>
> It exceeds the heavy changes of the light.

The "difference that we make in what we see" is more transforming than any rhetoric, so that as one of the three theories propounded in "Metaphors of a Magnifico" suggests, there are as many realities as observers. The word Stevens uses for the difference made by the subject in the object is description, which is "a little different from reality"; it is neither what is described nor an imitation of it, but rather something artificial that exists in no place, only in the spirit's universe, that intangible "locale" of all seeming. This somewhat elusive view of appearance is elaborated upon in the fifth section of "Description without Place": about the restricted meaning he gives to *description,* Stevens here says:

> It is an expectation, a desire,
> A palm that rises up beyond the sea,
>
> A little different from reality:
> The difference that we make in what we see
>
> And our memorials of that difference,
> Sprinklings of bright particulars from the sky.

The term Stevens makes synonymous with such description is *revelation,* the biblical connotations of which he underlines in the sixth part of the poem; there, too, he speaks of description as the double, though not too closely the double, of our lives—artificial, visible, intense.

The fullest illustration of "the difference that we make in what we see" is the early and widely anthologized lyric "Sea Surface Full of Clouds," the various sections of which ring a single setting through five changes. The setting in question is a November seascape near Tehuantepec, at daybreak. Arranged in six tercets, each part of the poem delineates a view of the ocean that reflects the highly colored Mexican sky; Stevens works out his five-paneled picture with exquisite balancing of syntax, delicately adjusted shadings of diction, using for every twelfth line an explanatory sentence in French to indicate how the shifting selves of the observer remodel this "fluent mundo" of sea and cloudy heavens, how in turn they evolve protean cloud-blossoms in marine gardens.

One of the poet's finest accounts of the process of perception is in "Woman Looking at a Vase of Flowers":

> It was as if thunder took form upon
> The piano, that time: the time when the crude

And jealous grandeurs of sun and sky
Scattered themselves in the garden, like
The wind dissolving into birds,
The clouds becoming braided girls. . . .

Hoot, little owl within her, how
High blue became particular
In the leaf and bud and how the red,
Flicked into pieces, points of air,
Became—how the central, essential red
Escaped its large abstraction, became,
First, summer, then a lesser time,
Then the sides of peaches, of dusky pears.

. . . The crude and jealous formlessness
Became the form and the fragrance of things
Without clairvoyance, close to her.

To the subject of the lyric, the bouquet becomes thunder, summer, the
sides of peaches and pears; the abstract red and blue turn into particulars. Colors and shapes powerfully stir the woman; she is conscious
of related impressions, which have a metamorphic nature: "The wind
dissolving into birds,/The clouds becoming braided girls. . . ." These
comparisons point out that the mind as well as the eye has its metamorphoses.

The spectator walking about New Haven on an ordinary evening regards certain chapels and schools as transformed men, openly displaying
in their new identities the secrets they hid while human:

It is as if
Men turning into things, as comedy,
Stood, dressed in antic symbols, to display

The truth about themselves, having lost, as things,
That power to conceal they had as men. . . .

In Ovid's *Metamorphoses* trees frequently are not really trees but victims
of love; stones, rivers, stars, not actually inanimate settings of man's life
but men and women removed to lower realms of existence. Stevens adapts
the principle of mutation to accord with the exigencies of his twentieth
century world by making the buildings of a Connecticut city exterioriza-
tions of its inhabitants, at least in the mind of one beholder.

Besides the transformations effected by perception, things are changed
by the words used to refer to them; nomenclature adds to the image on
the retina, the vibrations on the ear drum. In "Certain Phenomena of
Sound" Sister Eulalia is created of her name, just as is the dark-syllabled
Semiramide:

> You were created of your name, the word
> Is that of which you were the personage.
> There is no life except in the word of it.
> I write Semiramide and in the script
> I am and have a being and play a part.
> You are that white Eulalia of the name.

Earlier in this poem the Roamer, telling to the background of music what things he has seen as he wanders through the redwoods, constructs what he speaks of: "A sound producing the things that are spoken." The same process, creation through music, occurs in "The Auroras of Autumn":

> As if the innocent mother sang in the dark
> Of the room and on an accordion, half-heard,
> Created the time and place in which we breathed. . . .

The subjunctive mode in this poem, and the use of the verb *seem* in "Certain Phenomena of Sound," prevent one from ascribing to Stevens such a thorough-going idealism as might otherwise be warranted by these passages. "A Post-card from the Volcano" declares that what is said about a mansion becomes a part of it. Stevens affirms the same belief in "An Ordinary Evening in New Haven": "The poem is the cry of its occasion,/ Part of the res itself and not about it." These are, perhaps, extreme instances of reification, but they serve to show his conviction that the perceiving agent greatly alters reality.

Some objects, on the other hand, resist the catalysts of language and sense; among these are

> The weight of primary noon,
> The ABC of being,
>
> The ruddy temper, the hammer
> Of red and blue, the hard sound—
> Steel against intimation—the sharp flash,
> The vital, arrogant, fatal, dominant X.

From the testimony of this poem ("The Motive for Metaphor") Stevens apparently considers summer as a fullness of expression too much itself to need or sustain metaphor, unlike the half-seasons of autumn and spring, which some persons prefer to a complete reality. Certain roses in sunlight are

> Too much as they are to be changed by metaphor,
> Too actual, things that in being real
> Make any imaginings of them lesser things.

Although ordinarily man can, at least in theory, make things over, some objects, like the two pears in a lyric from *Parts of a World*, impose their own qualities so violently that they "are not seen/As the observer wills," but as they are. Other examples wherein two forces pull in opposite directions, victory going to the real over the fictive, are the rising sun, calm sea, and moon hanging in the sky of "Notes toward a Supreme Fiction," which Stevens declares "are not things transformed./Yet we are shaken by them as if they were." The perceiving agent is symbolized often by the wind, called Jumbo in the poem of that name, a "companion in nothingness" who although a transformer is himself transformed.

In the poem significantly called "Metamorphosis" the wind plays around with the names of the months, which are as vitally connected with their referents as are the names of characters in a Jonsonian comedy:

> Yillow, yillow, yillow,
> Old worm, my pretty quirk,
> How the wind spells out
> Sep - tem - ber. . . .
>
> Summer is in bones.
> Cock-robin's at Caracas.
> Make o, make o, make o,
> Oto - otu - bre.
>
> And the rude leaves fall.
> The rain falls. The sky
> Falls and lies with the worms.
> The street lamps
>
> Are those that have been hanged,
> Dangling in an illogical
> To and to and fro
> Fro Niz - nil - imbo.

From the very start the wind is shown taking liberties with its autumn world, altering yellow to yillow as illustration of how September leaves lose their clear yellow to the brown stains of decay. Of summer, only the skeleton is left; the robin, symbol of summer, has migrated to Venezuela. At the end of stanza two, the sound of September is distorted by the wind to *Oto - otu - bre;* after evidences of seasonal change the word finally becomes *Niz - nil - imbo,* a blending of *frozen, nil,* and *limbo,* with of course a suggestion also of November. It is no shock to hear that leaves and rain fall, since this is their natural behavior, though the adjective *rude* as a modifier for leaves causes some surprise. But when the sky falls, to lie with the worms, one realizes that a meaningful universe where things happen according to expected patterns has been replaced by a surrealistic one, void of reason, as different as possible from things of August, a world where street lamps are crazily pushed to and fro by the wind, as if they were Villon's hanged men.

The relation of subject to object is a metaphysical problem Stevens likes to meditate upon, as shown by the sixty-page lyric, "An Ordinary Evening in New Haven." In the second section, he supposes that "these houses are composed of ourselves," with the result that New Haven becomes "an impalpable town," its bells, "transparencies of sound"; if this be true, then it follows that New Haven is "So much ourselves, we cannot tell apart/The idea and the bearer-being of the idea." Further on he advises us to consider "Reality as a thing seen by the mind,/Not that which is but that which is apprehended." If these suppositions are valid, man might be regarded as a magician who makes phenomena real. The flowering Judas, dark-spiced branches of trees, cat-bird's gobble are "real only if I make them so." ("Holiday in Reality")

A final step in this tracing of the metamorphoses undergone by the objective world is the way in which a whole age takes character from one powerful figure. The term *Elizabethan* as applicable to the golden period of the sixteenth century is too dulled by use for flaming details of its origin to leap in the minds of average men, but Stevens, with characteristic alertness, looks afresh at the hackneyed phrase *Elizabethan age* and sees Elizabeth as a green queen in a summer of sun, the greenness and sunlight created by her own splendor:

> Her green mind made the world around her green.
> The queen is an example. . . . This green queen
>
> In the seeming of the summer of her sun
> By her own seeming made the summer change.

There are various kinds of queens—red, blue, green, argent—each of whom bestows an identity upon her *milieu*.

Just as metamorphosis links the objective and the subjective worlds, so it connects the realm of reality with the realm of the imagination. In fact these are not two realms at all, but one—the realm of resemblance. Everything in our environment is, in certain respects, like everything else, bound together in an inescapable relationship which is the basis of appearance. In "Three Academic Pieces" Stevens shows how this truth operates by analyzing the colors of a seascape:

> Take, for example, a beach extending as far as the eye can reach bordered, on the one hand, by trees and, on the other, by the sea. The sky is cloudless and the sun is red. In what sense do the objects in this scene resemble each other? There is enough green in the sea to relate it to the palms. There is enough of the sky reflected in the water to create a resemblance, in some sense, between them. The sand is yellow between the green and the blue.

In short, the light alone creates a unity not only in the recedings of distance, where differences become invisible, but also in the contacts of closer sight. So, too, sufficiently generalized, each man resembles all other men, each woman resembles all other women, this year resembles last year. The beginning of time will, no doubt, resemble the end of time. One world is said to resemble another.

It is easy to see how like things resemble each other (man and man, woman and woman, year and year); it is not so easy to apply this principle to dissimilar objects, such as sand and water, palm tree and sky. But Stevens' ingenuity in using color as a bond is persuasive enough to let the illustration stand as a foundation for his aesthetic theory.

Resemblance is omnipresent in Nature; poetry, however, must supply resemblances to its fictions if these are to be truly supreme. Fortunately, it has two ways of doing so denied to Nature, as the essay goes on to explain:

> In metaphor (and this word is used as a symbol for the single aspect of poetry with which we are now concerned, that is to say: the creation of resemblance by the imagination, even though metamorphosis might be a better word)—in metaphor, the resemblance may be, first, between two or more parts of reality; second, between something real and something imagined . . . and, third, between two imagined things.

For the second way, Stevens gives as an example music and that which music evokes in us; for the last he has in mind two abstractions.

The importance of equations in the critical prose of Wallace Stevens can hardly be overstated, a sign of intellectual exactitude found also in the criticism of Ezra Pound; indeed, Pound's Imagist tenets are the equivalent of Stevens' passion for finding metaphors that come ever closer and closer to the ideal resemblance. The first of the "Three Academic Pieces" is rich in equations: accuracy of literature is equated with accuracy of the structure of reality; reality, with the central reference for poetry; the desire for resemblance, with the desire to enjoy reality; and both these with the desire for elegance; false exaggeration, with the disturbance of balance between imagination and reality; life in metaphor, with the imagination. Stevens here discusses six topics: (a) poetry (b) metaphor (c) metamorphosis (d) resemblance (e) partial similarity between two dissimilar things (f) activity of the imagination. If these are considered anonymously, as letters, an analysis of the essay reveals that $a=b=c=d=e=f$. He clarifies his terms carefully, excluding identity and imitation from the meaning of resemblance, and hence from the meaning of five topics synonymous with it, for instance, from metamorphosis.

This is not the only instance in his criticism where Stevens uses metamorphosis and poetry interchangeably. In "Effects of Analogy," delivered at Yale as a Bergen lecture in 1948, he says:

Poetry is almost incredibly one of the effects of analogy. This statement involves much more than the analogy of figures of speech since otherwise poetry would be little more than a trick. But it is almost incredibly the outcome of figures of speech or, what is the same thing, the outcome of the operation of one imagination on another, through the instrumentality of the figures. To identify poetry and metaphor or metamorphosis is merely to abbreviate the last remark.

The same article elucidates an equation even more stimulating than those in "The Realm of Resemblance": the poet's sense of the world=the poet's world=the poet's subject=reality plus imagination. Such meditations in philosophy, carried on with an extraordinary seriousness, make the term hedonist, accorded to Stevens by more than one critic, hardly an appropriate one; they invalidate likewise the view that he is merely a strummer of nuances on a guitar, an exponent of preciosity, a dandy.

Four years before the Bergen lecture on analogy, another Stevens essay, "The Figure of the Youth as Virile Poet," laid the critical foundations for a metamorphic concept of poetry. After reviewing the difficulties of defining poetry, Stevens here remarks that at times we feel confident of reaching a center around which variations of the definition may cluster: "We say that poetry is metamorphosis and we come to see in a few lines descriptive of an eye, a hand, a stick, the essence of the matter." The "matter" which Stevens is referring to here is the *vis* or *noeud vital* which might constitute the center of poetry, discovery of which is a prerequisite for any valid definition. The philosopher, relying only upon reason, can never come to such a definition. Can the poet? Enigmatically, Stevens puts his answer to this question in a suppositional manner, confusing us by his introduction of the indicative form *was* into the conditional clause:

Suppose the poet discovered and had the power thereafter at will and by intelligence to reconstruct us by his transformations. He would also have the power to destroy us. If there was, or if we believed there was, a centre, it would be absurd to fear or to avoid its discovery.

This dangerous nature of poetry finds further articulation in "Poetry Is a Destructive Force":

> That's what misery is,
> Nothing to have at heart.
> It is to have or nothing.
>
> It is a thing to have,
> A lion, an ox in his breast,
> To feel it breathing there.
>
> Corazon, stout dog,
> Young ox, bow-legged bear,
> He tastes its blood, not spit.

He is like a man
In the body of a violent beast.
Its muscles are his own. . . .

The lion sleeps in the sun.
Its nose is on its paws.
It can kill a man.

One might imagine these lines as describing one of Ovid's transformations, since in these, when human beings were made beasts, reason was
always transferred into the body of the irrational creature. The last six
lines might almost apply to Hippomenes in Book Ten of the *Metamorphoses,* when after his successful wooing of Atalanta he meets doom at
the hands of Venus, whose temple he has defiled; he is turned into a lion,
together with his bride, and condemned to roam the Caledonian forest.
Stevens is not content to state that poetry is metamorphosis; he must also
write a poem wherein it shows itself to be so.

There are different degrees of excellence in poetry considered as metamorphosis, depending upon the things compared. To return to "The
Realm of Resemblance," if these are two unlike things of adequate
dignity, the resemblance transfigures, sublimates them. The common
property is made brilliant. When the human mind moves from some
exquisite earthly scene, such as a moonlit evening on a Caribbean island,
to the thought of Paradise, both ideas gain in glory. In such a manner
poetry transfigures, though not always so ambitiously. About this, Stevens
says:

> The images in Ecclesiastes: "Or ever the silver cord be loosed, or the golden
> bowl be broken, or the pitcher be broken at the fountain, or the wheel
> broken at the cistern"—these images are not the language of reality, they are
> the symbolic language of metamorphosis, or resemblance, of poetry, but
> they relate to reality and they intensify our sense of it and they give us
> the pleasure of "lentor and solemnity" in respect to the most commonplace
> objects.

The silver cord, golden bowl, pitcher, and wheel are parts of the tangible
world though used in this passage as symbols to effect metamorphosis or
resemblance or poetry—here Stevens makes no attempt to differentiate
among the three. The destruction of the body, which these represent
figuratively, borrows an imaginative glory from them, just as they, inanimate creatures, acquire a new luster from their association with human
death. Poetry satisfies our desire for resemblance but more than that,
by the activity of the imagination in discovering likeness, it intensifies
reality, enhances it, heightens it.

One more point, in a discussion of how poetry is metamorphosis in the
writing of Wallace Stevens, is that art, by erasing the defects of its

original, results in the ideal, in the universal unlimited by the particular, though drawn from it. In his most complete poetic statement on aesthetics, "Notes toward a Supreme Fiction," which concludes *Transport to Summer*, Stevens presents the poem as transmuting life to Eden-like perfection: "The poem refreshes life so that we share,/For a moment, the first idea. . . ." Later in the same work he rephrases the proposition thus: "The freshness of transformation is/The freshness of a world." Stevens works in the opposite direction from the Platonic theory. For Plato a poetic figure about a plum (A) was a copy of a real plum (B) which might perhaps have a bad spot on its underside and which itself was copied from the perfect plum (C) existing in the world of ideas. For Stevens, C drops out and A is superior to B. He is, indeed, closer to Aristotelian imitation, in spite of his repugnance for the term *imitation* as expressed in "The Realm of Resemblance." To Aristotle mimesis was not a mere copying of the object as it existed in nature; it was a resemblance worked out into perfection in so far as the maker was able to do so. All aspects of the object extraneous to its perfection were eliminated. The supreme fiction must give pleasure, it must change, but it must also be abstract—the Stevensian word for ideal.

One characteristic of the world of Wallace Stevens is the fluidity of essence. Besides the union of opposites in Nature, there is also a mysterious transference of essences. Now that the concept of essence is no longer taken for granted—at least in several schools of modern philosophy—this interference with quiddity requires less suspension of disbelief than it would have in earlier periods. One instance of such mutation occurs in the middle section of "Notes toward a Supreme Fiction": the water of the lake, says the poet, was "Like a momentary color, in which swans/Were seraphs, were saints, were changing essences." In "Variations on a Summer Day," the rocks of the cliffs are heads of dogs that turn into fishes and plunge into the sea; this, of course, happens only in the imagination though the desideratum is "To change nature, not merely to change ideas."

"The Apostrophe to Vincentine" begins with the poet's imagining Vincentine as a small, nude, nameless creature between single-colored earth and dark blue sky; then he actually sees her, and she changes to a warm, clean girl in a whited green dress (green standing as it usually does in Stevens for reality); when she approaches, talking, he adds her emotions to his conception of her, since what others feel makes a difference in what we see:

> And what I knew you felt
> Came then.
> Monotonous earth I saw become
> Illimitable spheres of you,
> And that white animal, so lean,

> Turned Vincentine
> Turned heavenly Vincentine
> And that white animal, so lean,
> Turned heavenly, heavenly Vincentine.

The monotonous earth metamorphoses into illimitable spheres of Vincentine, and she herself has turned from the lean white animal with which the poem started to just the opposite of animality—to *heavenly* Vincentine, the adjective here heightened by repetition and by the ambiguity of its first use. Stevens has meticulously chosen his heroine's name, for reasons of sense as well as of sound, since Vincentine means *conquering;* the word not only serves as a rhyme for *between, lean, clean,* and *green,* but signifies the victory of consciousness over inanimate being.

Still one more illustration of the fluidity of essence is the poem "The House Was Quiet and the World Was Calm," in which "The reader became the book; and summer night/Was like the conscious being of the book," a progression which identifies the reader with the summer night. Again Stevens surprises by using the indicative where accepted grammar would demand the subjunctive, as if to obliterate the distinction between wish and fulfillment; the scholar hears the words of the book spoken "as if there was no book." The poet goes on to say that truth itself is summer, the night, the reader—a blending of essences reminiscent of Eliot's "music heard so deeply that you are the music" in the *Quartets.* The entire lyric is but another phrasing of the exchanges between man and his environment, a topic which Stevens has been experimenting with since the 1917 publication of his play, "Carlos among the Candles." This brief drama opens with the entrance of Carlos, carrying a lighted taper. His first speech includes in embryo all that Stevens has later enunciated on the instability of essence:

> How the solitude of this candle penetrates me! I light a candle in the darkness. It fills the darkness with solitude, which becomes my own. I become a part of the solitude of the candle . . . of the darkness flowing over the house and into it. . . . Just to go through a door, and the change . . . the becoming a part, instantly, of that profounder room . . . equally to feel it communicating, with the same persistency, its own mood, its own influence . . . and there, too, to feel the lesser influences of the shapes of things, of exhalations, sounds. . . .

Whatever the shortcomings of this piece as theater, its epistemological foreshadowings are noteworthy.

To disbelieve in the separateness of things is to court pantheism. Wordsworth, to whom Stevens has been compared, is popularly (whether justifiably so or not) associated with this type of thinking. Amidst the irritations, tedium, and discouragements of life, the desire to become some unsusceptible object is not an uncommon one, the desire to be, for example, a sun-drenched rock on a sweep of Hawaiian beach, a thinking stone soothed by sea-wind and palm-shadows, detached from all burdens of humanity. Such tales as Niobe's are perhaps due to the longing to escape from grief; escapism, incidentally, is a term to which Stevens has never objected. No one can better suggest this imaginary metempsychosis. After commenting on how closely Stevens approaches Romantic pantheism, John Malcolm Brinnin, in his contribution to the Stevens issue of VOICES (Spring 1945), goes on to say: "If it is possible to understand how it feels to be a pear, a green light on the sea, a bowl of flowers, Stevens manages, with necromantic conviction, to say that he does."

Once man understands the nature of his world and of poetry he will, particularly if he is an artist, refashion reality in such a way as to achieve happiness in what will then become a terrestrial paradise. Adam was capable of something close to this:

> His mind made morning,
> As he slept. He woke in a metaphor: this was
> A metamorphosis of paradise,
>
> Malformed, the world was paradise malformed.

According to this view, imaginative activity is a way of rendering man divine, in the sense that he shares God's creative power: the "Pastoral Nun" in the last year of her age feels she has discovered this to be true and that if she lives in harmony with her faith in the oneness of poetry and apotheosis:

> Everything becomes morning, summer, the hero,
> The enraptured woman, the sequestered night,
> The man that suffered, lying there at ease,
>
> Without his envious pain in body, in mind,
> The favorable transformations of the wind
> As of a general being or human universe.

In "The Figure of the Youth as Virile Poet," Stevens also makes poetry synonymous with apotheosis. He characterizes the creative process thus:

The way a poet feels when he is writing, or after he has written a poem that completely accomplishes his purpose is evidence of the personal nature of his activity. To describe it by exaggerating it, he shares the transformation, not to say, apotheosis, accomplished by the poem.

The relevance of this to the Stevensian doctrine of resemblance, or metamorphosis, is obvious. In "A Pastoral Nun" Stevens underlines the connection of poetry, apotheosis, and resemblance by pointing out that the first two resemble each other in that "Each matters only in that which it conceives."

Remolding reality is not confined to men; even a rabbit can create through imagination a more satisfactory world than that of actuality, or so Stevens would convince us in one of his empathetic excursions into other than human consciousness, "A Rabbit as King of the Ghosts." Here the rabbit reduces the cat from a monument to a bug in the grass, little and green, whereas he himself grows to "a self that fills the four corners of the night." Everything in his environment now exists only for him —the trees, the vastness of night; he becomes more and more important in the cosmos until his head rises beyond the atmosphere of earth into space itself. The poem as a whole is a satiric expression of anthropomorphism.

This creative power, this sorcerer's gift capable of producing a terrestrial paradise, does not function automatically; it is an act of will, since imagination is the will of things. Nowhere is the conscious striving to effect a mutation of *milieu* more concretely brought out than in "Human Arrangement": on a rainy evening the speaker projects an imagined wooden chair into the sky, so that it becomes

> . . . the clear-point of an edifice,
>
> Forced up from nothing, evening's chair,
> Blue-strutted curule, true—unreal,
>
> The center of transformations that
> Transform for transformation's self,
>
> In a glitter that is a life, a gold
> That is a being, a will, a fate.

This imaginary chair in the real rainy sky reminds one of Marianne Moore's imaginary gardens with real toads in them and serves much the same purpose in emphasizing the interpenetration of the actual and the fictive in any true work of art.

At the present time, realization of the resources of the imagination is intermittent, confined to "moments of awakening,/Extreme, fortuitous, personal," which correspond to Eliot's intuitional flashes in the *Quartets*. But the day will come when earth will constitute all the heaven that a savage race hungers for, a primal paradise regained through courage. It does not seem to bother Mr. Stevens that he probably will not be around to enjoy it; for him, there is always the solace of the blue guitar. Yet he is not entirely without misgivings in thus fashioning his *Weltanschauung*:

> A little while of Terra Paradise
> I dreamed, of autumn rivers, silvas green,
> Of sanctimonious mountains high in snow,
>
> But in that dream a heavy difference
> Kept waking, and a mournful sense sought out,
> In vain, life's season or death's element.
>
> ("Montrachet-le-Jardin")

In the disorders which war causes, consciousness and fact replace imagination and fiction. War's tremendous impacts, just like the forces of Crispin's sea, cannot be managed:

> We are confronting, therefore, a set of events, not only beyond our power to tranquillize them in the mind, beyond our power to reduce them and metamorphose them, but events that stir the emotions to violence, that engage us in what is direct and immediate and real, and events that involve the concepts and sanctions that are the order of our lives and may involve our very lives; and these events are occurring persistently, with increasing omen, in what may be called our presence.

But metamorphosis, at least in times of peace, rebuilds our universe. Man is indeed the captain of his soul, the master of his fate, though he seldom acts as if he were; if he did, he would achieve freedom, as Stevens declares in "The Latest Freed Man."

The freed man is tired of metaphysics, of trying to explore essences. His desired emancipation is presented thus:

> For a moment on rising, at the edge of the bed, to be,
> To have the ant of the self changed to an ox
> With its organic boomings, to be changed
> From a doctor into an ox, before standing up,
> To know that the change and that the ox-like struggle
> Come from the strength that is the strength of the sun. . . .
> It was how he was free.

"On the Road Home," the next poem in *Parts of a World,* accentuates Stevens' relativism by saying that freedom comes only after man discovers there is no absolute truth. After the denials of the speaker and his companion, the grapes grow fatter, the tree changes from green to blue ("Then the tree, at night, began to change/Smoking through green and smoking blue"), the night becomes warmer, closer. Everything takes on a new plenitude of being, as the six superlative adjectives in the last four lines indicate: *largest, longest, roundest, warmest, closest, strongest.*

Set against the imagination as shaping spirit is the desire of Stevens, expressed with equal vividness, to face things as they are. Indeed, his devotion to things as they are is hard to reconcile with his wish to remold them to what they should be. It may be that these two contradictory views are merely another instance of his Heraclitean opposites which fuse into a third and perfect singular—but on the other hand their incompatibility may constitute a crucial lack of clarity in his aesthetic, though perhaps the clash might better be described as a sign of countries of the mind yet to be explored. Subtle as Stevens' propositions are and admirable as is the intricacy with which he has devised them in over a quarter of a century, there appear to be basic difficulties in his position, which suggest that the center which he seeks is still in the future tense.

On the side of things as they are, Stevens advocates a complete acceptance of the present, not an evasion such as that practiced by the "metamorphorid" Lady Lowzen of "Oak Leaves Are Hands":

> In Hydaspia, by Howzen
> Lived a lady, Lady Lowzen,
> For whom what is was other things.
>
> Flora she was once. She was florid
> A bachelor of feen masquerie,
> Evasive and metamorphorid.
>
> MacMort she had been, ago,
> Twelve-legged in her ancestral hells,
> Weaving and weaving many arms. . . .
>
> So she in Hydaspia created
> Out of the movement of few words
> Flora Lowzen invigorated
>
> Archaic and future happenings,
> In glittering seven-colored changes,
> By Howzen, the chromatic Lowzen.

Under this witty treatment is serious criticism: nothing but the past and the future exists for Lady Lowzen, who is adept at making these come alive and take on shimmering iridescence but who has no distinctive character of her own, as well as no belief in the reality of her Indian (Hydaspia, Howzen) environment. Stevens shows her metamorphorid nature by distorting *Flora* to *florid,* by using the word *bachelor* to keep even her sex from definiteness, by parodying *ancestral halls* to *hells*. As Miss MacMort, Flora had waited, spider-like, preoccupied with the splendid past of her family as symbolized in heraldic designs. A subtle overtone here is the etymology of Flora's maiden name: MacMort, the son (daughter) of death. Now, unsatisfied with being Lady Lowzen, she still dreams of the romantic past and the exciting future, her imagination a prism through which these two tenses pass. In the present she has no interest; her metamorphic powers do not touch it.

The problems raised by conflicting aspects of Stevens' theory of the imagination are not minor ones, though since their solution is "work in progress" one cannot at the present time criticize the theory with any conclusiveness. It would appear to be indisputable, however, that Stevens is a meliorist in the sense that he considers the human race to be moving forward toward a time when the faculties which comprise the psyche will be understood fully and will be used to the maximum of their powers. Then statements about the "change immenser than/A poet's metaphors in which being would/Come true" can be made in the indicative rather than in the subjunctive.

Is such a Utopian position tenable? The philosopher by profession would probably answer that one cannot (and never will be able to) think by imagining, since nothing is more unsuccessful in philosophy than an attempt to obliterate the distinctions between the abstract and the concrete. Poetry, he would say, deals with the concrete, the particular; philosophy, with the abstract, the universal—to which Stevens might reply by quoting from his description of the primitive man, held up as paragon, who "Imagines, and it is true, as if he thought/By imagining, anti-logician, quick/With a logic of transforming certitudes." ("Sombre Figuration") And perhaps the philosopher in refutation might then point to the description of heaven in "Sunday Morning"—an oriental paradise characterized by suspended motion except for the plucking of lutes—as an example of what happens when one demands that the suprasensible be clothed in sensory images. Despite Plato, Lucretius, Santayana, the marriage of poetry and philosophy is ordinarily not a happy one.

However, there is every reason to believe that one of Stevens' delicately testing intelligence will never rest content with his discoveries, whether in aesthetics or metaphysics; his mind is too fine to turn to stone by regarding all questions as answered. Undoubtedly the present stage of inquiry is "a moving contour, a change not quite completed." The spirit of Wallace Stevens is the spirit described in the tenth section of "An Ordinary Evening in New Haven": "It resides/In a permanence composed of impermanence." This is as it should be in one whose thought has metamorphosis at its heart. A mosaic of a man, even a major artist, is like a mosaic of the weather; in the very fluidity of both there is permanence of a sort:

                    See how
        On a day still full of summer, when the leaves
        Appear to sleep within a sleeping air,
        They suddenly fall and the leafless sound of the wind
        Is no longer a sound of summer. So great a change
        Is constant.

                              ("The Statue at the World's End")

Yet, like the weather, a man can only be described from day to day.

A Central Poetry

by C. Roland Wagner

In contemporary poetry it is not the fashion to have a philosophy and to believe in it; a sweeping theoretic vision of life is considered a positive threat to the artistic truthfulness of the sovereign poem. It is a rare pleasure, therefore, to breathe the atmosphere of confidence and wholeness which distinguishes the world of Wallace Stevens. Here, for a change, we are refreshed by certainty without fragmentariness, by joyous possibilities without dishonesty. Here we find a moral and philosophical center through which reality may be repossessed and recreated with each new poetic act. To those who claim that moral order is unnecessary for the making of great poetry, Stevens replies that actual poetry is the embodiment of a theory of poetry, and that a theory of poetry is identical with a theory of life. The moral and theoretic unity of his own poetry is the outcome of the moral and theoretic unity of his beliefs; and so the poetry "helps us to live our lives." The essays collected in *The Necessary Angel,* though at times characteristically elusive and tentative, help us to understand the beliefs. They prove Stevens to be the master of a remarkably precise and clear-sighted doctrine which, over the years, his poetry has been actualizing with increasing assurance.

In "Effects of Analogy" Stevens writes that "The poet is constantly concerned with two theories" of poetry. In the first, the imagination is seen as an absolute power enabling the poet arbitrarily to put reality to his own uses. Sensing that "his imagination is not wholly his own but that it may be part of a much larger, much more potent imagination . . . [the poet] pushes on and lives, or tries to live, as Paul Valéry did, on the verge of consciousness." The "marginal" poetry that results from a surrender to pure imagination, contrasts with the "central" poetry that results, or ought to result, from the second theory. This "relates to the imagination as a power within [the poet] to have such insights into reality as will make it possible for him to be sufficient as a poet in the very center of consciousness." Now the *effect* of Stevens' own poetry on some readers may very well be marginal, over-abstract and, in a sense, even too "mystical";

"A Central Poetry," a review of *The Necessary Angel*, by C. Roland Wagner. From *The Hudson Review*, V, No. 1 (Spring 1952), 144-148. Copyright 1952 by *The Hudson Review*, Inc. Reprinted by permission of *The Hudson Review*.

but its *intention* (and its effect on other readers), though it makes poetic use of the theory of pure imagination, is to contain that purity and "to press away from mysticism toward that ultimate good sense which we term civilization."

Stevens' concern with consciousness places him unmistakably in our time. But his apparent over-concern with consciousness, his incessant and even repetitious celebration of its possibilities, marks him as not wholly of our time. Most modern writers—at least those who, unlike Valéry, aim at the "disclosures of the normal"—admit (though often under protest) ideality and abstraction, but few are willing to withdraw themselves as far as Stevens does. Even Proust, for example, whose vision of art and life is almost identical with Stevens', had the novelist's greater enthusiasm for the dignity of commonplace truth. Certainly everything that happens to Marcel is explicitly a reiterated spiritual joy for the detached narrator, but for the reader that perpetual joy is always enmeshed with concrete experience. Now Stevens is perfectly at home in the world of solids and movables, but his eye, especially in the later poems, is always directed upward to the spiritual flowering of the "never-ending meditation." With the increasing nobility of his old age, he has approached the viewpoint of Proust's liberated narrator, uttering "this endlessly elaborating poem," this "ever-never-changing same," throughout a diversity of particular poetry. Like Proust's Vinteuil, he pronounces with a single unalterable "accent," the crowning "prayer" of personality—"the same prayer, poured forth before different risings of the inward sun." And it is in his recent volumes that we hear Stevens' "accent" in its most virile, almost naked form. To be sure, this favorable estimate of the later phase is not a popular one in some quarters. Mr. Randall Jarrell, for example, regrets that the early sense of "immediacy and precision and particularity, the live touch of things" has been sacrificed to the "elaboration and artifice and contrivance" of the later work. Poetizing, Mr. Jarrell moans, has given way to "philosophizing . . . alas! philosophizing." Well, the critic is free to enjoy what is given to him to enjoy and free to believe that Stevens is a better poet in *Harmonium* than in *Auroras of Autumn;* but if we, like Stevens, care to regard philosophy as something more than the poet's chief occupational hazard, the later central poetry may actually be enjoyed for what it is, a total human response to "the live touch of things."

Stevens' philosophy begins and ends with an acceptance of chaos without submission to chaos. And by chaos I do not mean merely the non-poetic material for poetry. Stevens accepts chaos in the final sense and without evasion—"I name you flatly"; reality has, at bottom, no meaning and no value. It is true, of course, that imagination "perceives the opposite of chaos in chaos," and the resulting imagined reality is also named flatly; but this *valuable* reality—this old world suddenly made new when transformed by the "supreme fiction"—is entirely at the mercy of the reality of chaos. The text of the world in which we read our lives is "A text of intelligent men/At the center of the unintelligible. . . ."

Central poetry is created out of the interweavings of pure imagination and bare reality. To attain this moral (or artistic) synthesis, a series of rejections is necessary. The most important of these is the rejection of traditional religion. This is constantly implied in Stevens, though it is true that he rarely states his lack of belief without some ambiguity, preferring, no doubt, to remain rather "beyond" rejection of a faith to which he extends considerable sympathy. Unlike Kafka, in whose "deliberate exploits of the abnormal" men are everlastingly metamorphosed into cockroaches, Stevens writes of men momentarily metamorphosed into angels. But he does not believe in angels, *necessary* though they may be as symbols for the moral life. When he speaks of God as "this world's capital idea" or declares that "God and the imagination are one," it seems evident that for Stevens God is a being whose essence does not involve His existence. And only a man who has surrendered all residual belief in religion could suppose that poetry and the arts are a genuine alternative to religion, that they offer, "in their measure, a compensation for what has been lost." The "invisible" truths which men have upheld on faith must give way to truths of the "visible" in acts of disciplined imagination: we must believe that "the visible is the equivalent of the invisible." Then the "false imagination" will be destroyed and religion may be judged as we judge poetry: "not so much that it is actually so as that it must be so"—not so much that God actually exists, as that He is a moral necessity based on contingent experience.

But to Stevens the imagination is endangered less by traditional religion than by its three familiar modern detractors—the romantic, the Freudian and the positivist. Here, perhaps because he is rejecting a fundamental moral outlook (rather than literal beliefs), his criticism is more straightforward. The romantic attitude is unsatisfactory, he tells us, since it "belittles" the great power of the imagination. "The imagination is the liberty of the mind. The romantic is a failure to make use of that liberty . . . The achievement of the romantic . . . lies in minor wish-fulfillments and it is incapable of abstraction." It errs, Stevens intimates, through a tendency to identify the ideal life of imagination with the whole life of reality. But the life of imagination is forever *transcending* the reality from which it obtains its life, forever composing and constantly outliving an ideal that is not quite life—"and yet the ideal itself remains alive with an enormous life."

But "if we cleanse the imagination of the taint of the romantic, we still face Freud." Freud discounted the healthy influence of religious illusions in particular, and so implied an unqualified rejection of imaginative illusions in general: "The object of [*The Future of an Illusion*] was to suggest a surrender to reality." Freud looked forward to a primacy of the intelligence in the life of the psyche, but since he admitted that we are now still far from able to live in a state of absolute disillusion, how are we to redeem the time as we await the triumph of the supreme science? —"what have we, if we do not have science, except the imagination?" The rejection of positivism follows. The positivist overlooks the imagination because its existence is not empirically verifiable. He ignores, even more deliberately than Freud, the fact that the imagination is the very instrument of verifiability and must employ illusions for analysis. Both Freud and the positivist fail to realize that consciousness is invincibly imaginative; by discrediting its illusions they tend to reduce consciousness itself to an ethically fruitless entity. Stevens would agree that consciousness (and imagination) is incapable of altering human nature: "Like light, it adds nothing, except itself." But it is precisely this added "nothing," this "savage spirit," which has made all the difference.

A passage from "An Ordinary Evening in New Haven" lays bare the skeleton of Stevens' human philosophy:

> Inescapable romance, inescapable choice
> Of dreams, disillusion as the last illusion,
> Reality as a thing seen by the mind. . . .

Summed up here are Stevens' answers to the four attitudes we have considered. *Religion* calls to us to worship God as the existent ideal: Stevens replies that God is "the supreme poetic idea," the ultimate illusion to which we must come when we have achieved disillusion with respect to all false ideals—when we have made of disillusion our central discipline.[1] The *romantic* ideal offers us complete freedom of the spirit by identifying spirit with the "poem" of reality: Stevens replies simply that "We live in the mind," that reality includes that which is not mind, and that the newly perfected reality which we eventually apprehend is an unreal appearance to the mind. *Freud* advises us to face the grimmest reality grimly unafraid: Stevens replies that reality can be faced truly only when we face it imaginatively; and to face reality imaginatively, or poetically, is to escape it—for "the poetic process is psychologically an escapist process. . . ." The *positivist* holds that the imagination as metaphysics cannot express the *literal* truth about reality; it can only image the emotions of the metaphysician: Stevens observes that "the imagination as metaphysics, from the point of view of the logical positivist, has at least *seeming* values" (italics mine), and that literal truth itself is valueless until, through the imagination, it issues in a concrete seeming for the mind.

---

[1] This could be Stevens' answer to Harcourt-Reilly's observation in *The Cocktail Party:* "Disillusion can become itself an illusion/If we rest in it." For Stevens there is no other place to rest.

Stevens' poetry sets forth his theory of reality and speaks to us of the human need to master reality; and that theory and that need become a theoretic vision for the reader, incarnate, let us say, in "An Ordinary Evening in New Haven." This poem (or even the isolated passage quoted above) is a new object of moral imagination: insofar as it is successful, it confronts reality anew and transcends reality. The spirit is drawn forth and liberated by the moral power of the poetry; so that each initiated reader is like "a man returning from Nowhere to his village . . . which he has come to cherish and wants to be near"—like Marcel returning to Combray after tasting the madeleine dipped in tea. "He sees without images. But is he not seeing a clarified reality of his own?" And is not this clarified reality, suffused with the colors of moral feeling, the end and justification of all art? Is this not the consummation of life itself? It would be tragic, Stevens believes, not to realize the extent of man's dependence on the arts: "The kind of world that might result from too exclusive a dependence on them has been questioned, as if the discipline of the arts was in no sense a moral discipline."

Notes toward a Supreme Fiction:
A Commentary

by Harold Bloom

> . . . to me I feel
> That an internal brightness is vouchsafed
> That must not die, that must not pass away.
> Why does this inward lustre fondly seek
> And gladly blend with outward fellowship?
> Why do *they* shine around me whom I love?
> Why do they teach me, whom I thus revere?
>
> Wordsworth, *The Recluse*

Stevens had the radiant fortune that attends only the great poets: his most ambitious poem is his best. The six hundred and fifty-nine lines of *Notes toward a Supreme Fiction* constitute his central attempt to relieve the imaginative poverty of his time, and they establish him as I think the central poet of that time, bringing to us the consolations of a healing poetic humanism as Wordsworth brought them to his contemporaries. Nothing else in twentieth century poetry written in English matches the magnificence of Stevens' *Notes,* for Stevens has all that Yeats sorely lacked, the wisdom and love whose absence renders the powers of poetry inadequate to the firm dignity of merely natural man. One reads and studies Yeats with growing wonder at the talents that could transform so much that was prose nonsense into genuine poetry, and yet with growing distaste for the vision of man that informs a play like *Purgatory* or a poem like *The Gyres.* One turns with relief to Stevens, whose gifts as a poet were as immense as those of Yeats, but who remained always a man speaking to men, and never sought to become an oracle with mummy truths to tell.

The tentativeness of Stevens' title is neither humility nor irony, for the poem is an attempt at a final belief in a fiction known to be a fiction, in the predicate that there is nothing else. The fiction is broadly poetry itself, and poetry is necessarily the subject of Stevens' poem. The *Notes* move toward the creation of a fictive hero who quite simply will become the real, and thus bring to a climax the whole movement of poetry in the Romantic tradition. In the closing sections of the third part of *Notes*, Stevens is able to gather together, in an astonishing splendor of integration, all the major themes of Romantic poetry, and so brings to a present perfection everything that is most vital in the imaginative legacy of Blake and of Wordsworth.

Notes opens with eight lines of dedication, appropriately celebrating the relationship of loving friendship, for in the mutuality of such confrontation there appear all the characteristics of the Supreme Fiction. The love of friends, as a marriage of reality and the imagination, depends upon an abstraction in Stevens' sense of that word, and clearly is subject to the necessities of change and of pleasure that serve further to define Stevens' version of the Romantic Imagination. The moment of communion caught in the dedication is one of the enlargements of life, bringing a central man into being through two men sitting at rest together, peaceful in a world still undergoing the living change of natural process, yet made vividly transparent by the light of common day.

It Must Be Abstract

Stevens gives the first part of *Notes* the admonitory title *It Must Be Abstract*. Elsewhere in his work the idea of abstraction is what more usually would be called "fabrication." The possible poet has the power to abstract or withdraw himself from outworn conceptualizations of reality, and to live in the world, yet outside the existing conceptions of it, and he can do this only by fabricating his fictions. When these fictions become supreme, in the work of a central poet, a Wordsworth or a Stevens, it is because the abstracted reality has been married to the possible sublimities of the imagination. To follow the poet by so halting a paraphrase leads to another kind of abstracting tendency, from which only the experience of reading his poem can save us. It is because *Notes* creates an extraordinary actuality that the attentive reader is able to capture a state of so being in the poem's presence as to feel that consciousness has taken the place of imagination.

Yet the poem's gift of such consciousness is properly deferred, in the exuberant premise that the reader is a "prodigious scholar" of the imaginative quest, an ephebe entering upon poetic maturity. Even as *The Comedian as the Letter C* mixed the modes of allegorical romance and spiritual autobiography (a thoroughly Romantic mixture) so the *Notes* mixes quest romance with the poetry of vision, again according to Romantic precedent. Stevens presents us with a long poem whose continuity is utterly dependent upon the impatient obsessions of an imagination determined to possess reality without altering it. He therefore declines the normal chronology of quest; the ephebe seeks, does not find, and finds, but all in a simultaneity. Stevens has no truth to make us free except the truths that together define the Supreme Fiction: the truth of separation or withdrawal of the imagination from its worn coverings and reality from its stale disguises; the truth of mutability and natural renewal; and the great truth of *Harmonium,* a humanism of love liberated through pleasure.

It Must Be Abstract begins by adjuring the ephebe to see the sun as it is, without evasion by a single metaphor. Yet the sun, in one of Stevens' most compelling and pervasive metaphors, is identified with man, or rather that brave man, our idea of the sun, is at one with the major abstraction or first idea, our idea of the human. The poet's first abstraction or saving withdrawal of the real from the unreal must be to divest the sun of its mythologies. As a modern humanist the poet begins by a rejection of invisibles: God, "a voluminous master folded in his fire," is dead, and since "the death of one god is the death of all," then "Phoebus is dead, ephebe." What remains is the project which was and is the joint venture of man and the sun, to "be in the difficulty of what it is to be."

The verbal play of the first poem of *It Must Be Abstract* warns the ephebe against taking himself too seriously. This warning is made explicit in the second poem, which deals with the ennui that lurks in our awareness of the first idea. The ravishments of truth are fatal to the truth itself, and a poem seeking to widen consciousness must warn us against self-consciousness. Not to have the first idea is best, for to desire is the only way to know again that we are of the veritable sun, that we possess within us the sublime potential of the central man. The ephebe must begin then with a sense of loss, of poverty, and so throw away the unrealities of unimaginative existence "as morning throws off stale moonlight and shabby sleep."

This much is prologue; with the third poem of *It Must Be Abstract* Stevens touches on greatness as he considers how the poem refreshes life:

> We move between these points:
> From that ever-early candor to its late plural
>
> And the candor of them is the strong exhilaration
> Of what we feel from what we think, of thought
> Beating in the heart, as if blood newly came,
>
> An elixir, an excitation, a pure power.
> The poem, through candor, brings back a power again
> That gives a candid kind to everything.

The belief here is also that of Coleridge and Wordsworth; the rapture, authentic and heartening, is Stevens' own. The gift of candor is evidenced at the start of this poem, with the fine admission that poetry's refreshment of life allows us to "share, for a moment, the first idea." To share, not to appropriate for ourselves, and to confront the redeeming idea of the human only as a brief relational event: Stevens has grasped, with imaginative sureness, the honest despair of Romantic humanism. The ever-early candor is in the nakedness out of which poems or vividly transparent encounters come; the late plural ensues from the imagination's generosity in giving back to us a world of such mixed motion and such imagery that our essential nakedness is clothed by a fictive covering. In a primal chant of exuberant response, Stevens illustrates the candid kind that is the poem's gift:

> We say: At night an Arabian in my room,
> With his damned hoobla-hoobla-hoobla-how,
> Inscribes a primitive astronomy
>
> Across the unscrawled fores the future casts
> And throws his stars around the floor. By day
> The wood-dove used to chant his hoobla-hoo
>
> And still the grossest iridescence of ocean
> Howls hoo and rises and howls hoo and falls.
> Life's nonsense pierces us with strange relation.

One knows, from elsewhere in Stevens, that the wood-dove is the bird who represents "the interior paramour," the Blakean emanation or Shelleyan epipsyche, the Muse the poet creates and loves. Even without such knowledge, this spirited chant declares itself as a manifesto of the imagination, part of the late plural the poem bestows. The Arabian, as much as Wordsworth's Arab in *The Prelude,* is a figure of capable imagination, and his incantation helps save the visionary faculty for the poet, inscribing an order across the uncertainties of futurity, and munificently throwing the excess of his gift at random around the floor. If the wood-dove's chant is no longer present as external reminder of visionary potency to the poet, the ocean remains; and its very inadvertence constitutes another song of fixed accord between reality and imagination. The rise and fall, grossly nonsensical, pierces us to recognition of relationship, teaches us again to separate what we need from what seems to be beyond our need.

Stevens is more adept than most poets at creating a dialectic of distinctions, and proceeds in the next two poems to distinguish such visionary naturalism from any form of pantheism. Sections IV and V of *It Must Be Abstract* are as rigorous as Blake in disengaging the origins of imagination from unredeemed nature. The poem springs from our realization:

> that we live in a place
> That is not our own and, much more, not ourselves
> And hard it is in spite of blazoned days.

Even the first idea, of ourselves as man, was not our own, for "there was a muddy centre before we breathed." The myth of earth precedes the myth of major man, and the painfully thought "I am" of Adam is the muddy precedent to the sophistications of consciousness. Something of progressive alienation between man and earth, already expressed in the absence of the wood-dove's song, is emphasized in the movement from Eve, who "made air the mirror of herself," to ourselves, for whom "the air is not a mirror but bare board."

In Section V the elegant pathos of this alienation is transformed by an extravagance of color into a pitying mockery of minor man, the ephebe as he has become. The lion's roar, elephant's blare, and bear's snarl meet their antithesis in the ephebe's utterance:

> But you, ephebe, look from your attic window,
> Your mansard with a rented piano. You lie
>
> In silence upon your bed. You clutch the corner
> Of the pillow in your hand. You writhe and press
> A bitter utterance from your writhing, dumb,
>
> Yet voluble dumb violence.

With something beyond mere irony Stevens insists on this ephebe as one of "the heroic children whom time breeds against the first idea." It takes a kind of heroism to lash the lion, but to be bred against the idea of man is clearly to exhibit the lesser fortitude. Half-way through *It Must Be Abstract* Stevens has brought the ephebe's quest to a nadir.

We are made to start again where we must, "in the difficulty of what it is to be." Section VI subtly alters the entire tone of the work, as a gentler insistence on the continued possibility of relationship begins to draw the object-world and the poet together again. Stevens is very much a poet of the human seasons, like Keats, and Section VI of *It Must Be Abstract* is his hymn to the weather and the giant man the weather almost evokes. A quietly modulated chant salutes what the poet has "imagined well," and then touches near to a revelation, more moving for its candid confession that this presence of the human in weather is "not to be realized," is not wholly capable of a saving abstraction from falseness:

> My house has changed a little in the sun.
> The fragrance of the magnolias comes close,
> False flick, false form, but falseness close to kin.

It must be visible or invisible,
Invisible or visible or both:
A seeing and unseeing in the eye.

The weather and the giant of the weather,
Say the weather, the mere weather, the mere air:
An abstraction blooded, as a man by thought.

"We cannot write the order of the variable winds," Emerson remarked, and went on to question how the law of our shifting moods and susceptibility was to be penetrated, though the two orders differed "as all and nothing." If the giant of the weather could be confronted, then the first idea could be thought again, and wholly within the context of natural experience. But the giant has not yet been encountered on this imaginative quest; the weather, like the sun, must be met without evasion. The mere weather, the mere air, must be abstracted from the outworn idealizations that pass for reality. In such nakedness of withdrawal, of a separation that fabricates again, the abstraction is realized, as a man is blooded, when he has had time to think enough.

From here to the end of *It Must Be Abstract* the poet feels free to approach again, though very gently, his fiction of major man, the giant of imagination concealed within each ephebe. Section VII celebrates those "times of inherent excellence" which are Stevens' modest equivalents of the state celebrated by Wordsworth in *Tintern Abbey*. There is an instructive sadness in contemplating the exhaustions that attend the increases of self-awareness in Romantic tradition. Wordsworth, in the sublimity of his natural strength, could speak of his eye as being made quiet by the power of harmony and the deep power of joy. Stevens too speaks of a gift akin to that of seeing into the life of things, but the gift has become "extreme, fortuitous, personal," though it can still be described as "moments of awakening . . . in which we more than awaken." The movement between Wordsworth and his eloquent heir is that between "balances that we achieve" and "balances that happen," and the elevation achieved by Stevens is serenely precarious. From that height we "behold the academies like structures in a mist."

It is to one of these mistily perceived structures that the next section refers, the "castle-fortress-home" in which an expedient hypothesis of the major man might be housed. Section VIII is Stevens in the vitality of his ironic extravagance, which habitually precedes the direct presentation of what is hottest and purest in his heart, a vision of major man. So we proceed from the "crystal hypothesis" of the MacCullough, who remains merely MacCullough, to the major man who evades our tautologies. That imagined thing, the first idea, moves in on the MacCullough through a process of incarnation which is a contemporary equivalent to the Romantics' visions of the cyclic rebirth of the Poetical Character. Even the

MacCullough may be transformed into a figure of the youth as virile poet, the "beau linguist" conceived as a young god:

> If MacCullough himself lay lounging by the sea,
>
> Drowned in its washes, reading in the sound,
> About the thinker of the first idea,
> He might take habit, whether from wave or phrase,
>
> Or power of the wave, or deepened speech,
> Or a leaner being, moving in on him,
> Of greater aptitude and apprehension,
>
> As if the waves at last were never broken,
> As if the language suddenly, with ease,
> Said things it had laboriously spoken.

Under such conditions the MacCullough too would sing beyond the genius of the sea. From this chant of a possible incarnation, Stevens descends to deliberate the advent of a more probable version of the major man. We must put aside the idiom of apotheosis, "the romantic intoning, the declaimed clairvoyance" and be content plainly to propound a coming of the major man more subtly modest in its manner. So at least Stevens claims, though his poem partly refutes him. Stevens was at once curiously shy and passionately defensive in regard to the Romantic, and clearly apotheosis can be the origin of the major man, as the third part of *Notes* will show. But *It Must Be Abstract,* in its two final sections, seeks another tone, at once toughly reasonable and displaying a proud poverty, as befits a bad time for the imagination. It is the Stevens who wrote *The Man On The Dump* whose voice is heard as an undersong in Sections IX and X, yet the overt declaration is for the major man as an immediacy of vision:

> He is and may be but oh! he is, he is,
> This foundling of the infected past, so bright,
> So moving in the manner of his hand.
>
> Yet look not at his colored eyes. Give him
> No names. Dismiss him from your images,
> The hot of him is purest in the heart.

The gestures of the major man are visible in the here and now, free of the illnesses of history, but so dangerous is it to categorize vision that again the ephebe is urged to become an ignorant man, and to avoid the despotism of the eye. All these elaborations of a central theme are brought together in the last section of *It Must Be Abstract,* where major man makes his appearance, not the poet as a young god but the poet as an old tramp, the comedian:

> in his old coat,
> His slouching pantaloons, beyond the town,
>
> Looking for what was, where it used to be.
> Cloudless the morning. It is he. The man
> In that old coat, those sagging pantaloons,
>
> It is of him, ephebe, to make, to confect
> The final elegance, not to console
> Nor sanctify, but plainly to propound.

On that clear morning, abstracted into reality, the major man comes, seeking the difficulty of what was, and presenting in himself the difficulty of what it is to be. The ultimate elegance is the imagined land, to be fabricated by the ephebe out of this battered hero who is beyond loss. The whole burden of *Notes* rests upon those closing lines and their admonition; where Wordsworth could offer to console and sanctify, the maker of the Supreme Fiction for us has a more elemental task. He must render us able to conceive of the fresh possibility of life, yet he can show us nothing which is more fecund as particle than as principle. The natural man of Wordsworth and Keats, the visionary man of Blake and Shelley— these could be manifested in the singular, in the struggle of a poet to realize himself, whether by growth or rebirth. Our idea of man is a final belief in a last-ditch sense of finality; major man is "abler in the abstract than in his singular," a figure of capable imagination only when withdrawn from his not very fecund world. Confronted by this "inanimate, difficult visage," we know as ephebes that our hard obligation is "plainly to propound" what we have abstracted, to present without ornament the naked poem, the vulnerable confrontation.

It Must Change

There is much in *It Must Be Abstract* that grows into the reader's consciousness with the inevitability of greatness, yet one's experience of *Notes* is that the poem becomes better as it develops, *It Must Change* being superior to the first part, and *It Must Give Pleasure* finer still. *Notes* could therefore be judged an uneven poem, but the ascending intensity of the work is certainly a matter of design, a movement from the essential prose of our condition in *It Must Be Abstract* to the ecstatic celebration of the marriage between flesh and air in *It Must Give Pleasure*.

The principal Romantic vision of mutability stems from Spenser, who lamented natural change and yet found in the cycle of the months an augury of salvation, an eternal principle surviving amid the particles of decay. In Blake this hopeful view of natural cycle survives in the vision of the world of Los at the close of the first book of *Milton*, but the larger emphasis falls on mutability as ironic repetition, "the Orc cycle" of meaningless eternal recurrence from which man must learn to fight free. Shelley's later poems, particularly *Adonais* and *The Triumph of Life,* tend to share this dark vision, and a mocking analogue seems to lurk in Byron's treatment of nature in *Don Juan.* This negative judgment upon natural cycle, to be found again in the later Yeats, has no relevance to Stevens, who shares the more positive Spenserianism of Wordsworth and Keats, an attitude that recognizes the tragedy of mutable existence, but insists also on the necessity of celebrating the values of organic repetition. The heroic faith in the merely natural of Keats in particular, who praised as true humanists those who "seek no wonder but the human face," is carried on in Stevens, who could say that "the adventurer/In humanity has not conceived of a race/Completely physical in a physical world." One feels behind the exquisite fables of *It Must Change* the faithless faith of Keats's tragic naturalism, though the overt presence of Keats is not felt, as it certainly is in Stevens' rapturous *Credences of Summer,* or as Wordsworth is felt in *Sunday Morning* or Coleridge in the *Final Soliloquy of the Interior Paramour.*

The first two sections of *It Must Change* are devoted to a celebration of the advent of spring which is worthy to be compared with any similar celebration in English poetry. Even as the absence of imagination had itself to be imagined, so deadest winter is a tribute to the saving power of change:

> It means the distaste we feel for this withered scene
>
> Is that it has not changed enough. It remains,
> It is a repetition.

The booming of the returning bees, "as if they had never gone," defies our sense of things past, and comically defies also the pronunciamentoes by which we would invest nature with our shabby notions of immortality. Against our unimaginative denial of the reality of change, the booming of the bees asserts a beginning, not a resuming:

> Why, then, when in golden fury
>
> Spring vanishes the scraps of winter, why
> Should there be a question of returning or
> Of death in memory's dream? Is spring a sleep?
>
> This warmth is for lovers at last accomplishing
> Their love, this beginning, not resuming, this
> Booming and booming of the new-come bee.

Without this bee that never settles, without its generations that follow in their universe, the land we inhabit "would be a geography of the dead," to cite *Somnambulisma,* one of Stevens' most crucial shorter poems. Such a geography of the dead is exemplified in Section III of *It Must Change* by the great statue of the General Du Puy. This noble rider was "an inhuman bronze," a monument to the past so rigid as to divest the past of all reality, and so the General belonged:

> Among our more vestigial states of mind.
> Nothing had happened because nothing had changed.
> Yet the General was rubbish in the end.

From this ironic apprehension Stevens suddenly modulates to passionate directness in Section IV, in itself a complete and profoundly moving poem. The origin of change is proclaimed as a marriage of contraries, without which is no progression. But Stevens is offering us rapture, not dialectics:

> Winter and spring, cold copulars, embrace
> And forth the particulars of rapture come.
>
> Music falls on the silence like a sense,
> A passion that we feel, not understand.
> Morning and afternoon are clasped together
>
> And North and South are an intrinsic couple
> And sun and rain a plural, like two lovers
> That walk away as one in the greenest body.

Change, in this vision, is a sharing, the living antithesis to the death-in-life that is merely a remaining with oneself. Radiant by virtue of this truth, the poem raises itself to the pure and productive atmosphere in which the interior paramour is invoked:

> Follow after, O my companion, my fellow, my self,
> Sister and solace, brother and delight.

After this, the poem's midpoint, there are no flats or resting places in *Notes,* no section that is not poetry of the highest order. Section V of *It Must Change* is Stevens at his most characteristic, recalling *Sunday Morning* and other poems in *Harmonium.* The island solitude in a wide water without sound reappears, blue with the color of imagination, and "a green baked greener in the greenest sun" of summer's reality. The "possible red" of the autumnal vision is suggested also, preparing us for its full development later, in *It Must Give Pleasure,* Section III. The planter of *It Must Change,* Section V, is an imaginative brother to the woman who meditates on death and change in *Sunday Morning,* and like her he understands that death and change are the mothers of beauty. He is the man positively affected by change in a positive light, and he dies in the dignity of major man:

> An unaffected man in a negative light
> Could not have borne his labor nor have died
> Sighing that he should leave the banjo's twang.

This meditation on dying well is followed by an ecstasy of bird song, in a Shelleyan poem that traces the natural destiny of the relational event, from the dialogue of sparrow and crackled blade to the necessity of the dialogue's petrification. The vatic cry of Shelley to the west wind is heard again in this fresh confrontation of life by life:

> Bethou me, said sparrow, to the crackled blade,
> And you, and you, bethou me as you blow,
> When in my coppice you behold me be.
>
> Ah, ké! the bloody wren, the felon jay,
> Ké-ké, the jug-throated robin pouring out,
> Bethou, bethou, bethou me in my glade.

Together, "these bethous compose a heavenly gong," but the fate of these natural confrontations is such that they cannot be transformed into the living dialogue of change that exists between humans, as in the Dedication of *Notes*. Because their song cannot change it becomes:

> A single text, granite monotony,
>
> One sole face, like a photograph of fate,
> Glass-blower's destiny, bloodless episcopus,
> Eye without lid, mind without any dream—

This is the anatomy of monotony, that where man is not, nature is barren, as one of Blake's aphorisms phrases it. But Stevens ends more in Shelley's spirit than in Blake's, with the hint that all dialogue must fail at last:

> Bethou him, you
> And you, bethou him and bethou. It is
> A sound like any other. It will end.

Though it must change, though its personal exchange of words will end, the supreme relationship of love becomes the fiction of the following section, a defense of "the easy passion, the ever-ready love/Of the lover that lies within us." The easiness of this passion, condemned by moralists for the very mutability that marks it as genuine, is paralleled to the scholar's heat "for another accessible bliss." The lover too experiences:

> The fluctuations of certainty, the change
> Of degrees of perception in the scholar's dark.

This theme of lovers' confrontation is raised to its apotheosis in Section VIII, a passage at once comically grotesque and seriously moving. Ozymandias, Shelley's king-of-kings, whose shattered relics presided over a desert in ironic pride, is confronted by his interior paramour, the bride of his imagination, who bears the splendidly Stevensesque name of Nanzia Nunzio. Stripped more nakedly than nakedness, she demands of him that she be clothed "in the final filament," the fictive covering bestowed by the inflexible order of reality upon the imaginative vision it contemplates embracing. The works of Ozymandias, like all the pride of a reality seeking to deny change, are sunk in the sand, but:

> A fictive covering
> Weaves always glistening from the heart and mind.

The monument of Ozymandias, like his empire, could not bear change; the fictive covering of living relationship, woven by heart and head together, weaves always in the present, and glistens with the motion of its making. Since the poem is itself a fictive covering, it too must change, which is the central point of Section IX, following. Not only must the poem resist the intelligence almost successfully, but it must take on a different form with each fresh reading. That miracle Stevens does not accomplish, but he approaches it as nearly as any poet of our time. Haunting him in Section IX of *It Must Change* is the fearful question every poet in the Romantic tradition is compelled to ask: "Does the poet evade us, as in a senseless element?" The true Romantic Agony is the fear of solipsism, the horror of becoming a monster like Blake's Urizen, self-absorbed in the deathly perfection of silence. To avoid this fate the poet performs his difficult quest:

> He tries by a peculiar speech to speak
>
> The peculiar potency of the general,
> To compound the imagination's Latin with
> The lingua franca et jocundissima.

That Stevens achieves this will I think become increasingly more evident, though it seems clear that he has a larger proportion of the imagination's Latin in his compound than he might have hoped. That he has spoken something of the peculiar potency of the general is proved in the concluding section of *It Must Change,* where the joy of imagination is released in splendor:

> The casual is not
> Enough. The freshness of transformation is
>
> The freshness of a world. It is our own,
> It is ourselves, the freshness of ourselves,
> And that necessity and that presentation
>
> Are rubbings of a glass in which we peer.
> Of these beginnings, gay and green, propose
> The suitable amours. Time will write them down.

That necessity is the will to change, expressed by the west wind, still a potent Romantic image; that presentation is the way of change. The west wind transforms our world and ourselves, and we peer into a freshness, gay and green with the color of reality. If we cannot quite choose the suitable amours such freshness deserves, we can at least propose them. The proposers will not record the results, but the time which will write them down is a redemptive agent, and for the refreshment of transformation we can afford that certain toll.

It Must Give Pleasure

The third part of *Notes* gives us a continual though difficult greatness. Four of the sections, the Canon Aspirin group, V to VIII, are I think the height of Stevens' achievement, and can scarcely be matched in English poetry since the Romantics. They are to Stevens what the Byzantium poems are to Yeats, the central works of a clarified vision, but their difficulties are more subtly integrated with their themes than the complexities of Yeats's poems, and much more relevant to a reality centered in common experience. Like the Byzantium poems and Keats's odes, they concern the poet's stance in relation to his own poetry, and they render the teleology of the imaginative life with an appropriate intensity.

The Supreme Fiction, now seen as the poem of reality, or nature conceived as a general being and human universe, must begin and end in delight, in the poet's creative joy and the reader's exuberant response. Pleasure is the power that liberates vision, that shows us the new earth given to us by the great marriage between reality and imagination, specifically celebrated by Stevens in *It Must Give Pleasure,* Section IV, the prelude to the Canon Aspirin poems. The necessity of joy for the poet is of course the explicit theme of much of Coleridge and Wordsworth, but Stevens is again deliberately their poverty-stricken heir. The joy of the

Romantics elevates its possessor to the experience of a theophany, and becomes an intimation of immortality. The pleasure Stevens exalts is another rich confirmation of mortality, as indeed it was for Keats, and leads to a manifestation of major man, the real man slumbering within us.

The first section of *It Must Give Pleasure* is founded on a contrast between mediated and unmediated vision and their resultant songs, a contrast set forth to perfection in Keats's ode *To Psyche*. Stevens presents first the "facile exercise" of religious celebration: "To sing jubilas at exact, accustomed times." Opposed to this is "the difficultest rigor" of the humanist poet who sees the unmediated vision:

> On the image of what we see, to catch from that
>
> Irrational moment its unreasoning,
> As when the sun comes rising, when the sea
> Clears deeply, when the moon hangs on the wall
>
> Of heaven-haven. These are not things transformed.
> Yet we are shaken by them as if they were.
> We reason about them with a later reason.

The "doctrine," for want of a better word, of *Notes* is expressed in this passage with finality, persuasiveness, and an astonishing economy of verbal gesture. The "unreasoning" here is that nakedness of confrontation that yields only to "a later reason," the poet's imaginative broodings. In such directness of life meeting life, of two realities brought face to face, we are moved as if the everyday had been transformed, though no transformation exists. "Think of the earth," Moneta exclaims to Keats in *The Fall of Hyperion*, and that thinking is also part of Stevens' "later reason," which becomes the subject of Section IV of *It Must Give Pleasure* (where the first line is nearly identical with the final line of Section I). Between this first statement of a reality now beyond the necessity for abstraction, and the chant celebrating a marriage of reality and imagination, come two poems presenting the waiting bride and the heroic bridegroom. The bride is "the blue woman," or poetic imagination, of Section II; the groom is the "lasting visage" of Section III, red with the color of autumn reality. In the fourth poem they appear, respectively, as "the maiden Bawda" and "a great captain." Together the three sections serve to introduce the Canon Aspirin poems, at once the climax of *Notes* and the fulfillment of Stevens' poetic promise, his "theory of poetry" so fleshed as to rival Rilke's visions of the poet's adequacy.

The blue woman, interior paramour of the poet's creative desire, does not wish for more than sensuous reality; enough for her that she remembers the full sequence of the seasons. She too sees what is in the difficulty of what it is to be:

> The blue woman looked and from her window named
>
> The corals of the dogwood, cold and clear,
> Cold, coldly delineating, being real,
> Clear and, except for the eye, without intrusion.

She sees in "the harmonious heat of August," when the world is largest, and our attendant credences are most intense. The powerful chant of Section III brings into counterpoise with this summer of our content the red countenance of autumn, where the human visage falls back into the rock that is the gray particular of man's self:

> A lasting visage in a lasting bush,
> A face of stone in an unending red,
> Red-emerald, red-slitted-blue, a face of slate. . . .

In this landscape the human is seen from afar, and is weathered down, like "the spent feeling leaving nothing of itself." Yet, amid these "red-in-red repetitions never going away," where we would expect to find only "an effulgence faded," we find instead the possibility of an Orphic salvation:

> A dead shepherd brought tremendous chords from hell
>
> And bade the sheep carouse. Or so they said.
> Children in love with them brought early flowers
> And scattered them about, no two alike.

As the expression of a faith that sees repetition becoming revival, the soldier of reality growing deathless in his ruddy ancientness, this passage has many parallels elsewhere in Stevens' poetry. Here it leads us back to reasoning "of these things with a later reason," but now "these things" are not only the real seen plainly but also our sense of a perfection grasped and come again, the blue woman and her revived lover. Of what we have thus seen we make "a place dependent on ourselves," a marriage place between the blue air and the red flesh:

> There was a mystic marriage in Catawba,
> At noon it was on the mid-day of the year
> Between a great captain and the maiden Bawda.

They take one another as a sign "to stop the whirlwind, balk the elements," for this is a marriage between sun and moon, a natural meeting that shatters the context of nature. But it remains a confrontation in this world, the human making choice of a human self:

> They married well because the marriage place
> Was what they loved. It was neither heaven nor hell.
> They were love's characters come face to face.

From this marriage proceeds the Supreme Fiction, whose exponent, major man, now enters the poem in the exhilarating person of the Canon Aspirin, Stevens' finest invention. The Canon is the cure for our current headache of unreality, even as St. John prophesies the cure of the backache of our fallen history in a later poem by Stevens. In his activity the Canon first becomes the angel of reality, then is tempted too far in his benevolent impositions, and finally is surpassed by the poet himself, who discovers an order that his created angel could only impose. The Canon therefore has his limitations, but that is only to say that one instance of the Supreme Fiction is finally inferior to its maker's desires.

We begin with an introduction very much in the luxurious *Harmonium* manner, which rapidly modulates into a rhetoric of sensible ecstasy, to appropriate one of Stevens' happiest phrases:

> We drank Meursault, ate lobster Bombay with mango
> Chutney. Then the Canon Aspirin declaimed
> Of his sister, in what a sensible ecstasy
>
> She lived in her house. She had two daughters, one
> Of four, and one of seven, whom she dressed
> The way a painter of pauvred color paints.

No sequence of greatly ambitious poetry, one might have believed, could afford to open with such deliberate banality. It is because Stevens is daring so fiercely Romantic a vision that he begins in such deceptive inconsequence. The Canon, one soon understands, is not far from being "that brave man," our abstraction of the sun. His sister is an abstraction of the moon, mother of the months, and her two daughters make up the lunar cycle, as one is the four weeks and the other the seven days. Because we are exploring the real, "without intrusion," the daughters are seen in their essential poverty, our poverty:

> But still she painted them, appropriate to
> Their poverty, a gray-blue yellowed out
> With ribbon, a rigid statement of them, white,
>
> With Sunday pearls, her widow's gayety.
> She hid them under simple names. She held
> Them closelier to her by rejecting dreams.
>
> The words they spoke were voices that she heard.
> She looked at them and saw them as they were
> And what she felt fought off the barest phrase.

This is the most moving of Stevens' insistences on seeing the very thing itself and nothing else. The Canon's sister, coloring the existence of her children, sees that nothing must stand between them and the shapes they take. In tribute the Canon hums a fugue of praise, but in the sleeping nights his sister transcends all praise, demanding of sleep that it bestow on her children "only the unmuddled self of sleep, for them." With this last rejection of the illusions of moonlight, we are prepared for the angelic greatness of the Canon.

The Canon's apotheosis is the subject of Section VI, the first of three sections forming a miniature dialectic among themselves. In this triad, Section VI states the thesis of the Canon's quest toward an integration of all reality, fact and thought together. Section VII is the antithesis, presenting the Canon's surrender of his quest to the angelic impatience that imposes rather than discovers order. The synthesis is in Section VIII, which one does not hesitate to call Stevens' finest poem, where the poet's discovery of reality is both given and celebrated. Sections IX and X, following, are commentaries on this discovery, after which *Notes* concludes with an invocation of the soldier, who is man embattled in the real world even as the poet is man embattled in the fictive or verbal universe.

Section VI is at once the most Miltonic and the most strenuously heroic of Stevens' poems. At long midnight, when "normal things had yawned themselves away," the Canon sleeps himself into an awareness of naked reality, and reaches a point "beyond which fact could not progress as fact," and where thought must begin. The Canon therefore reconceives night, and in this conceptual effort becomes the angel of reality, joining fact and thought together at that point of nakedness where they meet:

> So that he was the ascending wings he saw
> And moved on them in orbits' outer stars
> Descending to the children's bed, on which
>
> They lay. Forth then with huge pathetic force
> Straight to the utmost crown of night he flew.
> The nothingness was a nakedness, a point
>
> Beyond which thought could not progress as thought.

The Canon's Miltonic flight brings him to that metaphysical point where fact and thought alike have reached their limits, where reality and the imagination join in desperation. The Canon's heroism is in the intensity of his integrating choice, his refusal to reject either order:

> He had to choose. But it was not a choice
> Between excluding things. It was not a choice

> Between, but of. He chose to include the things
> That in each other are included, the whole,
> The complicate, the amassing harmony.

This choice is Wordsworthian rather than Blakean, for it insists that the context of fact or nature can be harmonized with the more exuberant context of the poet's apocalyptic desires. The problem in such a harmonization is to cultivate the highly anti-apocalyptic virtue of patience. Like Wordsworth, the Canon needs to wait upon the initiative of nature, but instead "he imposes orders as he thinks of them," in Section VII. Though this "is a brave affair," the exhausted Canon has forgotten that "to impose is not to discover." The passion of Stevens slowly mounts in an extraordinary emotional progression as he states his own version of a Romantic faithless faith:

> To discover an order as of
> A season, to discover summer and know it,
>
> To discover winter and know it well, to find,
> Not to impose, not to have reasoned at all,
> Out of nothing to have come on major weather,
>
> It is possible, possible, possible. It must
> Be possible.

No desperation could be more dignified, for Stevens speaks out of the barrenness of the fertile thing that can become no more, the giant of the weather in his nobility and his essential poverty. Utterly vulnerable, except for the Supreme Fiction, the poet prepares to confront the real, and calls upon the angel he has created to be silent and listen to the ultimate poem:

> It must be that in time
> The real will from its crude compoundings come,
>
> Seeming, at first, a beast disgorged, unlike,
> Warmed by a desperate milk. To find the real,
> To be stripped of every fiction except one,
>
> The fiction of an absolute—Angel,
> Be silent in your luminous cloud and hear
> The luminous melody of proper sound.

After this it is only a question of a final belief, for all possible prologues are ended. Stevens rises to his own challenge and gives us his ultimate poem, the supreme achievement of post-Romanticism and the

culmination of Coleridgean and Blakean poetic theory. As much as with
Rilke's best poetry, we are convinced that this is "the luminous melody
of proper sound":

> What am I to believe? if the angel in his cloud,
> Serenely gazing at the violent abyss,
> Plucks on his strings to pluck abysmal glory,
>
> Leaps downward through evening's revelations, and
> On his spredden wings, needs nothing but deep space,
> Forgets the gold centre, the golden destiny,
>
> Grows warm in the motionless motion of his flight,
> Am I that imagine this angel less satisfied?
> Are the wings his, the lapis-haunted air?
>
> Is it he or is it I that experience this?
> Is it I then that keep saying there is an hour
> Filled with expressible bliss, in which I have
>
> No need, am happy, forget need's golden hand,
> Am satisfied without solacing majesty,
> And if there is an hour there is a day,
>
> There is a month, a year, there is a time
> In which majesty is a mirror of the self:
> I have not but I am and as I am, I am.

If Blake had taken this final step, he would have celebrated his own
Spectre of Urthona, the crippled temporal will of every man, as the
earthly maker of that heavenly maker, Los the Poetic Genius. Had
Wordsworth crossed into this desperately triumphant poetic humanism,
The Prelude would have been followed by a poem of the kind of *Notes,*
and there are hints of such a poem in the early *Recluse* fragment. A less
tragic Keats might have lived into so prodigious an exaltation of the
poetic self, but the pressures of ill fortune created instead the purgatorial
Fall of Hyperion. What the poet comes to believe, in Stevens' late plural
of Romantic tradition, is that his disinterested joy in his own creation
is more than a final good. In that profoundest of satisfactions, the stance
of the creator before his own isolated and splendid artifact, the poet
ceases to possess but is, at last in the full difficulty of what it is to be.
Most central is that he ceases to have the sense of possessing himself, but
is one with that self. In that heroic integration, what is outside the self
can be dismissed without fear of solipsistic self-absorption, for the self
has joined major man:

> These external regions, what do we fill them with
> Except reflections, the escapades of death,
> Cinderella fulfilling herself beneath the roof?

The rest of *Notes* is epilogue. The song of the birds rises again in Section IX, renewing the vast repetitions that both constitute and exalt our lives, "until merely going round is a final good." In the last section of *It Must Give Pleasure* the poet invokes the universe he has created, "my green, my fluent mundo," with a homely affection appropriate to his achieved peace.

Notes ends with an address to the soldier of reality, the brother to the poet as the soldier of imagination. An exact balance between the humility and the pride of poetry is attained in the poem's conclusion:

> The soldier is poor without the poet's lines,
>
> His petty syllabi, the sounds that stick,
> Inevitably modulating, in the blood.
> And war for war, each has its gallant kind.
>
> How simply the fictive hero becomes the real;
> How gladly with proper words the soldier dies,
> If he must, or lives on the bread of faithful speech.

Stevens was to create a tone of even greater simplicity and dignity than this in the best poem of his final period, *The Rock*, but at the expense of some of the human warmth of this conclusion. Here, the poet and the soldier make their dwelling in that place formed by the imagination, in which being there together is enough.

Wallace Stevens: The Image of the Rock

by Ralph J. Mills, Jr.

I

Poets in old age, feeling the steady approach of death, often tend to organize their attitudes, to seek out some representative symbols in which these may be embodied and preserved against the dissolution that, they fear, awaits their own persons. In such efforts they retrace the patterns of all their previous work, hoping to mount a worthy crown upon it, a final image which will suffuse each poem with a new light—an illumination wrenched from a struggle on the very threshold of annihilation. This activity is, of course, restricted by the nature of individual cases and also by the disposition of the writer's mind toward the question of last things.

The concluding section of poems which Wallace Stevens appended to the collected edition of his work contains, as Randall Jarrell points out, some of his finest pieces. Almost without exception, they are meditations on death or display premonitions of that event. The title given to the group, *The Rock*, figures also as a symbolic image in a number of the more important poems, and it becomes evident that this symbol is appointed a heavy burden. It is to lend a final character to the whole body of Stevens' poetry, issuing and receiving meaning in a ceaseless flow of reciprocal relations with that body. Again, the rock is a place of spiritual entombment:

> There it was, word for word,
> The poem that took the place of a mountain.
> He breathed its oxygen,
> Even when the book lay turned in the dust of his table.[1]

"Wallace Stevens: The Image of the Rock" by Ralph J. Mills, Jr. This essay was published in its original form in *Accent*, XVIII, No. 2 (Spring 1958), 75-89. Revised by the author. Copyright © 1958 by *Accent*. Reprinted by permission of the author and *Accent*.

[1] All quotations of poetry, unless otherwise indicated, are from *The Collected Poems* (New York: Alfred A. Knopf, 1954). Quotations from *The Necessary Angel* (New York: Alfred A. Knopf, 1951) are indicated in the text.

The work itself resists the treachery of time. Death is time's instrument and maintains everything within an apparently endless temporal round. There is no real departure from this cycle but merely changing relations in it. In order to understand the total significance of the rock as it appears in these late poems, we must look at some of its previous manifestations and see how they contribute to that prominence.

The first notable appearance of the rock comes in "How to Live. What to Do." from *Ideas of Order* (1936). In this poem a "man and his companion," in exodus from a land and a state of life which they have left far behind, stop before "the heroic height" of an enormous rock as it stands "impure" in a strange landscape under the pale light of the moon. The human pair, who certainly more than suggest Adam and Eve cast from the Garden of Eden, are explorers of the kind we encounter in Stevens' array of *dramatis personae* searching for a tenable view of the world:

> Coldly the wind fell upon them
> In many majesties of sound:
> They that had left the flame-freaked sun
> To seek a sun of fuller fire.

The wind's incessant and derelict motion, always a harbinger of flux and change for the poet, creates the unsettled climate they have found between an old order sacrificed and a new one as yet unknown. But the rock remains the irreducible focus of the scene, bathed with the remote glare of the pure imagination (the moon), and we are forced, along with the travelers, to accept it as *the* essential and imperfect fact:

> Instead there was this tufted rock
> Massively rising high and bare
> Beyond all trees, the ridges thrown
> Like giant arms among the clouds.
>
> There was neither voice nor crested image,
> No chorister, nor priest. There was
> Only the great height of the rock
> And the two of them standing still to rest.

The tone is one of awe, almost of veneration, before the austere and secret promise of the rock. There is also a mixture here of a primitive pantheism and an empiricist's recognition of the definite and physical, both circumscribed by the poet's mind. The first intimation we have of Stevens' idea of a *personal church* is contained in the imagery of these stanzas, along with the attendant god of the imagination and the notable absence of ritual or clergy.

Yet the rock cannot be bound to one meaning, and Stevens likes to clothe it in the garbs of the richest season, as he does in "Credences of Summer." In this context it turns into "the rock of summer," associated with the peak of earthly, physical existence, but once more, and from another angle, it is established as a form of objective certainty in the changing universe of Stevens' poetry:

> The rock cannot be broken. It is the truth.
> It rises from land and sea and covers them.
> It is a mountain half way green and then,
> The other immeasurable half, such rock
> As placid air becomes. But it is not
>
> A hermit's truth nor symbol in hermitage.
> It is a visible rock, the audible,
> The brilliant mercy of a sure repose,
> On this present ground, the vividest repose,
> Things certain sustaining us in certainty.

Distinguishing this symbol as real or factual in opposition to the philosopher's (the hermit's) occult conceptualization, the poet sees the rock as encompassing the natural ("green") world grasped through the sense in an intuition of sheer physical being. The "immeasurable half" of "placid air" contrasts with the shifting winds that destroy or alter things in so many of Stevens' poems and corresponds to the transparent medium in which perception and what is perceived are brought to fruitful completion. Without this transparent medium, of which the images of the "major," "glass," or "central" man are other and more concentrated instances, man falls short of his potential stature and fails to realize what has been given him—the possibilities of the created world. Outside of consciousness, the rock is his only *tangible* form of assurance: it is the layer of the actual, solid world in which he has his being. Stevens insists that we, like his two travelers, start from there. "Reality is the beginning not the end," he writes in "An Ordinary Evening in New Haven."

II

Since we are involved with questions of death and eschatology in Stevens' poetry, it is necessary to examine his theology. To say that this poet is a naturalist, rejecting the orthodox systems of Christianity or any other belief, is not to say that a certain type of theology would be irrelevant here. It is true that from *Harmonium* on Stevens frequently treats supernatural religions with irony or otherwise indicates his distrust of them, sometimes setting as his frame of reference a world not unlike Nietzsche's one of eternal recurrence, as we discover in poems such as "Description without Place," where that philosopher is briefly mentioned. Often, as C. Roland Wagner has said, the influence of Bergson is discernible. At any rate, though Stevens satirizes self-righteous and stiff-necked piety or militant puritanism (see, for example, his treatment of Cotton Mather), he further reveals his own misconceptions of traditional Christianity. If I read him correctly, he views it as purely spiritual, as inimical to creation. This notion seems to lie behind satires like "Cortège for Rosenbloom." However, much orthodox Christian thought stresses the unity of the person rather than an unconditional division of body and soul which diminishes the worth of the former.

Whether we accept it or not, the announcement made in Nietzsche's *The Gay Science* of the destruction of God has become an integral part of our modern experience; it is the air we breathe. While Stevens assuredly holds such an attitude and has set the human as his boundary, he is, at the same time, quite unwilling to wholly discard the idea of God. There is, though, no struggle in his verse with an older kind of orthodoxy which must be shed (unless we take "Sunday Morning" as a partial exception); Christianity is simply observed in retrospect. In "The Men That Are Falling" from *The Man with the Blue Guitar* he employs the *persona* of a sleeper awakening to a vision in the darkness of his "catastrophic room," a metaphor for the mind. Dominated by the fierce moonlight of the imagination, he finds the pillow on which he gazes "more than sudarium," and there confronts the tortured visage of a man who at once represents Christ and all other martyrs to an ideal cause. Though the intentions here are partially political, the value of the human redemption Stevens attaches to this sacrifice is not entirely clear. Nonetheless, we do see that it belongs to this world, not to another. The agony and triumph are man's rather than God's, while the ideal prompting these selfish actions is the noble vision of projected human "desire." We may be struck by the similarity in this to the *immanent transcendence* in the writings of Joyce or Yeats, a transcendence achieved within the natural world yet raising the participants above the range of time and space. Stevens concludes the poem: "This death was his belief though death is a stone./This man loved earth, not heaven, enough to die." Death in the shape of the stone is fixed within the physical order of which it is a part; beyond there is only the "blank," as we are told in "The Blue Buildings in the Summer Air." Taken as a confrontation of Christ, "The Men That Are Falling" ends in the poet's refusal to accept His divinity. Yet he places importance and value on such sacrificial acts, recognizing in them a pinnacle of heroic tragedy that still belongs to the ordonnance of human imagination.

At the same time, the extent to which the significance of mortal gestures reaches is symbolic and finds fulfillment in what Stevens calls "supreme fictions." These projected ideas by which we guide ourselves lead the poet to the borders of his own mysticism. Furthermore, the attitude toward the universe Stevens implies does not preclude deity. Not only the poetry but the more recently published prose "Adagia"— aphorisms and meditations from his notebooks—in *Opus Posthumous* disclose a preoccupation with "God." But, in keeping with the limitations he has set, Stevens maintains his deity as indwelling. The universe, there- fore, receives its structure from within, not by the will of an external and omnipotent God. In one of the adages from his collection he writes, "God is in me or else is not at all (does not exist)." Evidently then the existence of Stevens' God depends completely on the existence of man; and this God is, moreover, a creative force within him or, as the poet says, "God and the imagination are one." The transfer of generative power from the divine Logos of the Prologue of St. John's Gospel to the human spirit is accomplished in "Description without Place." The world is created, we are told in this poem, not out of nothing but, we might say, *in* depth or perspective through the description of it:

> Description is revelation. It is not
> The thing described, nor false facsimile.
>
> It is an artificial thing that exists
> In its own seeming, plainly visible,
>
> Yet not too closely the double of our lives,
> Intenser than any actual life could be,
>
> A text that we should be born that we might read,
> More explicit than the experience of the sun
>
> And moon, the book of reconciliation,
> Book of a concept only possible
>
> In description, canon central in itself,
> The thesis of the plentifullest John.

In that space, to use a convenient metaphor, between reality and the imagination, the flatly objective and the actively subjective, is created the "book" in which we should, Stevens says, seek our fullest being. For "the word is the making of the world," constructing out of the bare rudi- ments of our situation among earthly objects a richer climate of habita- tion. The lonely pair of "How to Live. What to Do." must write upon this naked rock of the world the meanings for life of which they are capable. With that act, which is the imagination's endeavor, they and the rock are drawn together and figured forth in a new identity.

In one respect, then, poetry is for Stevens something more than the written literature alone. It is a mode of the mind's working, a way of looking that demands the "interdependence of reality and the imagination as equals," he remarks in *The Necessary Angel*. This activity, we should understand, is not restricted to writers or artists, though craftsmanship may be; it is rather the exercise of what we have somehow received as the power to make over our situation and circumstance: "The true work of art, whatever it may be," Stevens notes in *The Necessary Angel*, "is not the work of the individual artist. It is time and it is place as these perfect themselves." Poetry is involved in the very instant of our contact with the real and factual, and serves as the agent of a new reality born of the fusion of the imagination with raw physical things: "The poem is the cry of its occasion,/Part of the res itself and not about it." God, or the divine attribute, has become man's innate ability to renew the world and to live by the abundance arising from his intercourse with the blunt facts of material being. What Stevens calls "bare fact" is transmuted into the limitless prospects offered the mind by "analogy." The scope of life's potentiality is determined by the pursuit of our ideal images, fixed in earthly distances and glittering in the sunlit air. Of his thesis the poems are "pages of illustrations" giving a human meaning to an otherwise indifferent, often hostile, world. Following this in detail, we see Stevens developing the persistent terms of his "revelation" from the elemental parts of the universe: moon, sun, stars, sea, stones, rivers, trees and vegetation, wind and rain, the cycle of the seasons—all come through frequent use to operate as heavily weighted symbols. From such disciplined repetition there arises a gospel of the natural man, as we gather in "Esthétique du Mal":

> And out of what one sees and hears and out
> Of what one feels, who could have thought to make
>
> So many selves, so many sensuous worlds,
> As if the air, the mid-day air, was swarming
> With the metaphysical changes that occur,
> Merely in living as and where we live.

This kind of man charts his explorations, visualizes his horizon, from his experience of participation in the physical world and what the expansive movements of his mind can make of that.

III

The two primary components of Stevens' poetic cosmos, the brute material fact and the imagination which lends it meaning and value, are joined in the image of the rock. These interdependent parts are plainly visible in "Credences of Summer," where the physical level of creation—

and this implies all of nature—is surmounted by the curious transparent glaze of imagination, bringing our focus to bear on a central point of things in a vision of celestial majesty. Here the eye, chief organ of the imaginative faculty, projects its ideal representations and thus provides the harmonious conditions under which things become their utmost selves:

> It is the rock of summer, the extreme,
> A mountain luminous half way in bloom
> And then half way in the extremest light
> Of sapphires flashing from the central sky,
> As if twelve princes sat before a king.

This image of the gods is the inhuman center or idea from which everything radiates outward. Such immaterial deities are, however, human productions and are necessary to what R. P. Blackmur has called Stevens' "platonism," for these remote, inhuman figures of the mind comprise embodiments of man's ultimate desires: they are the absolutes he fashions —impermanent ones—out of his earthly experience. It is finally the rock that receives this celestial illumination and seizes the religious sense with its brilliance and splendor—and that is exactly what Stevens wishes. The rarefied realm of ideal beings exists only to enhance life in a tangible and very human world. And so we find the rock appearing as a radiant image in some of Stevens' latest pieces, for example, "The Poem That Took The Place of a Mountain" and, naturally, "The Rock" itself.

Before we examine these last and most fully developed uses of the rock, we should understand that Stevens has also assigned this symbol a relationship to death. To help us we shall have to introduce another passage from an earlier poem; this one is from "Esthétique du Mal," VII:

> How red the rose that is the soldier's wound,
> The wounds of many soldiers, the wounds of all
> The soldiers that have fallen, red in blood,
> The soldier of time grown deathless in great size.
>
> A mountain in which no ease is ever found,
> Unless indifference to deeper death
> Is ease, stands in the dark, a shadow's hill,
> And there the soldier of time has deathless rest.

The soldier, whose full title indicates the temporal order to which he properly belongs, becomes symbolic of all human life and the unavoidable conclusion awaiting it. Since it is really the dark or shadow side of the rock, the "mountain" of this passage seems an image of the burial mound, of earthly solidity and unity, and as the poet's version of the underworld. Though Stevens defines here a kind of survival, it is one which depends upon the continuity of life (and imagination) and the world rather than on any belief in God other than that already discussed. The levels of death intimated by the poem may identify "deeper death" with the doctrine of immortality held by Christians and unacceptable to the poet. The "concentric circles of shadows," derived from the traditional imagery of circles and rings associated with the idea of self-containment and eternity, take on greater clarity as we proceed in the poem:

> The shadows of his fellows ring him round
> In the high night, the summer breathes for them
> Its fragrance, a heavy somnolence, and for him,
> For the soldier of time, it breathes a summer sleep . . .

This ceremony, so close to that of the funeral rituals of seasonal gods, brings us back to "Sunday Morning" with its "ring of men" dancing and singing "on a summer morn" the glory of the sun, the joys of an earthly existence viewed as paradisiacal. Stevens says of these celebrants that "They shall know well the heavenly fellowship/Of men that perish and of summer morn." Apparently, if we fit the common properties of the two poems together, the living and the dead are connected with one another in some final and unbroken relation which escapes close definition but which is deeply involved with their mystical attachment to the earth— the fecund and voluptuous queen of so many of the poems, and the "earthly mothers waiting, sleeplessly" of "Sunday Morning." The two circling groups of men in "Esthétique du Mal" and "Sunday Morning" are in a sense one and the same; we merely observe them from a different point of view in each poem. Life and death, as both Richard Ellmann and Northrop Frye have said in reference to Stevens' personal eschatology, belong to each other and flow into each other. It is not surprising, then, to discover the poet writing in *The Necessary Angel*, "What a ghastly situation it would be if the world of the dead was actually different from the world of the living . . ." In Stevens' notions of how we construct and reconstruct our world there can be no difference because the imagination is "the will of things."

The interpenetration of life and death takes place through the only agent possible for such metamorphoses in Stevens' scheme—the mind itself. In a poem called "The Owl in the Sarcophagus" we are offered a somewhat heavy prophecy of "the mythology of modern death" through a trio of representative figures. There are "two brothers" in this oddly devised pantheon; one is "high sleep," the other, "high peace." They share the company of that archetypal woman, the queen of many disguises, who is here "the mother of us all,/The earthly mother and the mother of/The dead." The three apparitions, like the gods before them, receive their validity as projections through the imagination of human wishes. Under their aegis death brings no radical alteration to the essential nature of man's condition or the limits of his world. The earth, we are told, is the eternal feminine which enfolds us and gives us endless repose. If Yeats sometimes thought that man created all he knew and experienced, Stevens could play him a close second:

> Compounded and compounded, life by life,
> These are death's own supremest images,
> The pure perfections of parental space,
>
> The children of a desire that is the will,
> Even of death, the beings of the mind
> In the light-bound space of the mind, the floreate flare . . .
>
> It is a child that sings itself to sleep,
> The mind, among the creatures that it makes,
> The people, those by which it lives and dies.

The multiple voices of the "Interior Paramour," the voices that imagination adopts, return us to the problems attendant on the poet's separation of reality from this faculty.

Reality, or the physical, factual world, is a closed system in Stevens' cosmology, conditioned by "generations of the imagination" and bounded by the returning seasonal periods whose importance in the poetry we have previously mentioned. In "The Auroras of Autumn" the serpent, we gather, imposes both order and limitation for this world in the figure of his coiling length: "the master of the maze/Of body and air and forms and images." The snake encircles the cosmos, and so repeats that pursuit of his tail which has so long symbolized the eternal ring. Stevens again relies on the circle to suggest the completeness of our earthly being.

The imagination, though restricted in the individual person by the span of human existence, imposes itself on brute reality and extends the possibilities of what would otherwise remain a "basic slate." To account for the origins and goals of this reality and the life within it the imagination introduces figurations and images that are the spirit's interpretations and comfort. Through them the reality which is the foundation of life undergoes a radical transformation that leaves man dominating it through his images. The fundamental reality is what it was, but has now become something more too. In time these images will fade away or be destroyed and new ones will have to replace them. Stevens believes himself to be in a transitional period: old images and beliefs have died out; others are needed. The mind's labors swell, augmented by what must be included when there is no other support. Little wonder that, lacking an external God, Stevens deified the imagination. More of the scope of this work of the mind can be seen in a late poem, "The Sail of Ulysses," from *Opus Posthumous:*

> His mind presents the world
> And in his mind the world revolves.
> The revolutions through day and night,
> Through wild spaces of other suns and moons,
> Round summer and angular winter and winds,
> Are matched by other revolutions
> In which the world goes round and round
> In the crystal atmospheres of the mind,
> Light's comedies, dark's tragedies,
> Like things produced by a climate, the world
> Goes round in the climates of the mind
> And bears its floraisons of imagery.

The mind also resembles a circle, for it matches the conditions of the cycling seasons, the coiled snake, the rings of the living and the dead. This circular cosmos is the mind's own territory. Thus Stevens can remark in *The Necessary Angel,* "We live in the center of a physical poetry, a geography that would be intolerable except for the non-geography that exists there . . ." By "non-geography" Stevens means the spirit or mind or imagination and its activities.

The attainment of a true center of this world, both necessary and desirable under the poet's arrangement of things, is related to death and the rock in "The Owl in the Sarcophagus," III, and in "Things of August," IX, we learn that such a center of reality is the place from which meanings are perceived and made:

> A text of intelligent men
> At the center of the unintelligible,
> As in a hermitage, for us to think,
> Writing and reading the rigid inscription.

The earth itself composes the "text" of secular revelation announced earlier in "Description without Place." Created by the exercise of imagination on tangible things this sacred book preserves the ordered meanings bestowed by the mind upon a rather bleak chaos of sensory impressions. These notions are drawn together more closely in "The Hermitage at the Center" and "The World as Meditation" from *The Rock;* and in both the figure of the earth queen serves to unify life and death.

"The Irish Cliffs of Moher" in the poem of that title stand out for Stevens as another version of the rock and the ground of our being:

> This is my father or, maybe
> It is as he was,
> A likeness, one of the race of fathers: earth
> And sea and air.

In this poem we come to the farthest backward reach of Stevens' thought about the genesis of earth, a stony foundation, seemingly without origin, permeated by the psyche's most tenacious images. To the genealogy of the fathers all will be returned, for, as we read elsewhere, "the spirit comes from the body of the world." The center toward which life always moves and whence it reappears is at the heart of the symbolic circles we have seen. The unity of the real and the imagined is caught in the anticipated embrace of Penelope and the voyager Ulysses, the "form of fire" (he is the generative sun, she the fecund earth too), never fully achieved yet forever, through the reflective mind, coming nearer and nearer in "The World as Meditation." The closing of that ring, like the knitting of the circles already discussed, makes a wholeness that includes life and death, earth and the heavens, imagination and reality, the animate and the inanimate. Stevens' belief "beyond belief," his vision of what endures, is in the persistence of this totality.

IV

The space around which the serpent winds in "The Auroras of Autumn" and which the closed circle marks is the periphery of the rock; and in the poem of that title Stevens makes an effort to give a final explanation to his attitudes. There are three sections: the first begins the course of meditation from an autobiographical basis; the second discloses the rock itself and the meanings it brings together; and the last part once again places the rock in relation to death (and here we may perhaps think of Stevens' own, so closely following) which leads the poem back to the point where it began, only on a new level.

The opening section, "Seventy Years Later," has that peculiar flavor, almost a bitterness, of old age as it examines a past which no longer appears to have any ties with the present person and his situation. Indeed, the poet gazes at this earlier self with some astonishment and disbelief; they hardly seem to be attached to one another, or care to be:

> It is an illusion that we were ever alive,
> Lived in the houses of mothers, arranged ourselves
> By our own motions in a freedom of air.

With lines of defiant beauty Stevens claims that love and human relationships, at this remove in time, are grotesque: "an embrace between one desperate clod/And another . . ." But this "queer assertion of humanity," he realizes, is a block against "nothingness," and it forms at least "an impermanence/In its permanent cold." The barren rock is itself the substance of this negation, until human assertions—the acts of imagination—come to bear the "green leaves" upon it. The rock stands alone, as we first saw it in "How to Live. What to Do." an inhuman world, and it remains meaningless, a raw fact, without the invasion of the mind and senses. The responsibility for bringing about any change lies with the lonely couple of that poem, which is to say, with man himself. The gates of Eden have opened and, for Stevens, God is gone; divinity is man's attribute now and the world his task. In this coming forth there is a spring birth that is at once both purge and blossom, we are told in "The Rock": "the lilacs came and bloomed like a blindness cleaned,/Exclaiming bright sight . . ." Within the range of the eye the rock is made over, a rock upon a rock, and looms out now as a newly won ground on which the "incessant being alive" flourishes.

Whether Stevens intended it or not, the appropriation of the image of the rock is in keeping with his general adoption of biblical vocabulary for secular or private purposes. The rock is, of course, for a Christian associated with the origins of the Church in Christ's delegation of spiritual authority to Peter; from this event there has developed an identification of the rock symbol with the Church. We have pointed to several other uses Stevens makes of orthodox religious terminology and concepts. Inseparable from this practice, the vision of redemption and reconstruction—the creation of unified being—is then allied with the harmonious function of the rock in man's connection with it. The blossoms of green are insufficient by themselves, we find in "The Rock," Part II, "The Poem as Icon," and man must be "cured" or transformed himself, that is, identified with the "fiction of the leaves" he has made. Stevens' narcissism is revealed here, not as morbid egoism or self-concern, but as the contemplation of our projected images, in whose midst we live. Perhaps we might best think of a set of mirrors (imagination and reality) facing each other, which in-between themselves make a habitable world out of their blending reflections. The rock is the space of that world, and the wholeness it comes to imply in this late poetry contains sacramental meanings for Stevens. These meanings are bodied forth in the images of the leaves to suggest a kind of sanctification: "the figuration of blessedness,/And the icon is the man." In the lines that follow three successive seasons are taken up as properties of the rock, and together with it they are viewed against the backdrop of nothingness, involving the fourth season, winter, which is omitted from the ideal seasonal pattern:

> The pearled chapelet of spring,
> The magnum wreath of summer, time's autumn snood,

> Its copy of the sun, these cover the rock.
> These leaves are the poem, the icon and the man.
> These are a cure of the ground and of ourselves,
> In the predicate that there is nothing else.

Stevens means, I believe, that we should take "cure" in its sense of a spiritual charge or curacy, as well as remedy. In spite of his naturalism he is attempting to convey through the image of the rock a religious formulation to replace the Christian interpretation of life which, he feels, belongs to the past. The frequent conversion of the language of the Gospels and of biblical incident to his own poetic needs can only be understood in the light of some such intention. But the formulation brought about must be one that disavows doctrine or creed and, in the poet's idea of historical relativism, corresponds with any change, in fact, partakes of it.

At this point I think we may, borrowing from Richard Ellmann, speak of Stevens' personal "church of the imagination," mentioned in passing at the outset of this essay. By "church" I mean a composite of sacred values harbored by the rock and held within the compass of the mind. These include, most broadly, the life of the natural man and the work of the imagination therein. As such, it is, as we said before, a closed system, though an extensive one. Stevens discovers religiousness there in the desired fruition of existence:

> In this plenty, the poem makes meanings of the rock,
> Of such mixed motion and such imagery
> That its barrenness becomes a thousand things
>
> And so exists no more.

In one of the "Adagia" from *Opus Posthumous* he writes, "After one has abandoned a belief in god, poetry is that essence which takes its place as life's redemption." So the distinctive lines of aesthetics and theology merge in this church of the solitary imagination, a bulwark thrown up at the edge of an abyss. In one respect or another, the same tendency is noticeable in writers like Yeats and Rilke, in the Joyce of *Finnegans Wake*. The modern poet, often divorced from a stable religious faith or communal vision, is not only faced with the job of creating the reality of his art but finds himself inclined by the temptations of uncertainty to make of his art the single reality, an imagined one. If this is his choice, then the artist very likely becomes the inhabitant of his work. Joyce peers out at us from the figure of Steven Dedalus and later as Shem the Penman. Yeats continually—and successfully—dramatizes himself in his poetry, even imagines an eternity of art in which he might be enclosed. Because life and the poem are for Stevens ultimately interchangeable within the boundaries of the rock, he endows them with the same significance. In "The Poem That Took the Place of a Mountain" the rock appears as the final human resting place where the poet and his work will at last be joined with the perpetual ring of nature. Art and artist are identified with the rock they have transformed through the life of the imagination. Stevens apparently discovers in this prospect a substitute for the immortality of the soul and the resurrection of the person. Art is a vessel of the purified, essential human self; it carries that self back to the heart of reality at death. For in dying the poet will merely replace one relationship to the earth with another, more inexplicable bond.

Parallel to these notions Stevens locates Heaven and Hell, in "Esthétique du Mal," as integral areas of the mind developed from man's experience of the world rather than anything external to it. The rock is, finally, "the gray particular of man's life" and "The stone from which he rises up—and—ho,/The step to the bleaker depths of his descents . . ." These are first and last things mentioned in "The Rock," and later in the same poem the thought of death so near stirs the memory to recall the cycle of earthly life:

> The starting point of the human and the end,
> That in which space itself is contained, the gate
> To the enclosure, day, the things illumined
>
> By day, night and that which might illumines,
> Night and its midnight-minting fragrances,
> Night's hymn of the rock, as in a vivid sleep.

These stanzas draw together the circle of existence as Stevens envisages its certainty, a circle supported by the prevailing substance of the physical world and by the poem played upon that reality throughout a lifetime —a poem that remains after death (see, on this subject, "A Postcard from the Volcano"). Out of this encounter of the creative mind with concrete reality Stevens fashions his own religious image in the form of a chapel rising above the decay of an aged cathedral. The meaning is clear in this passage from "St. Armorer's Church from the Outside":

> Its chapel rises from Terre Ensevelie,
> An ember yes among its cindery noes,
> His own: a chapel of breath, an appearance made
> For a sign of meaning in the meaningless . . .

This breath is the warmth of life, the movement of the spirit, and the medium of poetic speech. Stevens' affirmation of them all makes the structure of the chapel where he is both priest and worshipper. Set in the teeth of time, it provides shelter against the unknown, the nothingness into which death threatens to catch us.

While Stevens admits, in *The Necessary Angel*, that "the imagination is able to manipulate nature . . . but it is not able to create a wholly new nature," we have seen what that manipulation involves. W. H. Auden, in a professorial address at Oxford on Robert Frost, prefaced his discussion by adapting two figures from *The Tempest* as metaphors for leading types of poetry, or perhaps we should say, poetic minds. These were, he said, "Ariel-dominated" and "Prospero-dominated." The latter category, in which he placed Frost, is representative of the search for wisdom; the former, which would include Rimbaud and Mallarmé, is best expressed by the attitudes of "Ode on a Grecian Urn" and seeks a "verbal earthly paradise." There can be little doubt, I think, that Stevens moves with Ariel. Poets of that kind hunger after the transformation which will bring a lost history full circle and restore to man the image and nature from which he once defected. Rilke's angels and Stevens' imagination are burdened with these crosses, however they try to twist away. In an age like ours such personal visions are doomed to heroic isolation, and poets must pursue them into the dark. Rejecting belief, they have still retained a notion of man's destiny from wreckage and abandonment. Stevens never withdrew his confidence from the idea of human regeneration, from the Just City, and from the earth in all its flower: each thing rooted in every other and opened deeply to the sun and sky—ripeness as it was meant to be.

Wallace Stevens: The Life of the Imagination

by Roy Harvey Pearce

. . . there is a war between the mind
And sky, between thought and day and night.

Coda to *Notes toward a Supreme Fiction*

One thing we can now surely say of the achievement of Wallace
Stevens: He has written, over some thirty years, a whole and continuing
poetry whose subject is the life, the form and function, of the imagination.[1] In the recently published *Transport to Summer*[2] that subject receives its broadest, most complex treatment, yet remains essentially as it
was in his first volume, *Harmonium:* in his language, a problem in the
relation of the imagined to the real; in more general language, of the
world as known to the world as outside knowing. From beginning to end
what has been basic is the predicament of the man who would know.
If, read in and of themselves, the poems in *Transport to Summer* contrast vividly with those in *Harmonium,* the contrast is as much an aspect
of continuity as of difference and opposition. It is a continuity that represents the growth and achievement which, for good and for bad, make the
total of Stevens' work greater than the sum of its parts. Viewed thus, the
poems in *Transport to Summer* are inevitable precisely as they show
Stevens trying to finish what he began in *Harmonium.*

"Wallace Stevens: The Life of the Imagination" by Roy Harvey Pearce. From *Publi-
cations of the Modern Language Association,* LXVI, No. 5 (September 1951), 561-582.
This essay appears in different form as part of a study of the whole of Stevens' poetry
(Chapter 9) in *The Continuity of American Poetry* by Roy Harvey Pearce, Princeton
University Press, 1961. Copyright © 1961 by Princeton University Press. Reprinted by
permission of the author, Princeton University Press, and The Modern Language Association of America.

[1] See particularly Marius Bewley, "The Poetry of Wallace Stevens," *Partisan Review,*
XVI (1949), 895-915; Bernard Heringman, "Wallace Stevens: The Use of Poetry," *ELH,*
XVI (1949), 325-336; Louis L. Martz, "The World of Wallace Stevens," in B. Rajan, ed.
Modern American Poetry: Focus Five (London, 1950), pp. 94-109; and William Van
O'Connor, *The Shaping Spirit: A Study of Wallace Stevens* (Chicago, 1950). All of these,
however, are most concerned with iteration and reiteration of subject and theme in
Stevens, rather than with continuity and development, as I am here.

[2] This was written before the publication of Stevens' *Auroras of Autumn* in Sept.
1950.

Treating of the relation of the imagined to the real—figured recently as the war between the mind and sky—Stevens is treating of our problem of belief. Unlike an Eliot, he has refused to move out of our culture into another and to seek a solution for the problem in the discovery of a "usable" form of belief. Rather, he has relied entirely on his own sensibility; he has tried to create the object of belief rather than discover it. This has been his strength and his weakness; this has been his risk. Always he has assumed, as he writes in "Esthétique du Mal," that the war between the mind and sky must be fought with what we have "as and where we are." What we have is the imagining self and a reality which is not part of that self, but which for the sake of belief must somehow be made part of it. We can believe only in a reality so known. To sketch a chronology: Stevens began by looking directly at our experience of the reality in which we are bound, continued by examining our predicament in being so bound, and has most recently been exploring the general implications of the predicament. Put another way, in terms of the problem of belief: He began by looking directly at the world which limits belief, continued by examining the possibility of belief and commitment in the face of that possibility, and has most recently been exploring the nature of possible belief. If the movement in the poems has been away from the descriptive and dramatic toward the discursive and dialectical, this is part of an immanent necessity rising out of a fixed subject matter and the poet's steadily maturing view of it. Essentially, the styles of *Harmonium* and *Transport to Summer* represent two modes of knowing. But the conception of the act of knowing, of the relation of the imagined to the real, remains constant. It is the degree of knowing, the complexity and inclusiveness of the knowledge, which grows. And it comes finally, in the major poems of *Transport to Summer,* to make for the possibility of mature, considered belief in the reality which we have "as and where we are."

I

What is central in the poems of *Harmonium* (1923, 1931) is an awareness of the texture of reality (in Stevens' sense of *Ding an sich*) as a factor at once for the enriching and for the limiting of experience. The driving concern of these poems is with the sensuously flowing aspect of reality as we come to know, to partake of, and thus to inform it and be informed by it. These are specifically poems of the creative imagination. In "Infanta Marina" we are given a picture of the consummately beautiful woman whose very motions become part of the beauty of her surroundings. The poem ends:

> And thus she roamed
> In the roamings of her fan,

> Partaking of the sea,
> And of the evening,
> As they flowed around
> And uttered their subsiding sound.

In "Domination of Black" we are moved "At night, by the fire," from a vision of leaves to a vision of peacock tails, so to the sound of peacock cries and to the sound of terror, and so to a knowledge of terror; each flows into the other, each becomes part of the other. And we are told that there are, after all, at least thirteen ways of looking at a blackbird; yet all these ways are perhaps dominated by this one:

> A man and a woman
> Are one.
> A man and a woman and a blackbird
> Are one.

The mode here is descriptive, for Stevens an act of a creative imagination, with the poet (as an implied speaker in a lyric) always bound up in what he would describe.

Thus in these poems, description is equated with perception, and perception with conception. The poet at once differentiates one segment of his reality from another and learns that in the process he has made every segment so differentiated part of himself. The "ancient star" addressed in "Nuances of a Theme by Williams" is admonished to "Lend no part to any humanity that suffuses/you in its own light," asked to "Be not an intelligence,/Like a widow's bird/Or an old horse." The point is that one asks and admonishes in vain, that the star is the *Ding an sich*, that one cannot know it as unsuffused by the light of humanity, that Stevens' own perceptions are so suffused.

Here the great example is "Sea Surface Full of Clouds":

> In that November off Tehuantepec,
> The slopping of the sea grew still one night
> And in the morning summer hued the deck
>
> And made one think of rosy chocolate
> And gilt umbrellas. Paradisal green
> Gave suavity to the perplexed machine
>
> Of ocean, which like limpid water lay.
> Who, then, in that ambrosial latitude
> Out of the light evolved the moving blooms,
>
> Who, then, evolved the sea-blooms from the clouds
> Diffusing balm in that Pacific calm?
> *C'était mon enfant, mon bijou, mon âme.*

In this opening section we are moved from the relatively bare statement which lets us know that the phenomenon of the sea exists, to a description of the sea as perceived, an account of how one comes to conceive of the sea. The green of the summer morning is known literally to have given all the self-sufficiency, quietness, and ease suggested by "suavity" to an ocean which has been known as something "perplexed." From whom does this and what follows rise? The line in French indicates as precisely as possible the specifically human source and the poet's attitude towards that source—"*enfant, bijou, âme.*" The rest of the description will follow from the quality of this attitude. And so it goes throughout the poem. The description is rich ("confected" is a word Stevens has recently used) because the very richness of the perceptive act differentiates the clearly from the dimly perceived, the imagined from the real. In being known, the ocean is given body, literally suffused with the light of humanity. The moral, if Stevens would draw it, would be the one toward the end of "Peter Quince at the Clavier" and would come as necessarily:

> Beauty is momentary in the mind—
> The fitful tracing of a portal;
> But in the flesh it is immortal.

Or, in the words of "The Emperor of Ice Cream," "be" must be "finale of seem." We are, for this Stevens, limited, even condemned, to rich perceptions.

For the Stevens of the *Harmonium* poems and those immediately after, the consequences of such limitation can be pathetic or amusing, hardly tragic. He traces such consequences in poems which are in mode essentially dramatic. They amount to portrayals of the interior conflict of men and women discovering that they must cling only to the world which their rich perceptions have given them. This is the imaginatively compounded world of "Sea Surface" and the rest. Here "Sunday Morning" is the received text—probably, since ours is an age which prefers not the poetry of ideas but rather the poetry of human response to ideas, the poem of Stevens which we have let ourselves know best.

The center of consciousness, the perceiving and informing imagination, in "Sunday Morning" is that of a woman intelligent and sensitive enough to be disturbed by her awareness of a "holy hush of ancient sacrifice" in which she cannot participate. She tries to break through the limits of her bright warm world and to achieve realization of that world of received religion, "Dominion of the blood and sepulchre." She tries to conceive of a divinity which is not immediate and palpable, which is entirely of the spirit. Yet "Divinity must live within herself"; for "All pleasures and all pains"—"These are the measures destined for her soul." So she struggles to break through her hard and sweet reality, to conceive of a God, a paradise, an eternity, which might be abstracted from that reality. We are made to follow each of her thoughts and questionings as one flows into another. We are placed at the center of her predicament; yet we know it as she cannot. Like her, we are bound in time, in the reality which is of time; yet seeing her thus, we may know that we must live and believe only in the light of the sun-as-reality, a light which, above all, may make us aware of experience as concrete and immediate and of infinitely delicate gradation:

> We live in an old chaos of the sun,
> Or old dependency of day and night,
> Or island solitude, unsponsored, free,
> Of that wide water, inescapable.
> Deer walk upon our mountains, and the quail
> Whistle about us their spontaneous cries;
> Sweet berries ripen in the wilderness;
> And, in the isolation of the sky,
> At evening, casual flocks of pigeons make
> Ambiguous undulations as they sink,
> Downward to darkness, on extended wings.

This is the way of the world of *Harmonium*. The elderly lover in "Le Monocle de mon Oncle" says at the end of his meditation:

> . . . I pursued,
> And still pursue, the origin and course
> Of love, but until now I never knew
> That fluttering things have so distinct a shade.

And the speaker in "To the One of Fictive Music" finds that that experience of music (thus, metaphorically, of all created beauty) perfects those who make it, involving them deeply in the intensely imaginative experiences from which, as modern men, they would flee. Here the plea is for acceptance of perceived reality as the very source of humanity:

> Unreal, give back to us what once you gave:
> The imagination that we spurned and crave.

The moods of "Sunday Morning," "Le Monocle," and "To the One of Fictive Music" are those of graceful and profound puzzlement, amused but peaceful resignation, and deep pleading. The mode of the poems is always dramatic and descriptive, marked by a richness and density of language and a tendency to let meaning arise from variations worked upon or out of a set of basic metaphors. These metaphors in turn let us know precisely how it is for the protagonist in each poem to feel as he does; for they represent the working of his sensibility on the reality which it must inform. Ultimately, meaning in all the poems stems from the situation of their protagonists, who are involved in a reality which is not theirs but which they yet must make theirs.

Stevens treats the general implications of this situation in the longest, most difficult, and, I think, most inadequate of the larger poems in *Harmonium,* "The Comedian as the Letter C." Here the protagonist, limited, once more, to a life of rich perceptions, is something of a poet, philosopher, and wit. Thus he is in a position to reflect learnedly and at length on his situation and generally to resolve it. As I understand it, the poem involves the protagonist's growth to artistic maturity.[3] The poet progresses from romantic subjectivism, to crude realism, to exotic realism, to a kind of local-colorism, to a disciplined, mature, and imaginative realism. He comes to know the potentialities and the limits of his own imagination. At this point he can face life squarely; he marries, begets children, and grows wiser. Yet at the end he is in a period of cautious skepticism, dubious about any acceptance of reality, however self-conscious and mature that acceptance may be. The point is that he has made a successful "adjustment." One needs expert guidance to gather this much; one needs more than one should need; for the very manner of the poetry will not allow for the release of such meaning; particulars get in the way of implicit generalization—the sense of detail, however much imaginatively informed, in the way of implicit dialectic. Here, for example, is part of the end of the third section—that which concerns the protagonist's sojourn in commonplace reality:

> He came. The poetic hero without palms
> Or jugglery, without regalia.
> And as he came he saw that it was spring,
> A time abhorrent to the nihilist
> Or searcher for the fecund minimum.
> The moonlight fiction disappeared. The spring,
> Although contending featly in its veils,
> Irised in dew and early fragrancies,
> Was gemmy marionette to him that sought
> A sinewy nakedness . . .

The overplus of language—parallels, appositions, repetitions, words unabsorbed into the whole, an overpowering concreteness—gets in the way of the developing analysis of the poet's situation. That which we like about the poem, the virtuosity and charming self-indulgence of language, can only obscure that which we should like as much—the argument and

---

3 Here I follow Hi Simons, " 'The Comedian as the Letter C': Its Sense and Its Significance," *Southern Review,* V (1940), 453-468.

the meaning. The poet-protagonist himself—with his powerful sensibility —gets between us and the poem. We never know the nature and quality of that final "adjustment" and his doubts about it. We can see here, as Stevens is trying to derive a general meaning from his materials, the emergence of a need for the mode of the later poetry—an expository, dialectical mode—if he is fully to understand and to resolve the predicament of this protagonist and the other perplexed ones who precede him in "Sunday Morning," "Le Monocle," and "To the One of Fictive Music."

II

The poems in *Ideas of Order* (1935, 1936), the volume after the second edition of *Harmonium* (whose texts I have followed), are for the most part written from the point of view of such a one as the protagonist in "The Comedian as the Letter C": that of a man trying to understand his involvement in the war between reality and imagination. In these later pieces Stevens is mainly concerned to demonstrate, largely in poems of situation, the interpenetration of the one by the other. As poet, he is, as he writes in a jacket note, an "exponent of the imagination." But, as human being, he finds that he must hold the imagination to concrete reality. In "Sad Strains of a Gay Waltz" and "Botanist on Alp (No. 1)," for example, he treats the failure of the imagination to come alive. And then in "Farewell to Florida," "Lions in Sweden," and "Mozart, 1935," he treats the need to hold the imagination to reality, and so indicates how it may come alive. Most important, in "The Idea of Order at Key West," he treats the work of the imagination as it gives to our reality whatever order we can be sure resides therein. In this poem he writes of the woman who sings beside the sea:

> It was her voice that made
> The sky acutest at its vanishing.
> She measured to the hour its solitude.
> She was the single artificer of the world
> In which she sang. And when she sang, the sea,
> Whatever self it had, became the self
> That was her song, for she was the maker. Then we,
> As we beheld her striding there alone,
> Knew that there never was a world for her
> Except the one she sang and, singing, made.

This is that "Blessed rage for order" by which we live.

What one misses in the poems in *Ideas of Order,* for all their competencies, is movement towards consideration of the more general implications of this view of man as caught between his imagination and his reality. There is, after all, a marked limitation to such poems of a descriptive-dramatic mode, poems one of whose uses should be to make us face our own special human predicament. It is something to tell us that the predicament exists and to make us aware of its every nuance, but critical hindsight makes us sense that this was and is not enough. Stevens himself comments generally on such a limitation in the poems in *The Man with the Blue Guitar* (1937) and *Parts of a World* (1942). Particularly, he writes in "The Poems of Our Climate" (in *Parts of a World*) a brilliantly descriptive account of "Clear water in a brilliant bowl,/Pink and white carnations"; and then he comments:

> Say even that this complete simplicity
> Stripped one of all one's torments, concealed
> The evilly compounded, vital I
> And made it fresh in a world of white,
> A world of clear water, brilliant-edged,
> Still one would want more, one would need more,
> More than a world of white and snowy scents.
>
> There would still remain the never-resting mind,
> So that one would want to escape, come back
> To what had been so long composed.
> The imperfect is our paradise.
> Note that, in this bitterness, delight,
> Since the imperfect is so hot in us,
> Lies in flawed words and stubborn sounds.

Poetry must be a means of grasping reality; but we must be aware of the process by which we grasp reality, however imperfectly; for in that process—which is the imaginative process—lies our humanity. What we need, in a phrase from "Of Modern Poetry" (also in *Parts of a World*), is "The poem of the act of the mind."

The greater part of the work in *The Man with the Blue Guitar* and *Parts of a World* consists of attempts to write such a poem. In the work in these volumes Stevens is concerned to get at the problem of reality and the imagination directly, not through a dramatic situation. As a result he begins to develop, particularly in *Parts of a World*, a mode adequate to such a direct approach to his problem. This, as I have noted, is the dialectical mode which is to be fully developed in *Transport to Summer* (1947): still and forever mannered, witty, and elegant—yet now discursive, centered on logical (and alogical) analysis; built out of a language which is as often abstract and nativist as it is richly concrete and exotic; with a syntactic and structural freedom which allows him to invent as he will, to explore the most general implications of his themes and still to return when he wishes to his local and particular starting point, which is, as always, the sensitive individual trying to satisfy simultaneously the claims of reality and the imagination. The poet-protagonist is now explicitly the philosopher, meditating abundantly and easily.

Yet the mode, and consequently the analysis, as developed in the poems in *The Man with the Blue Guitar* and in *Parts of a World*, is not made to do its proper job. It comes too easily, too casually; it represents, perhaps, an attempt to explore, and thus forecasts the later poems. As Stevens indicates—in another jacket note—the title poem in *The Man with the Blue Guitar* consists simply of a series of notes on "the incessant conjunctioning between things as they are and things imagined." This, for example, is the fifth in the series:

> Do not speak to us of the greatness of poetry,
> Of the torches wisping in the underground,
>
> Of the structure of vaults upon a point of light.
> There are no shadows in the sun,
>
> Day is desire and night is sleep.
> There are no shadows anywhere.
>
> The earth, for us, is flat and bare.
> There are no shadows. Poetry
>
> Exceeding music must take the place
> Of empty heaven and its hymns.
>
> Ourselves in poetry must take their place,
> Even in the chattering of your guitar.

The last nine lines are simply turned against the first three; discursive statement cancels out concrete realization and demonstrates the need for a poetry of ourselves. This is the role of the man with the guitar, the role of the poet, or (as Stevens makes explicit in his jacket note), of "any man of imagination."

Likewise, in *Parts of a World* there is everywhere the tendency simply to assert the place of the imagination and to demand of the poet that he do his proper work and conjoin imagination and reality. The themes of the earlier poems are restated and made to point explicitly to such a conclusion: "Sea Surface Full of Clouds," for example, is in "Variations on a Summer Day"; "Sunday Morning" is in "The Blue Buildings in the Summer Air," "Dezembrum," and "Bouquet of Belle Sçavoir"; and "The Idea of Order at Key West" is in "The Woman That Had More Babies Than That." The sameness of so many of the poems, developing at worst into flatness and at best into rich repetition, derives from Stevens' recognition of a situation and of a need, the precise nature and full implications of which he does not explore. "Landscape with Boat" and

"Asides on the Oboe" point toward "Notes toward a Supreme Fiction": "Extracts from Addresses to the Academy of Fine Ideas" points toward "Esthétique du Mal." But in each case the conjoining of imagination and reality is limited in scope because it results in a poetry of statement, not of analysis. Stevens does not move from recognition of a problem to an attempt to work out a solution.

Stevens will say in "Asides on the Oboe" that

> The prologues are over. It is a question, now,
> Of final belief. So, say that final belief
> Must be in a fiction. It is time to choose.

And he will show us clearly that whatever of our beliefs we have destroyed, we have not destroyed our belief in that

> impossible possible philosopher's man,
> The man who has had the time to think enough,
> The central man, the human globe, responsive
> As a mirror with a voice, the man of glass,
> Who in a million diamonds sums us up.

This is the man, ourselves, whom our imagination enables us to discover "without external reference" at the center of the reality which we have made. This is the reality in which we must believe, the point at which the texture of experience is given final form by the imagination. This is the point at which we discover, as Stevens says in a lecture delivered in 1947, "that poetry and reality are one, or should be . . ." [4] But we ask, if in this fragmented world we can finally discover and believe in ourselves, what does this discovery mean to us? What do *we* mean? Final belief demands, in short, complete philosophic and imaginative awareness. And the triumph of the major poems in *Transport to Summer*—to which the earlier poems are now literally a "prologue"—is the triumph of an elegantly individuated sensibility which has at last realized the possibilities of philosophic understanding and the moral imagination.

III

The title page of Stevens' most recent volume itself indicates the direction in which his poetry has moved. "*Transport to Summer,* by Wallace Stevens"; a journey on which we are carried to the clear light of the sun, to reality (and sun-as-reality is a favorite metaphor of Stevens) by a poet, "any man of imagination."

[4] "The Realm of Resemblance," *Partisan Review,* XIV (1947), 248.

The myriad small poems in *Transport to Summer* widen the possibility of a poetry of recognition and statement. Yet they have little existence of their own, being no more than introductions to the master poems in the volume, "Notes toward a Supreme Fiction" and "Esthétique du Mal." Glancing back toward the poems preceding them, they rush toward Stevens' masterworks. In these small poems, reality and the situation of the man hemmed in by his reality begin to be comprehended as well as accepted; liberation of the spirit seems possible; the mode, potentially complex and inclusive, is tentatively philosophic. Poetry begins to settle into its place in the world. We are told, for example, that "The Motive for Metaphor" is the need for recollection in tranquillity; so one must withdraw from reality, from "The weight of primary noon,/The ABC of being," from "The vital, arrogant, fatal dominant X"; and one must seek the pleasures of the imagination under an "obscure moon." Yet the lesson of such a piece as "The Bed of Old John Zeller" is that one must learn not to withdraw entirely, that one must learn "to evade/That habit of wishing and to accept the structure/Of things as the structure of ideas." That structure is, in the title of another poem, one of "Men Made Out of Words"; so, simply enough, "Life consists/Of propositions about life." Steadily and easily we move via words from the imagination to reality and back again; steadily and easily we are made to create our world. In "Credences of Summer" the creative process is thus briefly described. The "self," Stevens writes,

> having possessed
> The object, grips it in savage scrutiny,
> Once to make captive, once to subjugate
> Or yield to subjugation, once to proclaim
> The meaning of the capture, this hard prize,
> Fully made, fully apparent, fully found.

Yet such poems as these are merely notes for propositions about life. The propositions themselves, developed fully, are in "Notes toward a Supreme Fiction" and "Esthétique du Mal."

In these poems, which seem to me at once the most ambitious and the most important in his whole work, Stevens would finally conjoin reality and the imagination and would discover in such a conjoining the possibility of that ultimate belief which was denied to the protagonists of "Sunday Morning," "Le Monocle de mon Oncle," and "To the One of Fictive Music." So doing, he becomes explicitly philosophical—in the sense that he is concerned with realizing in esthetic form certain epistemological, ontological, and moral propositions. The relationship between the propositions and the poetry is this: that esthetic experience is the only means we have of initiating the inquiry by which we arrive at those propositions and is, moreover, the only means we have of realizing and believing in them. Thus Stevens' poetry is at once an expression and an exposition of a philosophical attitude. Since the authenticity of that attitude depends on origin in esthetic experience, it depends on the sensibility of the poet, a sensibility divorced—ideally—from any abstract system which would impose on it order from without; for order, esthetic order, "the structure of things," must be derived from a dynamic relationship between the individual imagination and the reality which it beholds. So the poet-esthete becomes the philosopher-moralist. To him a philosophical proposition fully realized is one realized as a poem. For propositions are statements involving the conjoining of the individual imagination and reality; and such a conjoining is the work of the poet, of "any man of imagination."

"Notes toward a Supreme Fiction" is a poem about belief. Nominally it turns on the nature of our Supreme Fiction, our supreme center of belief. Yet Stevens can describe the form of our Fiction only by indirection, in terms of what it must be, not of what it is. The three sections in the poem are headed "It Must Be Abstract," "It Must Change," and "It Must Give Pleasure." The "Must" in each of these headings is inferred dialectically as the poet describes and evaluates what it is for the man of imagination fully to live in reality and not to be overwhelmed by it. This is the argument:

"It Must Be Abstract." (I). We must begin with perceived reality, and argue from it to the *Ding an sich,* to "this invented world/The inconceivable idea of the sun"; yet we must not suppose that our perception of reality argues for our creation of reality. We must, in fact, dispose of the idea of any creator, even for the reality which exists outside our perception; for "Phoebus was/A name for something that never could be named." The sun, reality, simply was and is. (II). Still, we are driven by the very divisiveness of our lives to seek a unitive source of our idea of reality: ". . . not to have is the beginning of desire." (III). Poetry is our means to this source:

> The poem refreshes life so that we share,
> For a moment, the first idea . . . It satisfies
> Belief in an immaculate beginning
>
> And sends us, winged by an unconscious will,
> To an immaculate end.

(IV). Thus the origin of poetry, of our ideas of the world and of ourselves, is in our concrete past and present:

> From this the poem springs: that we live in a place
> That is not our own and, much more, not ourselves
> And hard it is in spite of blazoned days.

(v). The act of the poetic imagination is the source of human power over the world. (vi). Perception, knowledge, and feeling are interdependent— in origin, really one:

> Not to be realized because not to
> Be seen, not to be loved nor hated because
> Not to be realized.

And so we live by "An abstraction blooded, as a man by thought." (vii). Hence we must hold to reality if we are to hold to abstract truth; for, once more, the source of truth is reality. (viii-ix). It follows then that our hero, our "major man," will be man imagining—discovering a Supreme Fiction in the flux of reality and making it available to us; it follows, moreover, that his discovery will be that our Supreme Fiction is, in fact, "major man" (the abstraction) known through man (the concrete particular man). Analytic reason abstracts man from reality, but it is the creative imagination which reveals him to us. (x). Finally there is triumphant affirmation:

> The major abstraction is the idea of man
> And major man is its exponent, abler
> In the abstract than in his singular,
>
> More fecund as principle than particle,
> Happy fecundity, flor-abundant force,
> In being more than an exception, part,
>
> Though an heroic part, of the commonal.
> The major abstraction is the commonal,
> The inanimate, difficult visage. Who is it?
>
> What rabbi, grown furious with human wish,
> What chieftain, walking by himself, crying
> Most miserable, most victorious,
>
> Does not see these separate figures one by one,
> And yet see only one, in his old coat,
> His slouching pantaloons, beyond the town,
>
> Looking for what was, where it used to be?
> Cloudless the morning. It is he. The man
> In that old coat, those sagging pantaloons,
>
> It is of him, ephebe, to make, to confect
> The final elegance, not to console
> Nor sanctify, but plainly to propound.

The problem of "Sunday Morning" is faced and solved. Man, the Supreme Fiction, moves us as an abstraction, yet is known as a particular. The "major man" is the poet ("any man of imagination"), he who makes us know as the "final elegance" even that man whom our religionists and rulers see only as a poor bedraggled creature.

"It Must Change." (i). Change is part of the flow of reality; thus the Supreme Fiction must partake of Change. (ii). Growth and mortality—these are change and so are real. Immortality, which is not change, is not real:

> Spring vanishes the scraps of winter, why
> Should there be a question of returning or
> Of death in memory's dream? Is spring asleep?
>
> This warmth is for lovers at last accomplishing
> Their love, this beginning, not resuming . . .

(iii). Art which does not express the sense of change violates reality. (iv). Change originates, and we come to know it, in the opposites (man-woman, day-night, winter-summer, and so on) of which our world is constituted. (v). It is, in fact, growth and change which make life bearable. Here, in a poem strikingly in the manner and form of "Sunday Morning," Stevens again resolves the problem of *Harmonium*. He writes of his protagonist, a planter who had lived and died on a tropical island:

> An unaffected man in a negative light
> Could not have borne his labor nor have died
> Sighing that he should leave the banjo's twang.

The use of negatives here literally forces the positiveness of the statement on us. The point is that the planter who lived in a green land "baked greener in the greenest sun" took his abundant life from a positive light, in a positive land of growth and death, of change. He was not hemmed in, but was released by reality. (vi-vii). The positive existence of change is evidenced everywhere—in the beauty of sound which will end, in the earthbound quality of emotional experience. (viii-ix). Our knowledge, which is "never naked," has always a "fictive covering" involved in temporal reality; it is thus poetic knowledge. For the poem itself is of language, "The gibberish of the vulgate," which itself changes; in so being, the poem is of change and can make us know the Supreme Fiction. The poet, then:

> tries by a peculiar speech to speak
>
> The peculiar potency of the general,
> To compound the imagination's Latin with
> The lingua franca et jocundissima.

"Peculiar speech" and "peculiar potency"—the particular—make possible our knowledge of the general. Imagination's formal language finds expression in reality's "lingua franca et jocundissima." (x). Change thus is part of the movement of reality, movement which can be perceived everywhere. (This is the flow of reality celebrated in "Infanta Marina" and the rest.) Simply enough, "The freshness of transformation is/The freshness of a world." That which has baffled the poet of "The Idea of Order at Key West" no longer baffles him, because he accepts it for what it is. Man comprehends change by conceiving of the idea of order, by making poems which express that idea. For "The freshness of transformation" is "our own,/It is ourselves, the freshness of ourselves. . . ."

"It Must Give Pleasure." (I). To celebrate our belief regularly and ceremoniously, according to tradition—this is "a facile exercise." But the "difficultest rigor" is to celebrate our belief from moment to moment, in the very flux and disorder of reality—"to catch from that/Irrational moment its unreasoning." (II). What is needed is the pleasure of things-in-themselves. This is a pleasure in particulars, certainly; but yet we know the general, the Supreme Fiction, ourselves, in particulars. (This section is, once more, strikingly in the form of "Sunday Morning"; but the woman who is the protagonist here accepts her pleasurable reality as the woman in "Sunday Morning" cannot.) (III-VII). We are able to love things—particularized reality—because we take joy in them for their own sake. This is exemplified in (III) the love of children which gives beauty and life to the ugly, in (IV) the love of two persons for the portion of reality in one another, and negatively in (V-VII) the tale of the canon who would impose an alien order on reality and so drive delight from it, who does not know that "to impose is not to discover." (VIII). The poet affirms that he cannot believe in the abstract in and of itself; he can believe in it only as it is given delightful embodiment in informed reality: "I have not but I am and as I am, I am." (IX). Things-in-themselves, repeated, reexamined, perceived again and again—these are a final good. For through repetitions of things-in-themselves, we approach our Supreme Fiction:

> Perhaps
> The man-hero is not the exceptional monster,
> But he that of repetition is most master.

And it is "the vast repetitions final in/Themselves" which make for the Supreme Fiction. (x). The essential problem is to name one's world, to poetize it, to see it as a general structure of pleasurable particulars, and so to possess it. And inevitably, distortion is characteristic of this structure of particulars:

> That's it: the more than rational distortion,
> The fiction that results from feeling. Yes, that.

> They will get it straight one day at the Sorbonne.
> We shall return at twilight from the lecture
> Pleased that the irrational is rational,
>
> Until flicked by feeling, in a gildered street,
> I call you by name, my green, my fluent mundo.
> You will have stopped revolving except in crystal.

Here the poem ends, the possibilities of the reasoned abstract having been realized in the imagination which, as it works, adjusts itself to the distortions of reality, to change, and so adjusting, discovers the rich pleasure of existence. Belief in the world of "Sunday Morning" is not only possible but necessary. It is the exercise of the creative imagination, working out a set of epistemological and ontological propositions, which has made for that possibility and that necessity. After such knowledge there can come only belief.

So it is not so much the act of belief which concerns Stevens as it is preparation for that act—knowing the world which is to be faced, locating abstraction, change, and pleasure in the reality of that world. Stevens is Socratic enough to believe that full knowledge will call forth compulsive belief. When he comes further to examine imaginative experience of the world and finds pain and terror in that experience, he must posit evil as their source in reality. The Supreme Fiction must now also give pain. It is evil, thus, which Stevens studies in "Esthétique du Mal," a poem in which the lesson of the poet's life (the life of "any man of imagination") is most fully drawn. The final condition for belief in the Supreme Fiction is the acceptance of reality. The final condition for the acceptance of reality is the acceptance of the evil in reality. Epistemological and ontological understanding, having made for belief, now make for morality. Good and evil, pleasure and pain, are now comprehended, one with another.

The very title, "Esthétique du Mal," indicates clearly the location of positive evil in the texture of reality, the texture which is the stuff of esthetic experience. As a constituent of reality, however, evil cannot be known directly in itself, but rather must be known as it is shaped by the imagination: This is the source of pain. In Part I, the protagonist, another of Stevens' poets, is in Naples, "writing letters home/And, between his letters, reading paragraphs/On the sublime." As he reads, Vesuvius groans; there is for him in this groaning a knowledge of pain and terror, because he can conceive of such sound only as pain and terror imaginatively informed; the sound is his means of knowing pain and terror. And he sees that, for us, whatever of pain there is in the world is pain only as we know it imaginatively and, knowing it, are in part responsible for it. "This is a part of the sublime/From which we shrink." In Part II, the deep night and its sounds "At a town in which acacias grew," communicate to him "The intelligence of his despair, express/What meditation never quite achieved." He learns that pain is "indifferent" to reality, that reality is not painful except as the imagination is conjoined to it and makes it so. Nor does the imagination alone produce pain. Yet pain "never sees/How that which rejects it saves it in the end." This last contains a central paradox for man: Pain is "saved" in the end, in its human uniqueness, because it is not part of the imagination through which we come to feel it nor of the reality in which we feel it. This is a continuation of the paradox of the Supreme Fiction, which is independent of reality and the imagination, taken singly, but which comes into existence through that conjoining of both which marks the predicament of Stevens' man who would know. Another deceivingly simple way to put it is to say, as Stevens does in the middle of Part I, "Pain is human."

From Part III on, the propositions which give structure to the poem center less and less on the poet-protagonist and become more and more general. The truth ascertained in Part III is that "heaven and hell/are one," that even an "over-human god" discovered this, that "the health of the world," "the honey of common summer," the simple and direct experiencing of pleasurable reality, are not enough for us; paradoxically, we are continually pained to think that they might be, to long for a simpler life which we cannot have. The need is that we understand reality as we make (or remake) it for ourselves, with its portion of evil— here, in Part IV—even in the purity of music and painting. We cannot be sentimentalists. We must know ourselves as we know our world; and evil is of ourselves as much as of our world:

> The genius of misfortune
> Is not a sentimentalist. He is
> That evil, that evil in the self, from which
> In desperate hallow, rugged gesture, fault
> Falls out on everything: the genius of
> The mind, which is our being, wrong and wrong,
> The genius of the body, which is our world,
> Spent in the false engagements of the mind.

The rest of the poem develops in considerations of the "false engagements of the mind" toward which our genius directs us. In love for our kind in our world we can sustain ourselves against the evil in ourselves and in our world. This is the burden of Part V. Yet as Stevens makes clear, in Part VI, in a characteristically wild fable of a bird insatiably pecking at the sun, even love can never be fully satisfied, for our imperfections always characterize our desires. Then in a lyric of great tenderness, which is Part VII, he writes of evil and death:

> How red the rose that is the soldier's wound,
> The wounds of many soldiers, the wounds of all
> The soldiers that have fallen, red in blood,
> The soldier of time grown deathless in great size.

The soldier's wound is a metaphor for the suffering involved in living in this world; the metaphor is developed as the soldier is shown to be loved and sustained by his fellows in the very world which wounds him. So

> his wound is good because life was.
> No part of him was ever part of death.
> A woman smoothes her forehead with her hand
> And the soldier of time lies calm beneath that stroke.

So far as he is wounded by living in and of the world, he is not dead; living with evil-in-reality is not death, but the highest life. Part VIII is a meditation on the death of Satan, killed by disbelief. In denying and so losing him, however, we lost a means of grasping evil formally. We are left only with ourselves and our acceptance of our reality, and so of evil—with

> the yes of the realist spoken because he must
> Say yes, spoken because under every no
> Lay a passion for yes that had never been broken.

Part IX is a further exploration of the struggle of the "realist" to face evil imaginatively, without Satan. Part X is concerned with the vain nostalgia for escape from evil in the world, the hope to find escape in woman as a mother-wife. Part XI contrasts a reality truly known with one falsely known. It is the bitter reality which we need to know beyond any pleasure-principle:

> The tongue caresses these exacerbations.
> They press it as epicure, distinguishing
> Themselves from its essential savor,
> Like hunger that feeds on its own hungriness.

Parts XII-XIV, with logical analyses, meditations, and seeming-casual commentary, renew the richly informed view of a world of reality, with evil felt fully as "action moving in the blood." And Part XV forces this view of man in his world to its inevitable conclusion:

> The greatest poverty is not to live
> In a physical world, to feel that one's desire
> Is too difficult to tell from despair. Perhaps,

After death, the non-physical people, in paradise,
Itself non-physical, may, by chance, observe
The green corn gleaming and experience
The minor of what we feel. The adventurer
In humanity has not conceived of a race
Completely physical in a physical world.
The green corn gleams and the metaphysicals
Lie sprawling in majors of the August heat,
The rotund emotions, paradise unknown.

This is the thesis scrivened in delight,
The reverberating psalm, the right chorale.

One might have thought of sight, but who could think
Of what it sees, for all the ill it sees?
Speech found the ear, for all the evil sound,
But the dark italics it could not propound.
And out of what one sees and hears and out
Of what one feels, who could have thought to make
So many selves, so many sensuous worlds,
As if the air, the mid-day air, was swarming
With the metaphysical changes that occur
Merely in living as and where we live.

This is the morality of the major man: the need for living in an imagina-tively known reality; the need, moreover, to endure without despair the pain of having to live so. We can endure because we know that the "non-physical people, in paradise,/Itself non-physical" can know but weakly what we, the physical people, know strongly. Yet even we are not so completely limited by physicality as not to know of metaphysicals, the great abstractions, our fictions; these we know in terms of our physical reality—green, sprawling, and rotund. This had been Stevens' thesis in "Notes toward a Supreme Fiction." Here he discovers its final moral implications for us: This reality which we know imaginatively contains evil inseparably. Since our joy is to live in reality, we needs must live in evil and know it fully. The final statement is quiet, direct, deriving its strength from the emphasis on simple verbs of being. Being, in fact, is "living as and where we live."

"Esthétique du Mal," following on "Notes toward a Supreme Fic-tion," makes for a richly secular version of *felix culpa,* the Paradox of the Fortunate Fall. Richness and secularity are the essential qualities. But an outline such as this can only indicate propositions, lines of argu-ment, and conclusions—and so moves too far away from these essential qualities. What makes the argument stick, the poetry, is perhaps lost; but this is a chance that we must take. I think it is worth taking. For such a (temporary) cutting-down of the poems to the critic's size allows one to see them in all their richness and secularity, as growing inevitably out of the earlier poems and the earlier manner. It is indeed the development of a freely inventive, discursive mode that allows (or should one say, that forces?) Stevens fully to explore the general implications of "Infanta Marina," "Sunday Morning," and others like them. What emerges in "Notes toward a Supreme Fiction" and "Esthétique du Mal" is the possibility of belief in a world in which the conditions and forms of belief are themselves products of the interaction of the believer and his world, of the conjoining of the imagination and reality. It is a matter of created and recreated belief, not of belief given from the outside.

If such creativeness runs the danger of romantic irresponsibility, Stevens would avoid that danger by recognizing the strength and recalcitrance, even the evil, of the materials—the reality—on which creativeness must operate. Facing such a reality, all creation must be an act of violence. (In 1941, concluding that poetry was a means of self-preservation, Stevens could find in it "a violence within that protects us from a violence without." [5]) In the poetry it is a paradoxical violence; for it is a quality deriving from the very control which the poet exercises over his world. It is a violence which makes Stevens' dialectic not reasoned but hortatory; a violence which is at the heart of his special elegance, his fantasy, his invention, his exoticism, and his wit; a violence which makes for his tendency to move as often as not merely by association; a violence which allows him at his best to write only a long series of varyingly formed meditations, not a single thoroughly integrated poem. Such violence Stevens can never escape; for inevitably it too is a product of the conjoining of his imagination and his reality.

Such are the strengths and the weaknesses, results of a risk taken, which must rise naturally when a world without a received principle of order is considered by a man who refuses to accept any principle of order he cannot find authorized in the only thing he really knows, himself. If he is a man of rich sensibility, he will see his world as a green, fluent mundo, not as something out of Aquinas, Locke, Marx, or whoever currently dwells in the Apocalypse. He will improvise a principle of order out of the self. His strength will be his weakness; he will have taken his risk. He will be inadequate, paradoxically enough, when he sees, feels, and writes too much. But he will achieve form and wholeness, however amorphous, and maturity, however disaffected.

A recent poem, "The Lack of Repose," furnishes the proper gloss:

> A young man seated at his table
> Holds in his hand a book you have never written

---

[5] "The Noble Rider and the Sound of Words," in Allen Tate, ed. *The Language of Poetry* (Princeton, 1942), p. 125.

Staring at the secretions of the words as
They reveal themselves.

It is not midnight. It is mid-day,
The young man is well-disclosed, one of the gang,
Andrew Jackson Something. But this book
Is a cloud in which a voice mumbles.

It is a ghost that inhabits a cloud,
But a ghost for Andrew, not lean, catarrhal
And pallid. It is the grandfather he liked,
With an understanding compounded by death

And the associations beyond death, even if only
Time. What a thing it is to believe that
One understands, in the intense disclosures
Of a parent in the French sense.

And not yet to have written a book in which
One is already a grandfather and to have put there
A few sounds of meaning, a momentary end
To the complication, is good, is a good.

This is Stevens on received forms of belief, on forms which are not related to what he takes to be our immediate condition of belief. We know
in whom Andrew Jackson Something believes; we have recently been
told a great deal about his ghost and his grandfather. Yet we can move
from him and the southern traditionalists whom he represents to all
those who hold to forms of belief which are not primarily of our time,
of our place, and of ourselves; and we can turn to what in Stevens comes
to be a strongly individualistic antitraditionalism. Our problem, certainly, is to find a middle way between a too passive traditionalism and
a too active contemporaneity, between a dead reality and one super-
charged. With Stevens, at least, we can return to an overpoweringly
present reality and see how he tries to control it. Even if we cannot go
along with him, we can know fully the possibilities, the strengths and
weaknesses, and the risks, of *his* way. And we may pause at the last stanza
of "The Lack of Repose." It is indeed good, a good—a great good—the
service of a major man to men whom he would have live "as and where
[they] are."

IV

In the end, what issues from the poems is indeed a kind of estheticism,
but as Stevens defiantly insists, the highest estheticism. So it is more
than a coincidence that the later Stevens should herein resemble the

later James—locating, by means of the elegantly creative act, moral
order in the world that men must make and suffer to make. We should
remember, for example, the fate of Lambert Strether and of John
Marcher. We should remember the end of James's preface to *The Golden
Bowl:*

> We are condemned, . . . whether we will or no, to abandon and outlive, to
> forget and disown and hand over to desolation, many vital or social per-
> formances—if only because the traces, records, connexions, and the very
> memorials we would fain preserve, are practically impossible to rescue for
> that purpose from the general mixture. We give them up even when we
> wouldn't—it is not a question of choice. Not so on the other hand our really
> "done" things of this superior and more appreciable order—which leave us
> indeed all licence of disconnexion and disavowal, but positively impose on
> us no such necessity. Our relation to them is essentially traceable, and in that
> fact abides, we feel, the incomparable luxury of the artist.

Artist = poet = "any man of imagination." The price paid for the "really
'done' things" is suffering and pain. The reward, for Stevens as for
James, is knowledge and individuality—and a measure of freedom. This
is the meaning of the war between the mind and sky; this is, for Stevens,
the full life of the imagination.

Wallace Stevens: The World as Meditation

by Louis L. Martz

"In an age of disbelief," says Wallace Stevens in a late essay, "it is for the poet to supply the satisfactions of belief, in his measure and in his style." It is my purpose here to explore the nature of those satisfactions, to examine the measure and the style that Stevens achieved in his later poetry, and in this way to suggest the answer that Stevens found to his own blunt question: "What, then, is the nature of poetry in a time of disbelief?" [1]

The answer is implicit in the late poem that provides my theme and title here: *The World as Meditation* (1952) seems to sum up the poetical discoveries of Stevens since that time, some thirty years earlier, when his Paltry Nude started on her Spring Voyage through the world of *Harmonium,* to become at the close of that volume a complete Nomad Exquisite, fully attuned to the harmonies of nature, creating as nature herself creates:

> As the immense dew of Florida
> Brings forth
> The big-finned palm
> And green vine angering for life,
>
> .   .   .   .
>
> So, in me, come flinging
> Forms, flames, and the flakes of flames.

The World as Meditation, on the other hand, finds its central proposition, not in any text from the surface of things, but in certain words of a human composer, Georges Enesco: "J'ai passé trop de temps à travailler mon violon, à voyager. Mais l'exercice essentiel du compositeur—la méditation—rien ne l'a jamais suspendu en moi. . . . Je vis un rêve

---

[1] "Two or Three Ideas" (1951), in *Opus Posthumous,* ed. by Samuel French Morse (New York, 1957), pp. 206, 211 (cited hereafter as OP).

permanent, qui ne s'arrête ni nuit ni jour." With those words as epigraph, the poem presents as its symbol of human achievement the figure
of Penelope, awaiting the return of Ulysses. As the sun rises she awakens
to the meditation that has composed her life:

> A form of fire approaches the cretonnes of Penelope,
> Whose mere savage presence awakens the world in which she dwells.
>
> She has composed, so long, a self with which to welcome him,
> Companion to his self for her, which she imagined,
> Two in a deep-founded sheltering, friend and dear friend.
>
> . . . .
>
> But was it Ulysses? Or was it only the warmth of the sun
> On her pillow? The thought kept beating in her like her heart.
> The two kept beating together. It was only day.
>
> It was Ulysses and it was not. Yet they had met,
> Friend and dear friend and a planet's encouragement.
> The barbarous strength within her would never fail.

There is, we see, a "savage presence" outside her, the primitive force
of the sun, which arouses within her a "barbarous strength," some primitive human power that makes it possible for her to compose a self, with
the sun's encouragement; and so she dwells in a world of belief created by
her will. This sounds like the conception found at the close of Stevens'
essay "The Noble Rider" (1942), where he mentions a certain nobility
of mind that constitutes "a violence from within that protects us from a
violence without. It is the imagination pressing back against the pressure
of reality." Thus the violence of the sun might have aroused Penelope to
the violent, ugly pressure of those outward suitors; but her imagination
of Ulysses, her constant meditation of reunion with the man she constantly creates in her mind, this power presses back, composes within herself a world of value and order. Thus, as Stevens concludes in that essay,
imagination "seems, in the last analysis, to have something to do with
our self-preservation." [2]

I have used two terms, both prominent in Stevens' writings: *imagination, meditation;* they are not synonymous. Meditation is the essential
exercise which, constantly practiced, brings the imagination into play,
releases creative power, enables the human being to compose a sensitive,
intelligent, and generous self. It is the sort of self that Stevens has found
fully represented in the person of George Santayana, as he points out in
an essay of 1948. "Most men's lives," he regretfully concedes, "are
thrust upon them" by the outward violence; but he insists:

[2] *The Necessary Angel* (New York, 1951), p. 36 (cited hereafter as NA).

There can be lives, nevertheless, which exist by the deliberate choice of those that live them. To use a single illustration: it may be assumed that the life of Professor Santayana is a life in which the function of the imagination has had a function similar to its function in any deliberate work of art or letters. We have only to think of this present phase of it, in which, in his old age, he dwells in the head of the world, in the company of devoted women, in their convent, and in the company of familiar saints, whose presence does so much to make any convent an appropriate refuge for a generous and human philosopher. [NA, 147-48]

And so in his late poem *To an Old Philosopher in Rome* (1952) he finds the fulfillment of human existence in Santayana's reconciliation of flesh and spirit on the threshold of death:

> The sounds drift in. The buildings are remembered.
> The life of the city never lets go, nor do you
> Ever want it to. It is part of the life in your room.
> Its domes are the architecture of your bed.
>
> .   .   .   .
>
> It is a kind of total grandeur at the end,
> With every visible thing enlarged and yet
> No more than a bed, a chair and moving nuns,
> The immensest theatre, the pillared porch,
> The book and candle in your ambered room,
>
> Total grandeur of a total edifice,
> Chosen by an inquisitor of structures
> For himself. He stops upon this threshold,
> As if the design of all his words takes form
> And frame from thinking and is realized.

Such admiration for the power of *thinking,* for the constructive power of deliberate choice—this is not the sort of values that were being attributed to Stevens fifteen or twenty years ago. The central impact of Stevens' poetry up to about 1940 has been, I think, admirably summed up by Yvor Winters in his famous essay "Wallace Stevens or The Hedonist's Progress." There Winters, basing his thesis primarily on *Harmonium,* saw in Stevens the cultivation of "the realm of emotion divorced from understanding," the commendation of "the emotions as a good in themselves." It was, he felt, a point of view that had led Stevens from the great poetry of *Harmonium* into a "rapid and tragic decay" of style, the sad, inevitable progress of the hedonist, "unable to think himself out of the situation into which he has wandered." [3]

[3] *The Anatomy of Nonsense* (Norfolk, Conn., 1943), pp. 89, 91, 97.

Winters has made a brilliant diagnosis of the malady; but he underestimated the patient's will to live. Looking back now, with the immense advantage of all that Stevens has published since Winters wrote, and with the equally great advantage of the recent *Opus Posthumous*—looking back now, we can see that something quite different happened. We can see something analogous to the course of Yeats's poetry. We can see a poet, by a deliberate process of self-knowledge, rebuilding himself and his poetry, rebuilding himself through his poetry, and achieving, in *Transport to Summer* (1947), a volume of meditative poetry that is in every way the equal of his great, first volume of hedonist poetry. It is not a question of setting up divisions, but of watching recessive elements in the early poetry develop into dominance.

Let us try to sketch, now, this different progress. Stevens' second volume, *Ideas of Order,* appeared in 1935; its slimness, its dominant tone, and its title are all significant of a change in the poet's outlook. The buoyancy that gave forth the bounty of *Harmonium* is gone; that force within, like "the immense dew of Florida," that had brought forth "Forms, flames, and the flakes of flames" is subsiding, although here and there it reappears, the old gay defiance of Winters:

> But what are radiant reason and radiant will
> To warblings early in the hilarious trees
> Of summer, the drunken mother?

Or:

> What is there here but weather, what spirit
> Have I except it comes from the sun?

The trouble is that the younger Nomad Exquisite had lived by a view that the poet of the 1930's could no longer accept, for reasons he suggests in the late essay cited at the outset of this discussion: "If in the minds of men creativeness was the same thing as creation in the natural world, if a spiritual planet matched the sun, or if without any question of a spiritual planet, the light and warmth of spring revitalized all our faculties, as in a measure they do, all the bearings one takes, all the propositions one formulates would be within the scope of that particular domination"—as they were, for the most part, in *Harmonium*. "The trouble is, however, that men in general do not create in light and warmth alone," he continues. "They create in darkness and coldness. They create when they are hopeless, in the midst of antagonisms, when they are wrong, when their powers are no longer subject to their control. They create as the ministers of evil" (OP, 210). *Ideas of Order* moves in this different world; it is filled with the tones of evening: *A Fading of the Sun, Gray Stones and Gray Pigeons, Autumn Refrain, Winter Bells, Sad Strains of a Gay Waltz.*

> There is order in neither sea nor sun.
> The shapes have lost their glistening.
> There are these sudden mobs of men.

In this new atmosphere one poem stands out to control the chaos: the famous *Idea of Order at Key West.* Here the speaker, significantly, stands at the far edge of Florida, his back upon that world of flame and green. The physical world now offers none of its old "comforts of the sun," but exists here as

> The meaningless plungings of water and the wind,
> Theatrical distances, bronze shadows heaped
> On high horizons, mountainous atmospheres
> Of sky and sea.

The object of wonder and admiration is now a human figure, that singer by the shore whose voice made

> The sky acutest at its vanishing.
> She measured to the hour its solitude.
> She was the single artificer of the world
> In which she sang.

This is more than the Palace of Hoon, the solipsist of *Harmonium;* for the idea of order here resides in more than mental landscapes, in "More even than her voice, and ours": the idea of order is found in a unique conjunction of landscape, singer, and listener, a situation in which the listener's mind, exulting in the full strength of its powers, is able to assert the controlling force of consciousness, "Fixing emblazoned zones and fiery poles" upon the outer atmosphere, "Arranging, deepening, enchanting night"—while realizing fully that the outer universe goes its inhuman way.

The fierce strength of mind in that poem, its clipped and muted language before the final exultation, prepares the way for a striking addition to the volume *Ideas of Order,* when it appeared in a trade edition in the next year, 1936. The volume no longer opens with the curiously fatigued poem, *Sailing after Lunch,* where Stevens truly says, "My old boat goes round on a crutch/And doesn't get under way," and where he ends with the sentimental desire:

> To expunge all people and be a pupil
> Of the gorgeous wheel and so to give
> That slight transcendence to the dirty sail.

No, the volume now opens with the stirring *Farewell to Florida*, in which Stevens renounces all that "Florida" has symbolized in his earlier poetry: that world of vivid physical apprehension, where man created within the bounds of the natural order. "Her mind had bound me round," he says, but now he cries:

> Go on, high ship, since now, upon the shore,
> The snake has left its skin upon the floor.
> Key West sank downward under massive clouds
> And silvers and greens spread over the sea. The moon
> Is at the mast-head and the past is dead.
> Her mind will never speak to me again.

And he looks forward to his engagement with a new, a tough, bitter, and turbulent subject:

> My North is leafless and lies in a wintry slime
> Both of men and clouds, a slime of men in crowds.
> The men are moving as the water moves,
> This darkened water cloven by sullen swells
> Against your sides, then shoving and slithering,
> The darkness shattered, turbulent with foam.
> To be free again, to return to the violent mind
> That is their mind, these men, and that will bind
> Me round, carry me, misty deck, carry me
> To the cold, go on, high ship, go on, plunge on.

Stevens, it is clear, has determined to take his old boat out of *The Pleasures of Merely Circulating*, to plunge into the turmoil of the mid-thirties, to engage it somehow in his poetry. In fact, he had already begun the effort. The year before *Farewell to Florida* appeared he had already published the first part of what was to become his longest poetical effort, *Owl's Clover*, which appeared in 1936 in its original version of 861 lines. It is a poem that caused Stevens immense labor and, finally, intense dissatisfaction. In 1937 it reappeared with nearly 200 lines cut out; and in 1954 Stevens omitted it entirely from his *Collected Poems*, on the grounds that it was "rhetorical," Mr. Morse tells us (OP, xxiii). As a result of this drastic omission, the reader of the *Collected Poems* may emerge with a sense of the poet's steady self-possession, an ideal progress from the old gaudy style toward a sober, muted, thoughtful, pruned, and thoroughly remade poetry: for we move from *Ideas of Order* directly into *The Man with the Blue Guitar*, where

> The man bent over his guitar,
> A shearsman of sorts.

A shearsman indeed, a sort of tailor, cutting his cloth anew and shearing away the excess.[4] But the effect is too neat. We need *Owl's Clover*, preferably in its first version, to tell us all the trouble of the change; and fortunately we have it all now before us once again, in the new posthumous volume. It is not a successful poem, though it contains great passages and opens remarkably well, with the firmly controlled symbols of *The Old Woman and the Statue*. There the magnificent statue in the park represents the soaring, noble imagination of the past, "leaping in the storms of light": the statue is a work of art subtly and powerfully arranged for the human mind to grasp and be exalted. One thing, one thing only, the sculptor "had not foreseen": the old woman, "the bitter mind/In a flapping cloak," a woman so depressed that she cannot apprehend the statue's action:

> A woman walking in the autumn leaves,
> Thinking of heaven and earth and of herself
> And looking at the place in which she walked,
> As a place in which each thing was motionless
> Except the thing she felt but did not know.

That thing is the "harridan self," "Crying against a need that pressed like cold,/Deadly and deep." It is not simply physical poverty that tortures this suffering self: it is that she lives, as the second part tells us, amid "the immense detritus of a world"

> That is completely waste, that moves from waste
> To waste, out of the hopeless waste of the past
> Into a hopeful waste to come.

The hopeful waste of the future, I think, alludes to the sort of world proffered by Mr. Burnshaw, whose name adorns the original title of the second part: *Mr. Burnshaw and the Statue* (later altered to *The Statue at the World's End*). Stanley Burnshaw was the Marxist critic who in 1935 had reviewed *Ideas of Order* with considerable acuteness, though with a condescending tone: he had seen it as a book of "speculations, questionings, contradictions"—"the record of a man who, having lost his footing, now scrambles to stand up and keep his balance." [5] The critique, being so largely true, left the mark, as *Owl's Clover* shows in its derisive rejection of all mass-solutions that offer only "an age of concentric mobs."

---

[4] See Stevens' explanation of this figure in a letter to his Italian translator, Renato Poggioli: "This refers to the posture of the speaker, squatting like a tailor (a shearsman) as he works on his cloth." *Mattino Domenicale ed Altre Poesie* (Turin, 1954), p. 174.

[5] *New Masses*, Oct. 1, 1935, p. 42.

But what can be offered instead to the suffering self? The offering in this long second section turns out, in spite of its high rhetoric, to be surprisingly meager: it is simply the old pleasures of Florida, chanted in a weak imitation of the old hieratic style of *Sunday Morning,* as this passage (later removed) indicates:

> Dance, now, and with sharp voices cry, but cry
> Like damsels daubed and let your feet be bare
> To touch the grass and, as you circle, turn
> Your backs upon the vivid statue. Then,
> Weaving ring in radiant ring and quickly, fling
> Yourselves away and at a distance join
> Your hands held high and cry again, but cry,
> This time, like damsels captured by the sky,
> Seized by that possible blue.

But those waltzes had ended, long since. Clearly, the poet must try another way, and so, in his third section, Stevens turns to develop a contrast between two ways of life. One is the old way of religious meditation, where "each man,"

> Through long cloud-cloister-porches, walked alone,
> Noble within perfecting solitude,
> Like a solitude of the sun, in which the mind
> Acquired transparence and beheld itself
> And beheld the source from which transparence came.

And the other is something that seems to have arisen or to be arising in place of the old religious way, something he calls Africa, a world of dense, savage, mindless animality, where

> Death, only, sits upon the serpent throne:
> Death, the herdsman of elephants,
> To whom the jaguars cry and lions roar
> Their petty dirges of fallen forest-men,
> Forever hunting or hunted, rushing through
> Endless pursuit or endlessly pursued,
> Until each tree, each evil-blossomed vine,
> Each fretful fern drops down a fear like dew.

From here on, in the middle of the poem, *Owl's Clover* provides less and less sustenance for the troubled mind trying to feed in the dark. It becomes increasingly turgid and incoherent. The old religion cannot cope with "Africa," nor can the old art of the statue; nor can the problems be met by the believers in necessity, the nostalgic admirers of the old pioneer spirit, or the worshippers of the "newest Soviet reclame." "How shall we face the edge of time?"

> Where shall we find more than derisive words?
> When shall lush chorals spiral through our fire
> And daunt that old assassin, heart's desire?

"Lush chorals"—the backward glance toward the days of *Harmonium* —is ominous, and we are not surprised to find the poem ending with a Sombre Figuration in which the poet attempts to find refuge in a vague, semi-Jungian concept of the "subman." This subman is some inner man of imagination, who lies below the torments of thought: "The man below the man below the man,/Steeped in night's opium, evading day." But the subman has a precarious tenure, for he seems to reside only in a rhetoric of empty assertion:

> And memory's lord is the lord of prophecy
> And steps forth, priestly in severity,
> Yet lord, a mask of flame, the sprawling form
> A wandering orb upon a path grown clear.

It is a relief to turn from this evasive subman to the daylight figure who shears away this outworn pomp. The sounds made by *The Man with the Blue Guitar* (1937) show that Stevens, within a year's hard thought, has taken quick, firm strides toward the position thoroughly established in his prose essays and his later poetry: that "the poet must get rid of the hieratic in everything that concerns him," that he must abolish "the false conception of the imagination as some incalculable *vates* within us, unhappy Rodomontade" (NA, 58, 61)—i.e. the opium-drugged subman must be erased, along with the style in which he had been expressed. In his place we will have something like Picasso's clear, clean image of the old Guitar Player, a product of his "blue period" (though the guitar itself happens to be tan), which was, incidentally, exhibited in Hartford in 1934. We will have an image of life explored, discovered, and developed through a language made out of "things exactly as they are," a language moving now with a tough intent toward the discovery of a self:

> Ah, but to play man number one,
> To drive the dagger in his heart,
>
> To lay his brain upon the board
> And pick the acrid colors out,

> To nail his thought across the door,
> Its wings spread wide to rain and snow,
>
> To strike his living hi and ho,
> To tick it, tock it, turn it true,
>
> To bang it from a savage blue,
> Jangling the metal of the strings.

This is as far as we can get from the puzzled, ruminative ebb and flow of *Owl's Clover,* with its dissolving, eddying, and often turbid blank verse: note here the crisp common diction, the strict driving rhythm of the short couplets, subtly bound together by irregular rhymes and half-rhymes, all focused on one aim: a definition of the *self* as the only province of poetry:

> Ourselves in the tune as if in space,
> Yet nothing changed, except the place
>
> Of things as they are and only the place
> As you play them, on the blue guitar,
>
> Placed, so, beyond the compass of change,
> Perceived in a final atmosphere;
>
> For a moment final.

We have returned to the central position of the *Idea of Order at Key West:* man's inner rage for order as the ultimate constructive force in man's universe, and hence the never-ending effort of the mind to control, within the mind, that outer monster, the inhuman universe:

> That I may reduce the monster to
> Myself, and then may be myself
>
> In face of the monster, be more than part
> Of it, more than the monstrous player of
>
> One of its monstrous lutes, not be
> Alone, but reduce the monster and be,
>
> Two things, the two together as one.

From this effort, he says, "I shall evolve a man."

This sequence of thirty-three tightly argued, tightly ordered meditations on a theme establishes the altered style of the later Stevens. He has here, in a deliberate act of choice, sheared away the kind of writing that he later calls "The romantic intoning, the declaimed clairvoyance," since this, he says, is the "appropriate idiom" of apotheosis; and this is not at all his subject now. Apotheosis elevates the mortal to the stature of divinity; it glorifies; and the appropriate poetry of apotheosis is therefore the hymn, the ode, the celebration, the chant. In a peculiar sense, this had been the appropriate idiom of his earlier poetry, since he was there attempting to show, as he tells the lady in *Sunday Morning,* that "Divinity must live within" the human realm: "Passions of rain, or moods in falling snow." Hence he uses the idiom of romantic intoning to glorify the satisfactions of this earth, often with deliberate irony: the Comedian speaks of his "first central hymns, the celebrants/Of rankest trivia"; and indeed the whole mock-heroic effect of the Comedian arises from the application of such grand intoning to the achievements of this "merest minuscule."

But in his new effort to evolve a man, a new idiom must be invented, since "apotheosis is not/The origin of the major man" for whom the poet is now searching. "He comes," says Stevens, "from reason,/Lighted at midnight by the studious eye,/Swaddled in revery." He is the meditative man, master of the essential exercise, student, scholar, rabbi of a new idiom, which Stevens in *Of Modern Poetry* (1940) calls "The poem of the mind in the act of finding/What will suffice." There has never been a better definition of what might be called the genre of meditative poetry. It is not, we note, a poem celebrating what suffices; nor is it any lamentation for the lack of what suffices. The difference between the true meditative poem and other poetic genres seems to be exactly this: that it alone represents "The poem of the act of the mind," the poem of the mind, in the very act of finding. One thinks of Emily Dickinson, of Hopkins, of George Herbert, and especially of Donne, in his *Divine Meditations (Holy Sonnets).*

But further definition of the genre, if there is really such a genre, is necessary, and Stevens suggests it all in *Of Modern Poetry:*

> It has to be living, to learn the speech of the place.
> It has to face the men of the time and to meet
> The women of the time. It has to think about war
> And it has to find what will suffice. It has
> To construct a new stage. It has to be on that stage
> And, like an insatiable actor, slowly and
> With meditation, speak words that in the ear,
> In the delicatest ear of the mind, repeat,
> Exactly, that which it wants to hear, at the sound
> Of which, an invisible audience listens,
> Not to the play, but to itself, expressed
> In an emotion as of two people, as of two
> Emotions becoming one.

Let me expand, with only a little liberty, the possible implications of that text. This kind of poetry must know the common speech; it must make contact with men in their normal existence, through its language, its images, and its consideration of urgent problems, such as war, of whatever kind, whether between man and man, or between body and soul, good and evil, man and his environment—the "war between the mind and sky" that Stevens describes at the end of his "Notes toward a Supreme Fiction." It has to find what will suffice, but in order to do this, it must construct a stage on which an actor may enact the process of this finding. And as this actor speaks his meditated words, they find a growing response in a certain invisible audience, which is not simply us, the readers or listeners, but is first of all the larger, total mind of the poet himself, controlling the actor, who is some projected aspect of himself. Then, in the close, that actor and that audience, projected self and larger self, come together in a moment of emotional resolution—for a moment final. It is a process that Stevens describes thus in his *Adagia:* "When the mind is like a hall in which thought is like a voice speaking, the voice is always that of someone else." The voice is that of some projected self: the audience is the whole self. "It is necessary to propose an enigma to the mind," he says in another adage. "The mind always proposes a solution" (OP, 168). All this seems to describe something very like the action in *The Idea of Order at Key West:* the landscape is the stage, the singer by the shore is the actor, and the poet's larger mind is the audience. It is also very like the action that one finds in Donne's *Holy Sonnets,* which we may take as a prime example of pure meditative poetry, since they seem to arise directly from the rigorous meditative exercises commonly practiced by religious men of the seventeenth century. Recall how Donne projects some aspect of himself upon a stage: the deathbed, the round earth's imagined corners, the Cross; how he then allows that self to ponder the given situation; and how, at the close, the projected self makes a subtle union with the whole mind of the poet, concluding all in the finding of what will suffice.

One can only ponder the possibilities here, and pause to stress one point. In formal religious meditation, as developed during Donne's time and later practiced (certainly) by Hopkins and (presumably) by Eliot, the process of meditation consists of something akin to that just described by Stevens. It begins with the deliberate creation of a setting and the placing of an actor there: some aspect of the self; this is the famous composition of place recommended by the Jesuit exercises. This is followed by predominantly intellectual analysis of some crucial problem pertaining to that self; and it all ends in a highly emotional resolution where the projected self and the whole mind of the meditator come together in a spirit of devotion. This threefold process is related to the old division of the soul into memory, understanding, and will; the exercise of meditation integrates these faculties.

How is it that a modern poet such as Wallace Stevens, so vastly different from the seventeenth century in the objects of his belief, should come to describe the need for a kind of poetry to which Donne's *Holy Sonnets* seem to belong: a kind that we might call the genre of meditative poetry? Donne's strenuous cultivation of this kind of poetry seems to be part of his lifelong effort to transcend and resolve his grievous sense of the fickleness, the dissolution, the transiency and fragility of all physical things. In Stevens, I think, an analogous situation called forth the analogous discipline. Stevens, in mid-career, recognized the dissolution, or the inadequacy, of his old poetic self—a recognition recorded with a wry gaiety in *The Comedian as the Letter C.* His later poems represent a rigorous search for ways and means of evolving another kind of poetic self, in accord with the outlook expressed in the late essay dealing with the "time of disbelief": "There was always in every man the increasingly human self, which instead of remaining the observer, the non-participant, the delinquent, became constantly more and more all there was or so it seemed; and whether it was so or merely seemed so still left it for him to resolve life and the world in his own terms" (OP, 207).

Allusions in his prose essays indicate that in this effort Stevens engaged in broad reading among tough thinkers, while all his later poetry displays a new respect for the "radiant idea" and the "radiant will." This is clear in the first part of *Notes toward a Supreme Fiction* (1942), which insists that the fiction must be, in some sense, "abstract." Not, I think, abstract in the usual sense of a philosophical abstraction; Stevens has told us plainly what he thinks of this in his *Landscape with Boat,* where he decries the man who "wanted imperceptible air," who "wanted the eye to see"

> And not be touched by blue. He wanted to know,
> A naked man who regarded himself in the glass
> Of air, who looked for the world beneath the blue,
> Without blue, without any turquoise tint or phase,
> Any azure under-side or after-color.

By "abstract" Stevens seems rather to imply a quality of being taken out, abstracted in the root sense, from that world we call the outer universe: something concrete taken out of this and taken into the mind through a process of full, exact realization. From that "local abstraction" the turquoise tints and azure undersides can then radiate in all directions. This is the process that Stevens vividly describes in section vii of *Credences of Summer,* where he begins by scorning those who have found it too hard "to sing in face/Of the object," and have therefore fled to the woods, where they could sing "their unreal songs,/Secure." In a violent reversal of mood, he advocates a fiercely opposite process:

> Three times the concentred self takes hold, three times
> The thrice concentred self, having possessed
>
> The object, grips it in savage scrutiny,
> Once to make captive, once to subjugate
> Or yield to subjugation, once to proclaim
> The meaning of the capture, this hard prize,
> Fully made, fully apparent, fully found.

If this bears some resemblance to the old threefold process of formal meditation, it is only because Stevens has discovered for himself the same faculties, and has taught himself a way of using them for his own meditative ends. He has, in an essay of 1943, come to define the imagination as "the sum of our faculties," and has gone on to speak of "The acute intelligence of the imagination, the illimitable resources of its memory, its power to possess the moment it perceives" (NA, 61).

Indeed, it appears that Stevens has been thoroughly aware of the analogy I am suggesting, for in a newly published essay, written about 1937, we find him declaring: "The poet who wishes to contemplate the good in the midst of confusion is like the mystic who wishes to contemplate God in the midst of evil. . . . Resistance to the pressure of ominous and destructive circumstance consists of its conversion, so far as possible, into a different, an explicable, an amenable circumstance." And in this search, he adds, the poets "purge themselves before reality . . . in what they intend to be saintly exercises" (OP, 225, 227).

But if we accept Stevens' use of the term *meditation* as a proper description of his own secular exercises, we may appear to be stretching the word beyond any useful signification. Cannot any poem that contains any degree of hard thinking be thus called meditative? I do not think so, if we keep in mind the careful distinctions made by the old spiritual writer, François de Sales. "Every meditation is a thought," he says, "but every thought is not a meditation; for we have thoughts, to which our mind is carried without aim or design at all, by way of a simple musing. . . . And be this kind of thought as attentive as it may be, it can never bear the name of meditation." On the other hand, he says, "Sometimes we consider a thing attentively to learn its causes, effects, qualities; and this thought is named study." But "when we think of heavenly things, not to learn, but to delight in them, that is called to meditate; and the exercise thereof meditation." "So that meditation," he concludes, "is an attentive thought repeated or voluntarily maintained in the mind, to arouse the will to holy and wholesome affections and resolutions." [6]

It seems valid to adapt this definition to the meditation of earthly

---

[6] François de Sales, *A Treatise on the Love of God* (1616), Book VI, chap. ii; adapted from the translation of 1630.

things, since meditation is a process, not a subject. If we do this, then Stevensian meditation becomes: attentive thinking about concrete things with the aim of developing an affectionate understanding of how good it is to be alive. We can see the process working everywhere in his later poetry, but nowhere better than in *The World as Meditation,* which now needs to be read entire as an example of the full development of Stevens' meditative style. Note first how far the poem's range extends beyond the "comforts of the sun": the verbal beauty of Enesco's French draws in the cosmopolitan world of the musician, as the figure of Penelope draws in the ancient world of legend. Yet the sun exists as first cause; without it there would be nothing. Thus the poem is phrased to allow a double reference: the sun is Penelope's companion, along with Ulysses. Note too how the poem fulfills all of Stevens' requirements for this modern poetry: common speech, common images, common problems; the establishment of a stage, the placing of Penelope as actor on that stage, the imputed working of her meditative thoughts, along with the constant presence of the poet's larger mind, controlling all, and concluding all with an affectionate understanding of what will suffice.

Is it Ulysses that approaches from the east,
The interminable adventurer? The trees are mended.
That winter is washed away. Someone is moving

On the horizon and lifting himself up above it.
A form of fire approaches the cretonnes of Penelope,
Whose mere savage presence awakens the world in which she dwells.

She has composed, so long, a self with which to welcome him,
Companion to his self for her, which she imagined,
Two in a deep-founded sheltering, friend and dear friend.

The trees had been mended, as an essential exercise
In an inhuman meditation, larger than her own.
No winds like dogs watched over her at night.

She wanted nothing he could not bring her by coming alone.
She wanted no fetchings. His arms would be her necklace
And her belt, the final fortune of their desire.

But was it Ulysses? Or was it only the warmth of the sun
On her pillow? The thought kept beating in her like her heart.
The two kept beating together. It was only day.

It was Ulysses and it was not. Yet they had met,
Friend and dear friend and a planet's encouragement.
The barbarous strength within her would never fail.

She would talk a little to herself as she combed her hair,
Repeating his name with its patient syllables,
Never forgetting him that kept coming constantly so near.

The world of *Harmonium* has not been discarded here, but its reliance on the natural force of "sensibility" has been modified, and the pleasures of that world have been included within a larger structure of existence. By 1951 Stevens could strongly question "the dogma that the origins of poetry are to be found in the sensibility," and could suggest "if one says that a fortunate poem or a fortunate painting is a synthesis of exceptional concentration . . . we find that the operative force within us does not, in fact, seem to be the sensibility, that is to say, the feelings. It seems to be a constructive faculty, that derives its energy more from the imagination than from the sensibility"—imagination being, as we have seen, the "sum of our faculties." But he adds, in his cautious way, "I have spoken of questioning, not of denying" (NA, 164). That is because the old dews of Florida have never ceased to affect him. One of his very last poems, *Prologues to What Is Possible,* suggests that the value of existence may have resided in

A flick which added to what was real and its vocabulary,
The way some first thing coming into Northern trees
Adds to them the whole vocabulary of the South,
The way the earliest single light in the evening sky, in spring,
Creates a fresh universe out of nothingness by adding itself,
The way a look or a touch reveals its unexpected magnitudes.

There is no inconsistency here. The look, the touch, the flick of feeling, the "times of inherent excellence," "incalculable balances," "not balances/That we achieve but balances that happen"—these are things worth recognizing, and Stevens never ceases to celebrate them as part of the wonder of human consciousness. But he is quick to recognize that "the casual is not/Enough": it does not attain the full "freshness of ourselves"; it does not satisfy the "will to make iris frettings on the blank." Beyond the casual apprehensions there lie the willed and reasoned structures of the mind, which Stevens presents in two forms. One structure occurs when the mind thoroughly and fully concentrates upon the realization of some composition that appears to be inherent in the external scene, as in *Credences of Summer.*

Let's see the very thing and nothing else.
Let's see it with the hottest fire of sight.
Burn everything not part of it to ash.

> Trace the gold sun about the whitened sky
> Without evasion by a single metaphor.

Thus:

> One of the limits of reality
> Presents itself in Oley when the hay,
> Baked through long days, is piled in mows. It is
> A land too ripe for enigmas, too serene.

This seems to be what Stevens means by seeing things in their "first idea," their "ever-early candor"; this is the adequacy of landscape—for a moment final. It exists beyond us, it is no metaphor, and yet, Stevens insists, "the first idea is an imagined thing," since it is achieved by a calculated effort of the mind. It is part, then, "of the never-ending meditation," a poem of the mind in the act of finding what will suffice. It may be, he says, "of a man skating, a woman dancing, a woman/Combing," a Woman Looking at a Vase of Flowers, a Dish of Peaches in Russia, or a Large Red Man Reading: it may be found "in the crackling summer night,"

> In the *Duft* of towns, beside a window, beside
> A lamp, in a day of the week, the time before spring,
> A manner of walking, yellow fruit, a house,
> A street.

They are acts available to any man, a sort of poetry, "an imaginative activity that diffuses itself throughout our lives" (NA, 149). You return, say, from a long vacation with your family in the mountains, dog-tired, addle-brained, and feeling the whole expedition was a huge mistake. Two weeks later, the snapshots return, developed in full color: you are amazed at the beauty, the order, the focus; the trip is a success, after all. Such a realization would be, in Stevens' terms, a poetic action.

And finally, beyond such compositions, there lies the inexhaustible "realm of resemblance," in which the faculties of the imagination, using all their powers, "extend the object" by analogy, by metaphor. It is a realm in which the whole mind, like Stevens' Penelope, uses the world of sensory experience as a base upon which to construct a total edifice involving and demanding the whole stretch of human experience. By the use of such analogies man connects the external and the internal; the action of analogy is the mind's ultimate way of establishing its dominant, controlling position amid the "moving chaos that never ends." And this, too, is an activity that Stevens sees as available to everyone.

You sit in a chair, say, admiring the beauty of your four-year-old daughter: you call to mind certain resemblances between her and her absent mother, between her and your imagined image of yourself, between her and your memories and pictures of grandparents. You think, too, of certain painted images of children by Renoir or Romney; you think of Andrew Marvell's *Picture of Little T. C. in a Prospect of Flowers;* you think of the dogwood that bloomed last Spring and of the zinnias now blooming outside. And for a moment the object toward which all these resemblances converge, or from which they infinitely extend—for a moment the object becomes a vital center through which the sense of life is composed, final: "completed in a completed scene," as Stevens says. Such is Wallace Stevens' *World as Meditation,* a world where the poet may adopt the words of Valéry's Architect and say, "By dint of constructing, . . . I truly believe that I have constructed myself."

Wallace Stevens and the Image of Man

by Morton Dauwen Zabel

Stevens' poetry was from the first distinguished by two elements in which he remained largely unrivaled among his contemporaries—the richness of his imagery and the sustained confidence of his rhetoric. The two qualities are, of course, mutually dependent; the first sustains and substances the other; but in an age which became generally suspicious of the values they embody, he gave them an authority that made his distinction isolated even beyond the independent integrity his career describes.

The sensory and symbolic properties of his verse—what Hopkins would have called its "keeping"—show, especially in *Harmonium* and the earlier collections, a wit and opulence that have come to seem extravagant in these later days of poetic realism and fact-facing: extravagant even when compared with the verbal shock-tactics of surrealism or the more ebullient pages of Dylan Thomas. In his first decade of publication, during the heyday of Imagism, his luxuriance of metaphor and allusion outran even the contrived fancies in which Amy Lowell and her disciples were trading; and when set against the austerity of Frost and Robinson or the spectral lights in Eliot, he showed an exoticism that made his art a case apart from the critical and anti-Romantic motives then in evidence. The prodigality of his materials and the sensuous capacities they implied, the Baroque indulgence, the riot of colors and flowers, the spectacles of sunlight and lustres and tropical splendor, the pomp of rich living and reckless luxury—these mounting festivals of the senses that could emphasize in Parisian art its tact and in the Oriental its austerity were tokens of an imagination radically at odds with the critical tendencies in modern verse. Accordingly Stevens was labeled a "dandy," a "connoisseur," a confecter of extravagant fictions, an exponent of the Romantic indulgence from which it had required the severest possible discipline to wean the American taste. One early critic set him down as a "conjurer," another as a "poetic Harlequin"; the Humanists fell on even so concentrated a poem as "Anecdote of the

"Wallace Stevens and the Image of Man" by Morton Dauwen Zabel. This essay was originally published, in a different form, in *The Harvard Advocate*, CXXVII, No. 3 (December 1940), 19-23. Copyright 1940 by *The Harvard Advocate* and, in the present revised and expanded form, © 1963 by Morton Dauwen Zabel. Reprinted by permission of *The Harvard Advocate* and Morton Dauwen Zabel.

Jar" as recklessly irresponsible in its meaning; and a younger English critic (Julian Symons) said that most of the poems in *Harmonium* "contain a slightly tittery joke" and that "The Comedian as the Letter C" amounted to "a piece of virtuosity, a literary curio."

No defender of Stevens' work will flatly deny the characterization implied in these criticisms, even where they are obviously unjust or wrong-headed; their prejudice helps fix his poetic character almost as usefully as the most enthusiastic favor. They also make it clear why Stevens was quick in winning a place among the poets—few in any age and rare in ours—who transport their readers to an unmistakable milieu of the imagination, to a characteristic atmosphere in which the special cast of the artist's taste, sympathies, and temperament becomes recognizable. His work carried the radical stamp of a personality that was able, merely by the phraseology and figurative devices in which he dealt, to win half the battle of words and meaning.

A poet's imagery is the individuating medium of his sensibility. So, of course, are his rhythm, his tonal quality, his particular vision and the idea or intuition it embodies. But the range of these in poetry is both more limited and more difficult to establish. They lack the atmospheric and dramatic force of imagery; they may be, for practical purposes at least, indistinguishable in large numbers of poets, sometimes even in poets of sharply contrasting temperaments and intentions. We find the clues to Baudelaire's world in his imagery of cats, clocks, courtesans, sumptuous rooms, ships, seas, islands, and stark Parisian streets. We are inducted into Mallarmé's researches by his symbolism of fans, fauns, stones, swans, bibelots, and hieratic artifacts and emblems. We enter the conscious as well as the secret parts of Hopkins' spirit through his metaphors of sensory miracle and shock, of "skeined stained veined variety" in nature, of the intimate sublimity and stupendous particles of Creation upon which he fastened for its meaning. Eliot depicted the history of the contemporary spirit in his *mise-en-scène* of vacant lots, cheap hotels, rat-infested alleys, refuse-choked rivers, stale-aired houses, and purgatorial drawing-rooms whose squalor and desolation, further emphasized by contrasts of past splendor or fallen glory, prepared the way for the penitential symbols of *Ash Wednesday* and the self-analyzing language and search for identity in "Burnt Norton," "East Coker," and the other *Quartets*. The types represented by Hardy, Yeats, Rilke, and Valéry are similarly indexed; Cummings and Auden are as unmistakably, even where more derivatively, marked. The serious poet who never finds this personal medium for his imagination is as likely to fall into indistinguishable anonymity as men of minor and indeterminate talent.

Among the modern poets who show a marked originality in this line, two orders of imagery predominate. They may be defined by the examples of Mallarmé and Hopkins. Mallarmé's imagism is absolute in its claims, irreducible and exhaustive in intention, refined and specialized in its

subtlety to the point of discovering the positive identity of its underlying concepts. It implies a final perfection in its correspondence with
idea. It resists rational sublimation except in terms of a total intuitive
synthesis (he translated "symbolism" as "synthesis") of concept and
object. To both the concept and its sensory analogy a special initiation
is required in the reader, and this initiation only the poem can realize
or effect. "The world has become, in Mallarmé's own expression, *'trans-
fusible en du songe,'* " said Charles Mauron; and it is only by participat-
ing in the "dream" and at the same time submitting to the cold control
of the penetrating sensibility of the poet that we enter into the processes
of Mallarmé's intuition. The general fault of poets who accept Mallarmé's
example is that their symbols may surpass his in boldness or singularity
but fail to establish the continuity of effect and reference, of pervading
and realizing intelligence, which reduces the arbitrariness of his usage
to a logical order. They either subtilize the image out of recognition or
depend on a framework of reference outside the poetry itself—upon
correspondences or arguments never fundamentally integrated by the
poetic experience. To imitate Mallarmé is usually to risk the defeat of
expression. He represents a standard of "purity" almost inhuman in its
demands, and many of his own poems succeed as intelligible art only by
falling short of it.

Hopkins' imagery, on the contrary, is realistic in basis—as exhaustively
but consistently realistic, at least in intention, as the threading of a
psychological maze in Henry James. Sometimes it is an almost baffling
or impenetrable complex of meaning that Hopkins attempts to elucidate,
as in the day-and-night figure at the close of "Spelt from Sibyl's Leaves";
often he seized his insight through an impulse voluntarily reckless and
violent, as in "The Windhover"; his characteristic effect is dramatic and
immediate, not analytical and deliberate. His imagery is recognizably
concrete in spite of its exorbitant sharpness of perception or obsessive
differentiation of detail. It suggests the inadequacy of metaphor or allegory to cope with intuition. Yet it remains finally capable of realistic
sublimation, and the reader's reward comes when he masters the patience
to join the poet in his intense exercise of the empathetic and scrutinizing
faculties. Hopkins had his reasons for shrinking from the structural
rationality and logical process of Aquinas and finding a greater support
for his particular temperament in the pages of Augustine and Duns
Scotus.

Mallarmé, whatever the allegory of the poet's ultimate defeat conveyed in the "Faune," maintains his intention of severe control, of
persistent and fathoming lucidity, of a concentrating rigor that seeks to
arrive finally at the perfect focus and penetration. Hopkins conveys a
sense of restive agony and search, of man as "law's indifference," of a
passion for certitude perpetually beset by human inadequacy and doubt,
of a failure to penetrate to his desired vision except in momentary and

miraculous flashes of intense lyric clairvoyance. Mallarmé's is the imagery of a severely disciplined intuitive intellection. Hopkins' is the imagery of experience, of emotional and instinctual actuality. The two poets surpass most of their followers by the intensity and scrupulous sincerity they brought to their radically different modes of defining the purpose and responsibility of poetry.

Stevens harmonized their methods in a way that gives him a particular role among his contemporaries. His images succeeded in bringing into balance the intellectual and the realistic functions of metaphor, and the limitation of his poetry, when compared with, say, that of Eliot, Hart Crane, and other men of larger historical or moral vision, is relieved by an exceptional felicity and charm of imagistic artistry which those poets, whatever their superior capacities in scope and judgment, scarcely arrived at—often left, indeed, to stand at the level of an experimental or tentative statement.

He arrived at this success by a remarkable amenity and confidence of imagination. It was apparent in his early work in the continuous exhilaration of poems like "Ploughing on Sunday," "Disillusionment of Ten O'Clock," "The Emperor of Ice Cream," and "The Plot Against the Giant." It sometimes dwindled to the sleight-of-hand ingenuity of *jeux d'esprit* like "Thirteen Ways of Looking at a Blackbird" and the "New England Verses," or to the Baroque decoration of "Anecdote of the Prince of Peacocks," "Tea at the Palaz of Hoon," and "Frogs Eat Butterflies," in which the imputation of a "tittery joke" is perhaps inescapable. Sometimes it flowered into rootless blooms of sheer fantasy. But it shows at all times an easy, aristocratic self-assurance in grasping symbolic values, and ultimately it made it possible for him, with no stretching of phrases, straining of style, or forced intellection, to cover his astonishing amount of ground, in treating subjects of larger scope, with an effect of fluent and sustained authority, as in the successive stanzas of "Sunday Morning" and "The Comedian." No poet among his contemporaries was to surpass the effects of verbal luxuriance combined with rhetorical control in these works. They describe a continuous vitality of the senses; their imagery of aesthetic fastidiousness, tropical splendor, and privileged taste abounds on the page. It is a world of high living and indulgent pleasure, of surfeiting abundance, of Bakstian color and barbaric pomp, peculiarly symptomatic of the sensory decadence and moral license of the early-century years out of which this poetry and its radical theme grew. Melon-flowers, flaming birds, peacocks, parakeets, bananas, "barbaric glass," the "marguerites, coquelicots, and roses," the "rosy chocolate and gilt umbrellas," water-lights and fountains, "forms, flames, and the flakes of flames" come thick, and with these comes another order of richness—the effete elegance of privileged lives as indicated by rich furniture, yacht voyages, Florida and Caribbean winters, and luxurious houses, all of them implying, as Mr. Gorham

Munson said in an early essay, the "passionate American drive toward comfort." That drive figures in Stevens' special animus as a poet, as Marianne Moore took hers from her passionate enthusiasm for natural phenomena, social records, and scientific treatises, or Eliot his from his immersion in the phrases and figures of Classical and Renaissance literature. It is a world of

> visible, voluble delugings,
> Which yet found means to set his simmering mind
> Spinning and hissing with oracular
> Notations of the wild, the ruinous waste.

But that waste hems this world in. Chaos, confusion, and decadence are its threats. The mindless disorder of nature or the senses encroaches on the mind as it encroaches on the jar in Tennessee. The "droning of the surf," the "disturbing vastness of ocean," the mystery of foam and cloud in which "sultry moon-monsters are dissolving," set their mysterious dangers against any hope of passive content. The sinister forms of primitive superstition and terrifying fetish hover above the life of ease and self-indulgence as they weigh upon the Sunday-morning luxury of the emancipated modern woman; they make Crispin's journey a restive search for a way to live and to justify intelligence by. As the jar, imposed upon the wilderness, describes its principle of form and order, so the mind, eternally at odds with the vagaries of the imagination, imposes its principle of purpose, law, and reason.

> The imagination, here, could not evade
> In poems of plums, the strict austerity
> Of one vast, subjugating, final tone.

Sanity and the discipline of the mind thus assert their authority over "our bawdiness unpurged by epitaph" (i.e., by the meaning of death) and also over the "imagination which is the will of things." The "arrant spices of the sun" demand control if they are to yield "an image that is pure." That image became for Stevens the ultimate object of the poet's search.

He sought it first in the vitality of the imagination itself; then, in the name and instinct of intelligence, among the mysteries of the sensory and subconscious life; he finally came to extend his search to humane and ethical values in his effort to rescue from "this hoard of destruction, a picture of ourselves, now, an image of our society," the law of life and of the moral spirit which it is the duty of the artist (the man with the blue guitar) to rescue from the calamities and disorder of experience. Thus it was that Stevens came to condense into his poems the history of human privilege, luxury, aggression, and social wealth, and the struggle of man to find—in religion, in art, in moral and ethical disciplines, in philosophic order—the law of intelligence by which he may be rescued from his damnation. The overpowering vitality of nature is opposed by the rigors of taste, of order, and of the moral principle. Abundance is opposed by the anxiety of man's uncertain, disturbed, and dispossessed spirit. Surfeit is subjected to discrimination and analysis. The massive splendor of nature and the reckless life of the senses are laid under test by the imperative demands of sincerity, integrity, and reason. The motive of *Harmonium* had been expressed in the statement:

> Lend no part to any humanity that suffuses
> you in its own light.

But when that humanity came to be seen in its own desperate struggle against confusion, violence, and moral debilitation, the field of the poems widened. The whole agony of society was taken as a protest against the abstract theories and civilized confusions that threaten to defeat the purpose and dignity of man.

Stevens' poetry (the distinction is not peculiar to him; almost all serious poetry shows it and much of the genuinely valid in modern verse strongly emphasizes it) rests on a conscious antithesis of forces: of sentient man against unconscious nature, of animal existence against intelligence, of mind against passion and appetite, of order against chaos; and he took it as his task to concentrate these oppositions in "the image that is pure," and to set the "rage for order" against the confusions and aimlessness of man's phenomenal experience. The antithesis is capable of, and in a serious poet demands, wide application, and Stevens' later extension of its meaning took the form of setting the autonomous values of art against the conditions of modern ordeal, where personality dissolves into community, man into mass, intelligence into the heat of struggle and sympathy, aesthetic and intellectual judgment into the passions of social conflict. Yet the arc described by Stevens' development in these concerns was not allowed to remain a mere "up and down between two elements," and he resisted surrendering to "the malady of the quotidian." Where once he aimed to define the uses of privilege and the satisfactions of art or beauty, he later sought to compel art out of its superiority by demanding that its intelligence and value be conferred upon the disorder and desperations of society. The idea of order became subject and vulnerable to the tests and proof of human necessity.

The richness of Stevens' early images was saved from triviality and enervation by a balance of taste and judgment—by qualities of urbanity, wit, ironic humor, and an insistent compassion which even his excessive sophistication never wholly concealed. Thus the heat and extravagance of sensory experience were corrected, not by Hopkins' law of conscience and spiritual discipline, but by an ethic of prudence operating through the instruments of a civilized sense of human dignity and of a scrupulous diffidence of temper. This prudence was not artificially induced. It was guided by a sense of honor and intellectual sincerity, a habit of critical search and analysis. The method of Mallarmé became not so much a mode of discovering philosophical or conceptual essences as a means of refining the values of taste and of pride in order that they might become available to a larger humanity. Aesthetic absolutes were compelled out of abstraction and brought to terms with the real conditions of human existence and necessity.

Thus luxury met its test in a spiritual imperative; sophistication was checked by the claims of conscience. The universe itself, whether vast and ominous in its proportions or concentrated to the evidence of minute particulars, came to take on, for Stevens, an aspect of intimacy and confidence. It was man who was abstract and evasive, deprived by skepticism and disillusionment of his once heroic or divine capacity: an oddity, an enigma, an obscure homunculus. To make of man himself the instrument of knowledge through the transcendence of his imagination became Stevens' special task as a poet. He pursued it with the advantage of having seen in man his highest capacities for wit, pride, and sensibility —an image compelled to seek its highest potentialities, an homunculus fit to contain the whole meaning of creation. As his absurdity began to fall from him, his confusion about his destiny to wane, and his purpose in the universe to come clear, the doll showed itself capable of possessing more than mere brain, taste, and self-deprecating humor. It emerged as an image of a redeemed humanity.

It was thus that the imagination became for Stevens a source and principle of value, and something more: a mode of metaphysics. "When we consider the imagination as metaphysics," he said in one of the essays in his book *The Necessary Angel* in 1951, "we realize that it is in the nature of the imagination itself that we should be quick to accept it as the only clue to reality." Repudiating the imagination as licensed or romantic; rejecting the skepticism of the logical positivists; resisting the Freudian interpretation of fantasy, he made it his primary article of faith that in the absence of religious certitude or a faith in divine transcendence, it is only by means of an imaginative transcendence that "the Platonic resolution of diversity appears," and that "the world is no longer an extraneous object, full of other extraneous objects, but an image." "In the last analysis, it is with this image of the world that we are vitally concerned," he continued. "If the imagination is the faculty by which we import the unreal into what is real, its value is the value of a way of thinking by which we project the idea of God into the idea of man. It creates images that are independent of their originals. . . ."

Stevens' later poetry was dedicated to the creation of such images, and he defined his purpose in his volume of 1942, *Notes toward a Supreme Fiction:*

> The poem refreshes life so that we share,
> For a moment, the first idea. . . . It satisfies
> Belief in an immaculate beginning
>
> And sends us, winged by an unconscious will,
> To an immaculate end. . . .

As his verse advanced in this direction in the books of his last twenty years—*Ideas of Order, Parts of a World, Transport to Summer, The Auroras of Autumn*—it moved out of sensory realism toward speculative formulation, and so toward abstraction: out of the vividness and immediacy of imagistic statement toward conceptual definition and certitude. Perhaps necessarily it also declined in wit and invention as it advanced into philosophic ambition: the wit becomes increasingly contrived, the invention increasingly less spontaneous, thus betraying a familiar liability of speculative poetry. The poems seem unable to avoid the effect of becoming exercises on an idea, variations meant to test and exercise a prevailing theme. This resulted in a kind of virtuosity of language, aphorism, and logic from which "Sunday Morning" and the finest of his early verse had been free. It led to self-conscious ingenuities of metaphor; an element of intellectual deduction and process took the place of what were once direct strokes of instinctual vision and expression.

Stevens had, in fact, found his essential subject early. It is all in "Sunday Morning" (in another form in "The Comedian as the Letter C")—the loss of inherited faith, the desire to supplant it with faith in mind, "the need of some imperishable bliss," the failure of hedonistic satisfaction, and the recognition that

> Death is the mother of beauty; hence from her,
> Alone, shall come fulfillment of our dreams
> And our desires.

And in that poem the subject found its most searching pathos, its finest dramatic embodiment, and its purest music, perhaps its one complete and consummate expression in the whole range of Stevens' work. "For Stevens," as Edwin Muir remarked, "we live in the world and die in the world. . . . He believed this passionately and consequently he had to become a stoic though by nature he was a hedonist. Living in the world we know, which batters daily against our hearts and senses, he affirmed a world of beauty and aesthetic enjoyment, an autonomous world of poetry: a stoical affirmation." [1] But as that affirmation sought to justify itself in terms higher than the sensory or hedonistic, as it elevated imagination to a role of metaphysical authority, it inevitably lost its intimate contact both with the tragic memory of what had been lost and the physical reality of what was immediate. The result was an increasing attenuation of what had once been poetically vital in the early poems, and a movement toward a realm of idea superior to human test and necessity. It also meant a gradual subsidence of imaginative passion and the curtailment of one of the most remarkable energies that the American poetry of this century has seen.

Yet it cannot be denied that Stevens faced his problem, pursued and defined his argument, with a logic and sincerity rare among his contemporaries and remarkable even in a time of exceptional critical self-scrutiny among writers. The "supreme fiction" became for him a standard of responsibility in art, and the defining of it required an "engagement" that called for the fullest capacities of intellectual and moral search in the poet.

> I have compared poetry and philosophy [he said in another essay in *The Necessary Angel*]; and I have made a point of the degree to which poetry is personal, both in its origin and in its end, and have spoken of the typical exhilaration that appears to be inseparable from genuine poetic activity; I have said that the general progress from the incredible to the credible was a progress in which poetry has participated; I have improvised a definition of poetic truth and have spoken of the integrity and peculiarity of the poetic character. Summed up, our position at the moment is that the poet must get rid of the hieratic in everything that concerns him and must move constantly in the direction of the credible. He must create his unreal out of what is real.

This sufficiently defines the seriousness of his ambition and describes the process of his career in his art. It also serves to recall how genuinely his progress in thought was one "in which poetry has participated," and how much his contemporaries owe to him in their understanding of the serious philosophic purposes which poetry, as much today as in its more heroic ages, can serve. To look back on the whole body of his work today is to realize its progress in an empirical achievement: its development from a specific poetic character in which his finest powers in imagery, rhythmic and formal mastery, and expressive virtuosity arrived at an early fulfillment, toward the speculative and inductive responsibility that was implicit in those powers but which refused to remain

---

[1] Edwin Muir in *The Observer* (London), November 6, 1955. For the case against Stevens' development see Yvor Winters' essay "Wallace Stevens, or The Hedonist's Progress" in his *The Anatomy of Nonsense* (1943), reprinted in *In Defense of Reason* (1947); also J. V. Cunningham's essay "The Poetry of Wallace Stevens" in *Poetry*, December 1949, pp. 149-65.

satisfied at that level of mastery, even if the refusal meant risking the attenuation of the style and imaginative resources by which he won his early brilliance and success.

> It is a good light, then, for those
> That know the ultimate Plato,
> Tranquillizing with this jewel
> The torments of confusion.

This stanza from *Harmonium* may be taken as an epigram on Stevens' poetic purpose from its beginnings. Confusion is the surrender of mind and sensibility to the external; tranquillity derives from the knowledge and mastery of the self. The imagery of the external world in all its richness and splendor of outward appearance must be compelled to yield to the image of what man himself is, in his highest faculties of insight, of judgment, and of the purifying and discriminating intelligence. The self in this sense remains to most people the most "unreal" and unknown of existences: they shirk its imperatives, shun its discipline, and take refuge in what they assume to be an objective reality, material, social, or political. What they risk, however willingly, is a loss of identity, a surrender of their higher humanity to the seduction of phenomena. It became Stevens' obsession to rescue that humanity from confusion and defeat, and to make of its "unreality" a fiction—but a "supreme fiction" —in which the imagination brings idea and sense into the harmony of a full human intelligence—an intelligence which, denied appeal to superhuman authority, is compelled to make the human condition not only endurable but "credible." It was this image of man which Stevens made the ultimate goal of his poetic search; and if the search carried him from an early verse of what remains (in American poetry at least) an incomparable verbal brilliance, ironic wit, and metaphoric invention to a later verse of austere and even forbidding speculative rigor, it remains to his credit that before he ended his career he carried the meaning of the poems in *Harmonium* to its logical consequence in a philosophical enquiry which stands as one of the most impressive examples of poetic morality that can be found in the art he practised and, for his contemporaries, so seriously enriched. Whether he succeeded in making of his work an "ultimate Plato" is doubtless too much to ask or expect. It is enough to recognize that he brought into modern American verse a purpose which Goethe, Coleridge, Rilke, and Valéry exercised elsewhere, and which establishes him as one of the key figures in the line of poetics which concerns the poet's task and responsibility.

The Realistic Oriole:
A Study of Wallace Stevens

by Northrop Frye

Wallace Stevens was a poet for whom the theory and the practice of poetry were inseparable.[1] His poetic vision is informed by a metaphysic; his metaphysic is informed by a theory of knowledge; his theory of knowledge is informed by a poetic vision. He says of one of his long meditative poems that it displays the theory of poetry as the life of poetry (486), and in the introduction to his critical essays that by the theory of poetry he means "poetry itself, the naked poem" (*N.A.* viii). He thus stands in contrast to the dualistic approach of Eliot, who so often speaks of poetry as though it were an emotional and sensational soul looking for a "correlative" skeleton of thought to be provided by a philosopher, a Cartesian ghost trying to find a machine that will fit. No poet of any status—certainly not Eliot himself—has ever "taken over" someone else's structure of thought, and the dualistic fallacy can only beget more fallacies. Stevens is of particular interest and value to the critical theorist because he sees so clearly that the only ideas the poet can deal with are those directly involved with, and implied by, his own writing: that, in short, "Poetry is the subject of the poem" (176).

It has been established in criticism ever since Aristotle that histories are direct verbal imitations of action, and that anything in literature with a story in it is a secondary imitation of an action. This means, not that the story is at two removes from reality, but that its actions are representative and typical rather than specific. For some reason it has not been nearly so well understood that discursive writing is not thinking, but a direct verbal imitation of thought; that any poem with an idea in it is a secondary imitation of thought, and hence deals with

"The Realistic Oriole: A Study of Wallace Stevens" by Northrop Frye. From *The Hudson Review*, X, No. 3 (Autumn 1957), 353-370. Copyright © 1957 by *The Hudson Review*, Inc. Reprinted by permission of *The Hudson Review*.

[1] All references to Stevens' poetry are accompanied by the page number in *The Collected Poems of Wallace Stevens*, 1954, and all references to his critical essays by the page number in *The Necessary Angel*, 1951, preceded by the letters *N.A.* I am sorry if this procedure makes the article typographically less attractive, but the proper place for such references, the margin, has disappeared from modern layout.

representative or typical thought: that is, with forms of thought rather than specific propositions. Poetry is concerned with the ambiguities, the unconscious diagrams, the metaphors and the images out of which actual ideas grow. Poet and painter alike operate in "the flux/Between the thing as idea and the idea as thing" (295). Stevens is an admirable poet in whom to study the processes of poetic thought at work, and such processes are part of what he means by the phrase "supreme fiction" which enters the title of his longest poem. The poet, he says, "gives to life the supreme fictions without which we are unable to conceive of it" (*N.A.* 31), and fictions imitate ideas as well as events.

Any discussion of poetry has to begin with the field or area that it works in, the field described by Aristotle as nature. Stevens calls it "reality," by which he means, not simply the external physical world, but "things as they are," the existential process that includes ordinary human life on the level of absorption in routine activity. Human intelligence can resist routine by arresting it in an act of consciousness, but the normal tendency of routine is to work against consciousness. The revolution of consciousness against routine is the starting-point of all mental activity, and the center of mental activity is imagination, the power of transforming "reality" into awareness of reality. Man can have no freedom except what begins in his own awareness of his condition. Naturally historical periods differ greatly in the amount of pressure put on free consciousness by the compulsions of ordinary life. In our own day this pressure has reached an almost intolerable degree that threatens to destroy freedom altogether and reduce human life to a level of totally preoccupied compulsion, like the life of an animal. One symptom of this is the popular demand that the artist should express in his work a sense of social obligation. The artist's primary obedience however is not to reality but to the "violence from within" (*N.A.* 36) of the imagination that resists and arrests it. The minimum basis of the imagination, so to speak, is ironic realism, the act of simply becoming aware of the surrounding pressures of "things as they are." This develops the sense of alienation which is the immediate result of the imposing of consciousness on reality:

> From this the poem springs: that we live in a place
> That is not our own and, much more, not ourselves.

The "act of the mind" (240) in which imagination begins, then, is an arresting of a flow of perceptions without and of impressions within. In that arrest there is born the principle of form or order: the inner violence of the imagination is a "rage for order" (130). It produces the "jar in Tennessee" (76), the object which not only is form in itself, but creates form out of all its surroundings. Stevens follows Coleridge in distinguishing the transforming of experience by the imagination from the rearranging of it by the "fancy," and ranks the former higher (ignoring, if he knew it, T. E. Hulme's clever pseudo-critical reversal of the two). The imagination contains reason and emotion, but the imagination keeps form concrete and particular, whereas emotion and reason are more apt to seek the vague and the general respectively.

There are two forms of mental activity that Stevens regards as unpoetic. One is the breaking down of a world of discrete objects into an amorphous and invisible substratum, a search for a "pediment of appearance" (361), a slate-colored world of substance (15, 96) which destroys all form and particularity, symbolized by the bodiless serpent introduced in "The Auroras of Autumn" (411), "form gulping after formlessness." This error is typically an error of reason. The other error is the breaking down of the individual mind in an attempt to make it a medium for some kind of universal or pantheistic mind. This is typically an error of emotion, and one that Stevens in his essays calls "romantic," which is a little confusing when his own poetry is so centrally in the Romantic tradition. What he means by it is the preference of the invisible to the visible which impels a poet to develop a false rhetoric intended to be the voice, not of himself, but of some invisible super-bard within him (N.A. 61). In "Jumbo" (269), Stevens points out that such false rhetoric comes, not from the annihilation of the ego, but from the ego itself, from "Narcissus, prince/Of the secondary men." Such an attitude produces the "nigger mystic" (195, 265), a phrase which naturally has nothing to do with Negroes, but refers to the kind of intellectual absolute that has been compared to a night in which all cows are black, a world clearly no improvement on "reality," which is also one color (N.A. 26).

A third mode of mental activity, which is poetic but not Stevens' kind of poetry, is the attempt to suggest or evoke universals of mind or substance, to work at the threshold of consciousness and produce what Stevens calls "marginal" poetry and associates with Valéry (N.A. 115). Whatever its merit, such poetry for him is in contrast with "central" poetry based on the concrete and particular act of mental experience. Stevens speaks of the imagination as moving from the hieratic to the credible (N.A. 58), and marginal poetry, like the structures of reason and the surrenderings of emotion, seeks a "hierophant Omega" (469) or ultimate mystery. There is a strong tendency, a kind of intellectual deathwish, to conceive of order in terms of finality, as something that keeps receding from experience until experience stops, when it becomes the mirage of an "after-life" on which all hierophants, whether poets or priests, depend. But for the imagination "Reality is the beginning not the end" (469), "The imperfect is our paradise" (194), and the only order worth having is the "violent order" produced by the explosion of imaginative energy which is also a "great disorder" (215).

This central view of poetry is for Stevens based on the straight

Aristotelian principle that if art is not quite nature, at least it grows naturally out of nature. He dislikes the term "imitation," but only because he thinks it means the naive copying of an external world: in its proper Aristotelian sense of creating a form of which nature is the content, Stevens' poetry is as imitative as Pope's. Art then is not so much nature methodized as nature realized, a unity of being and knowing, existence and consciousness, achieved out of the flow of time and the fixity of space. In content it is reality and we are "Participants of its being" (463); in form it is an art which "speaks the feeling" for "things as they are" (424). All through Stevens' poetry we find the symbol of the alphabet or syllable, the imaginative key to reality which, by bringing reality into consciousness, heightens the sense of both, "A nature that is created in what it says" (490).

However, the imagination does bring something to reality which is not there in the first place, hence the imagination contains an element of the "unreal" which the imaginative form incorporates. This unreal is connected with the fact that conscious experience is liberated experience. The unreal, "The fabulous and its intrinsic verse" (31), is the sense of exhilaration and splendor in art, the "radiant and productive" atmosphere which it both creates and breathes, the sense of the virile and the heroic implied by the term "creative" itself, "the way of thinking by which we project the idea of God into the idea of man" (*N.A.* 150). All art has this essential elegance or nobility, including ironic realism, but the nobility is an attribute of art, not its goal: one attains it by not trying for it, as though it were definable or extrinsic. Although art is in one sense an escape from reality (i.e., in the sense in which it is an escape *of* reality), and although art is a heightening of consciousness, it is not enough for art simply to give one a vision of a better world. Art is practical, not speculative; imaginative, not fantastic; it transforms experience, and does not merely interrupt it. The unreal in imaginative perception is most simply described as the sense that if something is not there it at least ought to be there. But this feeling in art is anything but wistful: it has created the tone of all the civilizations of hisory. Thus the "central" poet, by working outwards from a beginning instead of onwards toward an end, helps to achieve the only genuine kind of progress. As Stevens says, in a passage which explains the ambivalence of the term "mystic" in his work: "The adherents of the central are also mystics to begin with. But all their desire and all their ambition is to press away from mysticism toward that ultimate good sense which we term civilization" (*N.A.* 116).

Such ultimate good sense depends on preserving a balance between objective reality and the subjective unreal element in the imagination. Exaggerating the latter gives us the false heroics that produce the aggressive symbols of warfare and the cult of "men suited to public ferns" (276). Exaggerating the former gives us the weariness of mind that bores the "fretful concubine" (211) in her splendid surroundings. Within art itself there has been a corresponding alternation of emphasis. In some ages, or with some poets, the emphasis is on the imaginative heightening of reality by visions of a Yeatsian "noble rider"

> On his gold horse striding, like a conjured beast,
> Miraculous in its panache and swish.   (426)

At other times the emphasis is ironic, thrown on the minimum role of the imagination as the simple and subjective observer of reality, not withdrawn from it, but detached enough to feel that the power of transforming it has passed by. These two emphases, the green and the red as Stevens calls them (340), appear in Stevens' own poetry as the summer vision and the autumn vision respectively.

The summer vision of life is the *gaya scienza* (248), the "Lebensweisheitspielerei" (504), in which things are perceived in their essential radiance, when "the world is larger" (514). This summer vision extends all over the *Harmonium* poems, with their glowing still lifes and gorgeous landscapes of Florida and the Caribbean coasts. Its dominating image is the sun, "that brave man" (138), the hero of nature who lives in heaven but transforms the earth from his mountain-top (65), "the strong man vaguely seen" (204). As "we are men of sun" (137), our creative life is his, hence the feeling of alienation from nature in which consciousness begins is really inspired by exactly the opposite feeling. "I am what is around me" (86), the poet says; the jar in Tennessee expresses the form in Tennessee as well as in itself, and one feels increasingly that "The soul . . . is composed/Of the external world" (51) in the sense that in the imagination we have "The inhuman making choice of a human self" (*N.A.* 89), a subhuman world coming to a point of imaginative light in a focus of individuality and consciousness. Such a point of imaginative light is a human counterpart of the sun. The poet absorbs the reality he contemplates "as the Angevine Absorbs Anjou" (224), just as the sun's light, by giving itself and taking nothing, absorbs the world in itself. The echo to the great trumpet-call of "Let there be light" is "All things in the sun are sun" (104).

There are two aspects of the summer vision, which might be called, in Marvellian language, the visions of the golden lamp and of the green night. The latter is the more contemplative vision of the student in the tradition of Milton's penseroso poet, Shelley's Athanase, and Yeats's old man in the tower. In this vision the sun is replaced by the moon (33 ff.), or, more frequently, the evening star (25), the human counterpart of which is the student's candle (51, 523). Its personified form, corresponding to the sun, is often female, an "archaic" (223) or "green queen" (339), the "desired" (505) one who eventually becomes an "interior paramour" (524) or Jungian anima (cf. 321), the motionless spinning Penelope (520) to whom every voyager returns, the eternal Eve (271) or naked bride (395) of the relaxed imagination. Here we are, of course, in danger of the death-wish vision, of reading a blank book. Some of the irony of this is in "Phosphor Reading by his Own Light" (267), as well as in "The Reader" (146). The bride of such a narcist vision is the sinister "Madame La Fleurie" (507). But in its genuine form such contemplation is the source of major imagination (387-8), and hence Stevens, like Yeats, has his tower-mountain of vision or "Palaz of Hoon" (65; cf. 121), where sun and poet come into alignment:

> It is the natural tower of all the world,
> The point of survey, green's green apogee,
> But a tower more precious than the view beyond,
> A point of survey squatting like a throne,
> Axis of everything.   (373)

From this point of survey we are lifted above the "cat," symbol of life absorbed in being without consciousness, and the "rabbit" who is "king of the ghosts" and is absorbed in consciousness without being (209, 223).

The autumnal vision begins in the poet's own situation. To perceive "reality" as dingy or unattractive is itself an imaginative act ("The Plain Sense of Things," 502), but an ironic act, an irony deepened by the fact that other modes of perception are equally possible, the oriole being as realistic as the crow (154), and there can be no question of accepting only one as true. It is a curious tendency in human nature to believe in dis-illusionment: that is, to think we are nearest the truth when we have established as much falsehood as possible. This is the vision of "Mrs. Alfred Uruguay" (248), who approaches her mountain of contemplation the wrong way round, starting at the bottom instead of the top. (Her name is apparently based on an association with "Montevideo.") The root of the reductive tendency, at least in poetry, is perhaps the transience of the emotional mood which is the framework of the lyric. In *Harmonium* the various elaborations of vision are seen as projected from a residual ego, a comedian (27 ff.) or clown (Peter Quince is the leader of a group of clowns), who by himself has only the vision of the *"esprit bâtard"* (102), the juggler in motley who is also a magician and whose efforts are "conjurations." When we add the clown's conjurations to the clown we get "man the abstraction, the comic sun" (156): the term "abstraction" will meet us again.

This *esprit bâtard* or dimmed vision of greater maturity, *un monocle d'un oncle,* so to speak, comes into the foreground after the "Credences of Summer" (372) and the "Things of August" (489) have passed by. In September the web of the imagination's pupa is woven (208); in November the moon lights up only the death of the god (107); at the onset of winter the auroras of a vanished heroism flicker over the sky, while in the foreground stand the scarecrows or hollow men of the present (293, 513).

To this vision belong the bitter "Man on the Dump" (201), the ironic "Esthétique du Mal" (313), with its urbane treatment of the religio-literary clichés, such as "The death of Satan was a tragedy/For the imagination," which are the stock in trade of lesser poets, and the difficult and painfully written war poems. It is more typical of Stevens, of course, to emphasize the reality which is present in the imaginative heightening of misery, the drudge's dream of "The Ordinary Women" (10) which none the less reminds us that "Imagination is the will of things" (84). The true form of the autumnal vision is not the irony which robs man of his dignity, but the tragedy which confers it ("In a Bad Time," 426).

At the end of autumn come the terrors of winter, the sense of a world disintegrating into chaos which we feel socially when we see the annihilation wars of our time, and individually when we face the fact of death in others or for ourselves. We have spoken of Stevens' dislike of projecting the religious imagination into a world remote in space and time. The woman in "Sunday Morning" (66) stays home from church and meditates on religion surrounded by the brilliant oranges and greens of the summer vision, and in "A High-Toned Old Christian Woman" (59) it is suggested that the poet, seeking an increase rather than a diminishing of life, gets closer to a genuinely religious sense than morality with its taboos and denials. For Stevens all real religion is concerned with a renewal of earth rather than with a surrender to heaven. He even says "the great poems of heaven and hell have been written and the great poem of the earth remains to be written" (*N.A.* 142). It is part of his own ambition to compose hymns "Happy rather than holy but happy-high" (185) which will "take the place/Of empty heavens" (167), and he looks forward to a world in which "all men are priests" (254). As this last phrase shows, he has no interest in turning to some cellophane-wrapped version of neo-paganism. He sees, like Yeats, that the poet is a "Connoisseur of Chaos" (215) aware that "Poetry Is a Destructive Force" (192), and Stevens' imagery, for all its luxuriance and good humor, is full of menace. From the "firecat" of the opening page of the *Collected Poems,* through the screaming peacocks of "Domination of Black" (8), the buzzard of "The Jack-Rabbit" (50; cf. 318), the butcher of "A Weak Mind in the Mountains" (212), the bodiless serpent of "The Auroras of Autumn" (411) and the bloody lion of "Puella Parvula" (456), we are aware that a simple song of *carpe diem* is not enough.

In the later poems there is a growing preoccupation with death, as, not the end of life or an introduction to something unconnected with life, but as itself a part of life and giving to life itself an extra dimension. This view is very close to Rilke, especially the Rilke of the Orpheus sonnets, which are, like Stevens' poetry in general, "a constant sacra-

ment of praise" (92). "What a ghastly situation it would be," Stevens remarks, "if the world of the dead was actually different from the world
of the living" (*N.A.* 76), and in several poems, especially the remarkable
"Owl in the Sarcophagus" (431), there are references to carrying on the
memories or "souvenirs" of the past into a world which is not so much
future as timeless, a world of recognition or "rendezvous" (524), and
which lies in the opposite direction from the world of dreams:

> There is a monotonous babbling in our dreams
> That makes them our dependent heirs, the heirs
> Of dreamers buried in our sleep, and not
> The oncoming fantasies of better birth.   (39)

In the poems of the winter vision the solar hero and the green queen
become increasingly identified with the father and mother of a Freudian
imago (439). The father and mother in turn expand into a continuous
life throughout time of which we form our unitary realizations. The
father, "the bearded peer" (494), extends back to the primordial sea
(501), the mother to the original maternity of nature, the "Lady Lowzen"
of "Oak Leaves Are Hands" (272). In "The Owl in the Sarcophagus"
these figures are personified as sleep and memory. The ambivalence of
the female figure is expressed by the contrast between the "regina of the
clouds" in "Le Monocle de mon Oncle" (13) and the "Sister and mother
and diviner love" of "To the One of Fictive Music" (87). The poet determined to show that "being/Includes death and the imagination"
(444) must go through the same world as the "nigger mystic," for a
"nigger cemetery" (150) lies in front of him too, just as the sunrise of
the early play, *Three Travellers Watch a Sunrise,* is heralded by a
hanged man. The search for death through life which is a part of such
recreation leads to a final confronting of the self and the rock (*N.A.* viii),
the identification of consciousness and reality in which the living soul is
identified with its tombstone which is equally its body (528). In this
final triumph of vision over death the death-symbols are turned into
symbols of life. The author of the Apocalypse prophesies to his "backache" (which is partly the *Weltschmerz* of the past) that the venom of
the bodiless serpent will be one with its wisdom (437). The "black river"
of death, Swatara (428), becomes "The River of Rivers in Connecticut"
(533), a river *this* side of the Styx which "flows nowhere, like a sea" because it is in a world in which there is no more sea.

If we listen carefully to the voice of "the auroral creature musing in
the mind" (263), the auroras of autumn will become, not the after-
images of remembrance, but the *Morgenrot* of a new recognition. As the
cycle turns through death to a new life, we meet images of spring, the
central one being some modification of Venus rising from the sea: the
"paltry nude" of the poem of that name (5); "Infanta Marina" (7);

Susanna lying in "A wave, interminably flowing" (92); "Celle qui fût Heaulmiette" (438) reborn from the mother and father of the winter vision, the mother having the "vague severed arms" of the maternal Venus of Milo. This reborn girl is the Jungian anima or interior paramour spoken of before, the "Golden Woman in a Silver Mirror" (460). She is also associated with the bird of Venus, "The Dove in the Belly" (366; cf. 357 and "Song of Fixed Accord," 519). It is also a bird's cry, but one outside the poet, which heralds "A new knowledge of reality" in the last line of the *Collected Poems*. The spring vision often has its origin in the commonplace, or in the kind of innocent gaudiness that marks exuberant life. Of the spring images in "Celle qui fût Heaulmiette" the author remarks affectionately, "Another American vulgarity"; the "paltry nude" is a gilded ship's prow, and the "emperor of ice-cream" presides over funeral obsequies in a shabby household (64). "It is the invasion of humanity/That counts," remarks a character in *Three Travellers Watch a Sunrise*. "Only the rich remember the past," the poet says (225) and even in "Final Soliloquy of the Interior Paramour" (524) there is still a parenthetical association of new vision with a poverty which has nothing to lose.

In "Peter Quince at the Clavier" beauty is called "The fitful tracing of a portal." Portal to what? The word itself seems to mean something to Stevens (*N.A.* 60, 155), and in the obviously very personal conclusion of "The Rock" it is replaced by "gate" (528). Perhaps Stevens, like Blake, has so far only given us the end of a golden string, and after traversing the circle of natural images we have still to seek the center.

The normal unit of poetic expression is the metaphor, and Stevens was well aware of the importance of metaphor, as is evident from the many poems which use the word in title or text. His conception of metaphor is regrettably unclear, though clearer in the poetry than in the essays. He speaks of the creative process as beginning in the perception of "resemblance," adding that metamorphosis might be a better word (*N.A.* 72). By resemblance he does not mean naive or associative resemblance, of the type that calls a flower a bleeding heart, but the repetitions of color and pattern in nature which become the elements of formal design in art. He goes on to develop this conception of resemblance into a conception of "analogy" which, beginning in straight allegory, ends in the perception that "poetry becomes and is a transcendent analogue composed of the particulars of reality" (*N.A.* 130). But nowhere in his essays does he suggest that metaphor is anything more than likeness or parallelism. "There is always an analogy between nature and the imagination, and possibly poetry is merely the strange rhetoric of that parallel" (*N.A.* 118).

Clearly, if poetry is "merely" this, the use of metaphor could only accentuate what Stevens' poetry tries to annihilate, the sense of a contrast or great gulf fixed between subject and object, consciousness and existence. And in fact we often find metaphor used pejoratively in the poems as a form of avoiding direct contact with reality. The motive for metaphor, we are told, is the shrinking from immediate experience (288). Stevens appears to mean by such metaphor, however, simile or comparison, "the intricate evasions of as" (486; cf. "Add This to Rhetoric," 198). And metaphor is actually nothing of the kind. In its literal grammatical form metaphor is a statement of identity: this is that, A is B. And Stevens has a very strong sense of the crucial importance of poetic identification, "where as and is are one" (476), as it is only there that one finds "The poem of pure reality, untouched/By trope or deviation" (471). Occasionally it occurs to him that metaphor might be used in a less pejorative sense. He speaks of "The metaphor that murders metaphor" (*N.A.* 84), implying that a better kind of metaphor can get murdered, and "Metaphor as Degeneration" (444) ends in a query how metaphor can really be degeneration when it is part of the process of seeing death as a part of life.

When metaphor says that one thing "is" another thing, or that a man, a woman, and a blackbird are one (93), things are being identified *with* other things. In logical identity there is only identification *as*. If I say that the Queen of England "is" Elizabeth II, I have not identified one person with another, but one person as herself. Poetry also has this type of identification, for in poetic metaphor things are identified with each other, yet each is identified as itself, and retains that identity. When a man, a woman, and a blackbird are said to be one, each remains what it is, and the identification heightens the distinctive form of each. Such a metaphor is necessarily illogical (or anti-logical, as in "A violent disorder is an order") and hence poetic metaphors are opposed to likeness or similarity. A perception that a man, a woman, and a blackbird were in some respects alike would be logical, but would not make much of a poem. Unfortunately in prose speech we often use the word identical to mean very similar, as in the phrase "identical twins," and this use makes it difficult to express the idea of poetic identity in a prose essay. But if twins were really identical they would be the same person, and hence could be different in form, like a man and the same man as a boy of seven. A world of total simile, where everything was like everything else, would be a world of total monotony; a world of total metaphor, where everything is identified as itself and with everything else, would be a world where subject and object, reality and mental organization of reality, are one. Such a world of total metaphor is the formal cause of poetry. Stevens makes it clear that the poet seeks the particular and discrete image: many of the poems in *Parts of a World,* such as "On the Road Home" (203), express what the title of the book expresses, the uniqueness of every act of vision. Yet it is through the particular and discrete that we reach the unity of the imagination, which respects individuality, in contrast to the logical unity of the generalizing reason, which destroys it. The false unity of the dominating mind is what Stevens condemns in "The Bagatelles the Madrigals" (213), and in the third part of "The Pure Good of Theory" (331-2), where we find again a pejorative use of the term metaphor.

When a thing is identified as itself, it becomes an individual of a class or total form: when we identify a brown and green mass as a tree we provide a class name for it. This is the relating of species to genera which Aristotle spoke of as one of the central aspects of metaphor. The distinctively poetic use of such metaphor is the identifying of an individual with its class, where a tree becomes Wordsworth's "tree of many one," or a man becomes mankind. Poets ordinarily do not, like some philosophers, replace individual objects with their total forms; they do not, like allegorists, represent total forms by individuals. They see individual and class as metaphorically identical: in other words they work with *myths,* many of whom are human figures in whom the individual has been identified with its universal or total form.

Such myths, "archaic forms, giants/Of sense, evoking one thing in many men" (494) play a large role in Stevens' imagery. For some reason he speaks of the myth as "abstract." "The Ultimate Poem Is Abstract" (429; cf. 270, 223 and elsewhere), and the first requirement of the "supreme fiction" is that it must be abstract (380), though as far as dictionary meanings are concerned one would expect rather to hear that it must be concrete. By abstract Stevens apparently means artificial in its proper sense, something constructed rather than generalized. In such a passage as this we can see the myth forming out of "repetitions" as the individual soldier becomes the unknown soldier, and the unknown soldier the Adonis or continuously martyred god:

> How red the rose that is the soldier's wound,
> The wounds of many soldiers, the wounds of all
> The soldiers that have fallen, red in blood,
> The soldier of time grown deathless in great size.   (318)

Just as there is false metaphor, so there is false myth. There is in particular the perverted myth of the average or "root-man" (262), described more expressively as "the total man of glubbal glub" (301). Whenever we have the root-man we have, by compensation, "The superman friseured, possessing and possessed" (262), which is the perversion of the idea of *Übermenschlichkeit* (98) into the Carlylean great man or military hero. Wars are in their imaginative aspect a "gigantomachia" (289) of competing aggressive myths. The war-myth or hero of death is the great enemy of the imagination: he cannot be directly fought except by another war-myth; he can only be contained in a greater and more genuine form of the same myth (280, section xv). The genuine form of the war-hero is the "major man" (334; 387-8) who, in "The Owl in the

Sarcophagus," is personified as peace (434), the direct opposite of the war-hero, and the third of the figures in "the mythology of modern death" which, along with sleep and memory, conquer death for life.

We thus arrive at the conception of a universal or "central man" (250), who may be identified with any man, such as a fisherman listening to wood-doves:

> The fisherman might be the single man
> In whose breast, the dove, alighting, would grow still.   (357)

This passage, which combines the myth of the central man with the anima myth of the "dove in the belly" (366), is from a poem with the painfully exact title, "Thinking of a Relation between the Images of Metaphors." The central man is often symbolized by glass or transparency, as in "Asides on the Oboe" (250) and in "Prologues to What Is Possible" (515). If there is a central man, there is also a central mind (298) of which the poet feels peculiarly a part. Similarly there is a "central poem" (441) identical with the world, and finally a "general being or human universe" (378), of which all imaginative work forms part:

> That's it. The lover writes, the believer hears,
> The poet mumbles and the painter sees,
> Each one, his fated eccentricity,
> As a part, but part, but tenacious particle,
> Of the skeleton of the ether, the total
> Of letters, prophecies, perceptions, clods
> Of color, the giant of nothingness, each one
> And the giant ever changing, living in change.   (443)

In "Sketch of the Ultimate Politician" (335) we get a glimpse of this human universe as an infinite City of Man.

To sum up: the imaginative act breaks down the separation between subject and object, the perceiver shut up in "the enclosures of hypothesis" (516) like an embryo in a "naked egg" (173) or glass shell (297), and a perceived world similarly imprisoned in the remoteness of its "irreducible X" (*N.A.* 83), which is also an egg (490). Separation is then replaced by the direct, primitive identification which Stevens ought to have called metaphor and which, not having a word for it, he calls "description" (339) in one of his definitive poems, a term to which he elsewhere adds "apotheosis" (378) and "transformation" (514; cf. *N.A.* 49), which come nearer to what he really means. The maxim that art should conceal art is based on the sense that in the greatest art we have no sense of manipulating, posing or dominating over nature, but rather of emancipating it. "One confides in what has no/Concealed creator" (296), the poet says, and again:

> There might be, too, a change immenser than
> A poet's metaphors in which being would
>
> Come true, a point in the fire of music where
> Dazzle yields to a clarity and we observe,
>
> And observing is completing and we are content,
> In a world that shrinks to an immediate whole,
>
> That we do not need to understand, complete
> Without secret arrangements of it in the mind.   (341)

The theoretical postulate of Stevens' poetry is a world of total meta-phor, where the poet's vision may be identified with anything it visu-alizes. For such poetry the most accurate word is apocalyptic, a poetry of "revelation" (344) in which all objects and experiences are united with a total mind. Such poetry gives us:

> . . . the book of reconciliation,
> Book of a concept only possible
>
> In description, canon central in itself,
> The thesis of the plentifullest John.   (345)

Apocalypse, however, is one of the two great narrative myths that expand "reality," with its categories of time and space, into an infinite and eternal world. A myth of a total man recovering a total world is hardly possible without a corresponding myth of a Fall, or some account of what is wrong with our present perspective. Stevens' version of the Fall is similar to that of the "Orphic poet" at the end of Emerson's *Nature:*

> Why, then, inquire
> Who has divided the world, what entrepreneur?
> No man. The self, the chrysalis of all men
>
> Became divided in the leisure of blue day
> And more, in branchings after day. One part
> Held fast tenaciously in common earth
>
> And one from central earth to central sky
> And in moonlit extensions of them in the mind
> Searched out such majesty as it could find.   (468-9)

Such poetry sounds religious, and in fact does have the infinite per-spective of religion, for the limits of the imagination are the conceivable, not the real, and it extends over death as well as life. In the imagination the categories of "reality," space and time, are reversed into form and creation respectively, for art is "Description without Place" (339) standing at the center of "ideal time" (*N.A.* 88), and its poetry is "even older than the ancient world" (*N.A.* 145). Religion seems to have a monopoly of talking about infinite and eternal worlds, and poetry that uses such conceptions seems to be inspired by a specifically religious interest. But the more we study poetry, the more we realize that the dogmatic limiting of the poet's imagination to human and subhuman nature that we find, for instance, in Hardy and Housman, is not normal to poetry but a technical *tour de force*. It is the normal language of poetic imagination itself that is heard when Yeats says that man has invented death; when Eliot reaches the still point of the turning world; when Rilke speaks of the poet's perspective as that of an angel containing all time and space, blind and looking into himself; when Stevens finds his home in "The place of meta-men and para-things" (448). Such language may or may not go with a religious commitment: in itself it is simply poetry speaking as poetry must when it gets to a certain pitch of metaphorical concentration. Stevens says that his motive is neither "to console/Nor sanctify, but plainly to propound" (389).

In *Harmonium*, published in the Scott Fitzgerald decade, Stevens moves in a highly sensuous atmosphere of fine pictures, good food, exquisite taste, and luxury cruises. In the later poems, though the writing is as studiously oblique as ever, the sensuousness has largely disappeared, and the reader accustomed only to *Harmonium* may feel that Stevens' inspiration has failed him, or that he is attracted by themes outside his capacity, or that the impact of war and other ironies of the autumnal vision has shut him up in an uncommunicative didacticism. Such a view of Stevens is of course superficial, but the critical issue it raises is a genuine one.

In the criticism of drama there is a phase in which the term "theatrical" becomes pejorative, when one tries to distinguish genuine dramatic imagination from the conventional clichés of dramatic rhetoric. Of course eventually this pejorative use has to disappear, because Shakespeare and Aeschylus are quite as theatrical as Cecil de Mille. Similarly, one also goes through a stage, though a shorter one, in which the term "poetic" may acquire a slightly pejorative cast, as when one may decide, several hundred pages deep in Swinburne, that Swinburne can sometimes be a poetic bore. Eventually one realizes that the "poetic" quality comes from allusiveness, the incorporating into the texture of echoes, cadences, names, and thoughts derived from the author's previous literary experience. Swinburne is poetic in a poor sense when he is being a parasite on the literary tradition; Eliot is poetic in a better sense when, in his own phrase, he steals rather than imitates. The "poetic" normally expresses itself as what one might loosely call word-magic or incantation, charm in its original sense of spell, as it reinforces the "act of the mind" in poetry with the dream-like reverberations, echoes, and enlarged significances of the memory and the unconscious. We suggested at the beginning that Eliot lacks what Stevens has, the sense of an autonomous poetic theory as an inseparable part of poetic practice. On the other hand Eliot has pre-eminently the sense of a creative tradition, and this sense is partly what makes his poetry so uniquely penetrating, so easy to memorize unconsciously.

In Stevens there is a good deal of incantation and imitative harmony; but the deliberately "magical" poems, such as "The Idea of Order at Key West," "To the One of Fictive Music," and the later "Song of Fixed Accord" have the special function of expressing a stasis or harmony between imagination and reality, and hence have something of a conscious rhetorical exercise about them. In "The Idea of Order at Key West" the sense of carefully controlled artifice enters the theme as well. In other poems where the texture is dryer and harder, the schemata on which "word-magic" depends are reduced to a minimum. The rhymes, for instance, when they occur, are usually sharp barking assonances, parody-rhymes (e.g., "The Swedish cart to be part of the heart," 369), and the meters, like the curious blank *terza rima* used so often, are almost parody-meters. A quality that is not far from being anti-"poetic" seems to emerge.

Just as the "poetic" is derived mainly from the reverberations of tradition, so it is clear that the anti-"poetic" quality in Stevens is the result of his determination to make it new, in Pound's phrase, to achieve in each poem a unique expression and force his reader to make a correspondingly unique act of apprehension. This is a part of what he means by "abstract" as a quality of the "supreme fiction." It was Whitman who urged American writers to lay less emphasis on tradition, thereby starting another tradition of his own, and it is significant that Whitman is one of the very few traditional poets Stevens refers to, though he has little in common with him technically. It is partly his sense of a poem as belonging to experiment rather than tradition, separated from the stream of time with its conventional echoes, that gives Stevens' poetry its marked affinity with pictures, an affinity shown also in the curiously formalized symmetry of the longer poems. "Notes toward a Supreme Fiction," for instance, has three parts of ten sections each, each section with seven tercets, and similarly rectangular distributions of material are found in other poems.

When we meet a poet who has so much rhetorical skill, and yet lays so much emphasis on novelty and freshness of approach, the skill acquires a quality of courage: a courage that is without compromise in a world full of cheap rhetoric, yet uses none of the ready-made mixes of rhetoric in a world full of compromise. Stevens was one of the most courageous poets of our time, and his conception of the poem as "the heroic effort to live expressed/As victory" (446) was unyielding from the beginning. Courage implies persistence, and persistence in a distinctive strain often develops its complementary opposite as well, as with Blake's fool who by persisting in his folly became wise. It was persistence that transformed the tropical lushness of *Harmonium* into the austere clairvoyance of *The Rock,* the luxurious demon into the necessary angel, and so rounded out a vision of major scope and intensity. As a result Stevens became, unlike many others who may have started off with equal abilities, not one of our expendable rhetoricians, but one of our small handful of essential poets.

Chronology of Important Dates

1879   Wallace Stevens born October 2 in Reading, Pennsylvania.

1897   Enrolled at Harvard as a special student.

1901   Entered New York Law School.

1904   Admitted to the bar in New York State.

1909   Married Elsie V. Kachel.

1914   First publication of Stevens' mature work, in the November issue of *Poetry: A Magazine of Verse;* see "Phases," I-IV in *Opus Posthumous,* pp. 3-5.

1916   Joined legal staff of New York branch of Hartford Accident and Indemnity Co.; transferred to Hartford.

1923   *Harmonium.*

1934   Elected Vice-President of Hartford Accident and Indemnity Co.

1936   *Ideas of Order.*

1937   *The Man with the Blue Guitar.*

1942   *Parts of a World.*

1946   Became a member of the National Institute of Arts and Letters.

1947   *Transport to Summer.*

1950   *The Auroras of Autumn.*
          Awarded the Bollingen Prize in Poetry.

1951   *The Necessary Angel: Essays on Reality and the Imagination.*

1954   *The Collected Poems* published on his 75th birthday.

1955   Received the Pulitzer Prize for poetry and the National Book Award.
          Died August 2.

1957   *Opus Posthumous.*

Notes on the Editor and Authors

MARIE BORROFF, the editor of this volume, is Professor of English at Yale University. As a critic and scholar, she is concerned with the style of poetry and the history of the English language. Her poetry has appeared in *The American Scholar, The Virginia Quarterly Review,* and *The Yale Review.* She has published articles on the poetry of Louis MacNeice and Marianne Moore, and is the author of *Sir Gawain and the Green Knight: A Stylistic and Metrical Study.*

HAROLD BLOOM is Associate Professor of English at Yale University. He is the author of *Shelley's Mythmaking, The Visionary Company: A Reading of English Romantic Poetry,* and *Blake's Apocalypse: A Study in Poetic Argument.*

NORTHROP FRYE is Professor of English and Principal of Victoria College at the University of Toronto. He is the author of *Fearful Symmetry: A Study of William Blake,* and *Anatomy of Criticism.*

LOUIS L. MARTZ is Douglas Tracy Smith Professor of English and American Literature at Yale University. He is the author of *The Poetry of Meditation: A Study in English Religious Literature of the Seventeenth Century.*

RALPH J. MILLS, JR., is Assistant Professor in the Committee on Social Thought at the University of Chicago. He has published a number of articles on contemporary poets.

ROY HARVEY PEARCE is Professor of English at The Ohio State University. He is the author of *The Continuity of American Poetry.*

Sister M. BERNETTA QUINN, O.S.F., is Chairman of the Department of English at the College of Saint Teresa. She is the author of *The Metamorphic Tradition in Modern Poetry.*

JOSEPH N. RIDDEL is Assistant Professor of English at Duke University. He has published a number of articles on Wallace Stevens.

The late HI SIMONS combined a career in business with an interest in literary criticism. His published essays were concerned mainly with the poetry of Wallace Stevens.

C. ROLAND WAGNER is Teaching Fellow in Philosophy in the New College at Hofstra.

MORTON DAUWEN ZABEL is Professor of English at the University of Chicago. He has published a number of articles on modern criticism, fiction, and poetry and is the author of *Craft and Character: Texts, Methods, and Vocation in Modern Fiction.* From 1927 to 1938 he was Associate Editor, then Editor in Chief, of *Poetry: A Magazine of Verse.*

Selected Bibliography

Note. This bibliography does not include critical articles. The reader is referred to the Bryer and Riddel *Checklist* in Section 1 below, the Brown and Haller anthology in Section 3, and the selected bibliographies provided in some of the other books listed in that section.

1. BIBLIOGRAPHICAL AIDS

Bryer, Jackson R. and Joseph N. Riddel. "A Checklist of Stevens Criticism." *Twentieth Century Literature*, VIII, Nos. 3-4 (October 1962-January 1963), 124-142. Divided into six sections: Books, Articles, Dissertations, Some Foreign Sources, Play Reviews, and Book Reviews. The most complete bibliography of writings on Stevens.

Morse, Samuel French. *Wallace Stevens: A Preliminary Checklist of His Published Writings, 1898-1954*. New Haven: Yale University Library, 1954.

2. BY WALLACE STEVENS

The Collected Poems. New York: Alfred A. Knopf, 1954.

The Necessary Angel: Essays on Reality and the Imagination. New York: Alfred A. Knopf, 1951.

Poems. Selected, and with an Introduction, by Samuel French Morse. New York: Vintage Books, 1959. Contains 95 poems, a 15-page introduction, and a list (pp. 171-173) of dates of composition.

Opus Posthumous. Edited, and with an Introduction, by Samuel French Morse. New York: Alfred A. Knopf, 1957. Contains poems omitted by Stevens from the 1954 collection and, beginning approximately with "The Dove in Spring," p. 97, those written after the publication of that volume. It also includes translations, plays, prose pieces, and the collection of notes and aphorisms called *Adagia*.

3. ABOUT WALLACE STEVENS

Brown, Ashley and Robert S. Haller. *The Achievement of Wallace Stevens.* Philadelphia: J. B. Lippincott, 1962. Contains 19 essays, including some important Stevens criticism of the 1920's and 1930's, as well as an introduction and an extensive bibliography. Also available in paperback as a Keystone Book.

Kermode, Frank. *Wallace Stevens.* Edinburgh: Oliver and Boyd, 1960; New York: Grove Press, 1961. (Evergreen Pilot Books.)

O'Connor, William Van. *The Shaping Spirit: A Study of Wallace Stevens.* Chicago: Henry Regnery, 1950.

Pack, Robert. *Wallace Stevens: An Approach to His Poetry and Thought.* New Brunswick, New Jersey: Rutgers University Press, 1958.

Tindall, William York. *Wallace Stevens.* University of Minnesota Pamphlets on American Writers, No. 11. Minneapolis: University of Minnesota Press, 1961.

TWENTIETH CENTURY VIEWS

Forthcoming Titles